T0285365

SUDS SERIES

SUDS SERIES

Baseball, Beer Wars, and the Summer of '82

J. Daniel

UNIVERSITY OF MISSOURI PRESS

COLUMBIA

Library of Congress Cataloging-in-Publication Data

Names: Daniel, J., 1967- author.
Title: Suds series : baseball, beer wars, and the summer of '82 / by J.
    Daniel.
Description: Columbia, MO : University of Missouri Press, 2023. | Series:
    Sports and American culture | Includes bibliographical references.
Identifiers: LCCN 2022047661 (print) | LCCN 2022047662 (ebook) | ISBN
    9780826222800 (hardcover) | ISBN 9780826222947 (paperback) | ISBN
    9780826274854 (ebook)
Subjects: LCSH: Baseball--United States--History--20th century. | St. Louis
    Cardinals (Baseball team)--History--20th century. | Milwaukee Brewers
    (Baseball team)--History--20th century. | Beer--Social aspects--United
    States--History--20th century. | Advertising--Beer--United
    States--History--20th century. | Popular culture--United
    States--History--20th century.
Classification: LCC GV863.A1 D35 2023 (print) | LCC GV863.A1 (ebook) |
    DDC 796.3570973/0904--dc23/eng/20221101
LC record available at https://lccn.loc.gov/2022047661
LC ebook record available at https://lccn.loc.gov/2022047662

Typeface: Bernina Sans and Minion Pro

Sports and American Culture

Adam Criblez, Series Editor

This series explores the cultural dynamic between competitive athletics and society, the many ways in which sports shape the lives of Americans, in the United States and Latin America, from a historical and contemporary perspective. While international in scope, the series includes titles of regional interest to Missouri and the Midwest. Topics in the series range from studies of a single game, event, or season to histories of teams and programs, as well as biographical narratives of athletes, coaches, owners, journalists, and broadcasters.

For Sue,

who consented to the playing of

"Take Me Out to the Ball Game" at our wedding,

and for Michael and Brady,

my two all-time favorite baseball players

Contents

ix

Acknowledgments

Book writing is very much a team effort, and I had a great one. In the spring of 2020, I was looking for a home for this project, and Dave Jordan suggested I contact the University of Missouri Press. Had he not made that suggestion, and added support along the way, this book may never have gotten off the ground.

Andrew Davidson, the editor in chief at the University of Missouri Press, answered my query immediately and looped in Adam Criblez, editor of the series Sports and American Culture. Between them, they made my idea for this book a reality, for which I'll be forever grateful.

Shawn Wintle served as a proofreader and cheerleader throughout the process of writing the draft for submission, and it was Sachin Waikar who got me started on the book-writing road. Thank you, gentlemen.

I want to give a special thanks to the guys I grew up with. They are the ones who lived the 1982 baseball season with me. We played wiffleball and Strat-O-Matic, traded baseball cards and insults, and remain great friends to this day. I won't name any at the risk of leaving someone out, but you know who you are.

My parents, Jim Sosnoski and Patricia Harkin, instilled in me a love of learning and the written word. I don't want to think where I'd be without them.

Finally, I want to thank my family, who allowed me to spend more than two years living back in 1982, gave me space, and patiently listened while I regaled them with tales of Robin Yount and Rickey Henderson.

SUDS SERIES

INTRODUCTION

> So much has been said to ridicule and belittle the attempt of several cities unable to get into the (National) League to organize an independent baseball association that the weak-kneed brethren have been particularly timid about indorsing (sic) the scheme. Still, the promoters of the undertaking were determined and had the opponents . . . of the new League witnessed the enthusiasm of the delegates who arrived (in Cincinnati) . . . their bitterness and mockery would have turned to astonishment.
>
> —*Cincinnati Enquirer*, November 2, 1881

The approximately twenty delegates, including sporting goods magnate A. J. Reach and J. H. Pank, president of the Kentucky Malting Company, who gathered at the Gibson House Hotel represented the cities of Cincinnati, Pittsburgh, St. Louis, Louisville, Baltimore, and Philadelphia. The astonishing result of their initial meeting was the creation of the American Association, a rival of the incumbent and decidedly conservative National League. Led by William Hulbert, who ruled with an iron fist, the National League forbade the sale of alcohol at games as well as playing baseball on Sundays. When teams or players ran afoul of Hulbert, he took swift and often draconian actions. In 1879, the Cincinnati Red Stockings ignored Hulbert's rules against alcohol sales and Sunday games only to find themselves kicked out of the league. Two years later, Hulbert officially blacklisted ten players from various teams for "confirmed dissipation and general insubordination,"[1] with offenses ranging from drinking to gambling.

Many of the team owners in the upstart American Association, which began play in 1882, had strong connections to alcohol, primarily beer, and the ability to sell it at games represented a windfall. By some estimates, teams could expect to add an additional $5,000 per season in revenue from alcohol sales, a figure equivalent to more than $125,000 in the twenty-first century. Additionally, tickets to American Association games were less expensive ($0.25 rather than $0.50) than tickets to National League games, and Sunday afternoon contests allowed people who worked six days a week the opportunity to take in a ball game on their day off. More people in the stands and the ability to attend a game any day of the week all equaled the chance to sell more alcohol, thus earning the league the derisive nickname "The Beer and Whiskey League."

Among its most colorful owners was Christopher Von der Ahe of the St. Louis Browns. Born in Prussia in 1848, the oldest of nine children, Von der Ahe immigrated to the United States in his late teens and eventually settled in St. Louis.[2] He took a job as a grocery store clerk in the city's West End on the corner of Sullivan and Spring, less than five miles from the site of current-day Busch Stadium. He soon advanced to become co-owner of a combination grocery store and saloon, and in 1872 he used his life's savings to buy out his partner and become the sole proprietor. Von der Ahe relocated the business to a larger building a block south and, over time, expanded his empire to include a butcher shop and a feed and flour store. He was not a baseball fan, but he quickly noticed that his saloon was busier on days that the St. Louis Browns played at nearby Grand Avenue Park, and his entrepreneurial spirit kicked in. If he could purchase the Browns, he could "double-dip" by earning money from both the games *and* the postgame celebrations. Before long he had secured the concession rights at Grand Avenue Park, which seemed like a boon at first, but when baseball began to slip in popularity due to a sagging economy and gambling scandals, his investment appeared to be in danger. A shrewd businessman, Von der Ahe saw what many did not. Professional baseball was not dying; it was in its infancy and dealing with the inevitable growing pains that accompany a fledgling enterprise. Rather than cut his losses and walk away, Von der Ahe opted to buy low and purchased the ballpark with an eye toward creating a vast entertainment complex that included not only baseball but also a running track, cricket fields, handball courts, and bowling alleys. "It took guts—some thought reckless stupidity—to invest in baseball in 1880, especially in St. Louis," wrote Edward Achorn in *The Summer of Beer and Whiskey*. "But however little or much he knew about baseball, the immigrant grocer knew this: to make a dollar in America, a man had to take a chance. 'If it sells beer, I'm all for it,' he told his fellow investors."[3]

Throughout the summer of 1881, Von der Ahe hosted exhibition games on Sundays featuring local amateur teams at his newly refurbished ballpark, and, after a slow start, the crowds began to grow. Working-class citizens of St. Louis attended mass in the morning and then headed to the ballpark for some entertainment and a few beers. "He took no interest in the game, but stood over his bartenders, watching the dimes and quarters that the crowd showered over the bar," recalled one player. "'Hear dem shouting out dere?' Von der Ahe reportedly said in his thick German accent. 'Tree thousand dem fools and one vise man, and that vise man is me, Chris Won der Ahe!'"[4]

Von der Ahe proved there was money to be made in baseball, especially when paired with alcohol sales. Soon, Cincinnati, Pittsburgh, and Louisville, all river cities who had hoped to one day join the National League, embarked on a new quest: creating their own baseball league. The American Association began play in the spring of 1882 and Von der Ahe's Browns were among its most successful franchises, posting the league's best record four years in a row, from 1885 through 1888, and winning the championship in 1886. The AA was derisively dubbed "The Beer and Whiskey League" by many in the National League and it eventually ran into problems with both finances and personnel, especially with the founding of a third professional league called The Players' League in 1890, which siphoned off many stars of the American Association. The demise of the Beer and Whiskey League did not end the relationship between baseball and alcohol, however. Some owners in the National League noticed that selling alcohol at baseball games equated to larger profits and the league eventually followed suit. Even though the American Association only survived a few seasons, four of its teams, Von der Ahe's Browns (who later became the St. Louis Cardinals), the Cincinnati Red Stockings (modern-day Reds), the Pittsburgh Alleghenys (Pirates), and the Brooklyn Atlantics, who entered the league in 1884 and later became the Dodgers, were absorbed in the National League.

Beer and baseball were a winning combination, and it seemed nothing could come between them. That was, until January 16, 1919, when the United States passed the Eighteenth Amendment to the Constitution, which banned the manufacture, sale, or transportation of alcohol.

Prohibition lasted until December of 1933, but once it was repealed, the relationship between beer and baseball was rekindled. By the 1940s it was forever solidified as breweries and teams entered into advertising agreements. The Fallstaff Brewing Company sponsored former pitcher Dizzy Dean's broadcasts of St. Louis Browns games, and Yankee fans heard Mel Allen describe home runs as "Ballantine Blasts" thanks to a sponsorship agreement with Ballantine Beer.

Breweries, or at least those owned by well-off brewers, naturally gravitated toward team ownership. When Fred Saigh, owner the St. Louis Cardinals, was convicted of tax evasion in 1953, he put the team up for sale, and Anheuser-Busch purchased the team to keep them in St. Louis and establish themselves as civic heroes, which led to increased sales. The following year, Jerold Hoffberger, president of National Brewing Company, led a group that purchased a newer version of the St. Louis Browns[5] and moved them to Baltimore, where they became the Orioles. As the decades rolled on, baseball games were full of beer advertisements as more teams formed relationships with breweries. Among them were the Red Sox, sponsored by Narragansett Beer, the Twins (Hamms), and Mets (Rheingold). Hudepohl, a longtime sponsor of the Cincinnati Reds, issued commemorative cans after the Reds won the World Series in 1975 and 1976, and Pittsburgh Brewing, makers of Iron City Beer, did the same when the Pirates won a World Series in 1979. But the relationship between beer and baseball did produce some unwanted results, one of most infamous of which took place in Cleveland in 1974 when the Indians hosted the Texas Rangers on "Ten Cent Beer Night." Spectators were permitted to purchase up to six ten-cent beers at a time, and many did just that, again and again, before things got ugly. One fan ran onto the field and tried to steal the hat of a Rangers player, who was then rescued by multiple bat-wielding teammates. The resulting riot ended in nine arrests and a Cleveland forfeit.

It was also in the 1970s that a used-car mogul named Bud Selig purchased the Seattle Pilots in bankruptcy court, moved them to Milwaukee, and renamed them the Brewers, an homage to Milwaukee's baseball (and brewing) past. The Beer and Whiskey League had a team called the Brewers in their final season, and the Brewers resurfaced in 1902 as a member of the minor league American Association (not affiliated with the former major league.) The 1902 version of the Brewers was owned by Otto Borchert, whose family also ran the F. Borchert and Sons Brewery. The team won eight championships between 1913 and 1952 while playing at Borchert Field, named after the team's founder who passed away in 1927. The Brewers ceased operations in 1953 when the Boston Braves moved to Milwaukee and began play in a brand-new ballpark named Milwaukee County Stadium. Despite some success, including a World Series title in 1957, attendance at Braves games began to decline in the early 1960s, and Lou Perini, who moved the team from Boston to Milwaukee, sold to a group in Chicago who relocated the franchise once again, this time to Atlanta, where they became the Braves.

Selig was a season ticket holder before the Braves moved to Atlanta, and was determined to bring Major League Baseball back to his hometown. When the Pilots became available, he pounced. The transaction took place so close to the beginning of the season that the team didn't have a chance to design new uniforms. As a result, the "new" Brewers adopted the blue and yellow color scheme of the Pilots, changed the name on the front of the jersey, and replaced the nautical-themed Pilots hats with a simple blue cap with a yellow M. The Milwaukee Brewers, Version 3.0, were born.

Ten years later, at the 1980 Winter Meetings, a trade between the team once owned by Von der Ahe to sell more beer and the team renamed the Brewers after the city's beer connections set in motion a chain of events that would ultimately lead to the two teams facing off in the 1982 World Series. On December 12, 1980, Cardinals manager/general manager Whitey Herzog approached Milwaukee Brewers general manager Harry Dalton with a simple question: "How'd you like to win the pennant next year?"[6]

Herzog grew up in tiny New Athens, Illinois, and used to skip school to hitchhike the thirty-three miles to St. Louis to attend major-league games. He would arrive early, watch batting practice, and collect home run balls hit into the stands. Once the game was over, he would sell the balls for bus fare home. His principal knew of his habit, but rather than punish him, he'd pull the young Herzog aside to get a report of the previous day's game. Herzog signed with the New York Yankees in 1949 and spent four years in the minor leagues, advancing as far as Triple-A. But when the Korean conflict arose, Herzog was pressed into duty in the Army Corps of Engineers. Once he returned, he found himself in spring training in 1958 competing for a spot in the Yankees outfield. Unfortunately, Herzog's competition was Mickey Mantle, and Herzog was dealt to the lowly Washington Senators in April. His stint in Washington lasted all of eight games before he was sold to the Kansas

City Athletics in May. By the spring of 1959, after three years in the major leagues, Herzog maintained just a .232 lifetime batting average. But his life, and the course of baseball history, was about to change.

Like many players, Whitey Herzog had trouble hitting a major-league curveball. Unlike many players, Herzog had a coach in Kansas City, former major-league pitcher Johnny Sain, who happened to still possess a nasty curveball and was willing to work with Whitey to make him a better hitter. On the back fields of spring training, day after day, Sain threw curveballs until Herzog began to time them. Once the regular season began, American League pitchers were unaware of Herzog's training at the hands of a master and continued to feed him curveballs. But this time, Herzog knew how to stay back on curveballs. Instead of lunging and taking off balance swings, Herzog was hitting line drives and they were falling in for hits. In his first eight games, Herzog hit .433 and finished the season at .293.

"I eventually realized that if I made it, it would be as a platoon-type guy," Herzog said in his 1999 book, *You're Missing a Great Game*. "I just wanted to hang on five years and get my major league pension. But if Johnny Sain hadn't stayed after school and slung me all those Uncle Charlies, I never would have."[7]

Herzog finished his playing career after the 1963 season and spent three years in the Kansas City front office, first as a scout and then as a coach. From there, he joined the New York Mets, where he became director of player development and excelled. Under his watch, the Mets signed players like Gary Gentry and Jon Matlack, who became key contributors to their 1973 National League Championship ballclub. But by the time the Mets reached the 1973 World Series, where they fell to the Oakland A's, Herzog was gone, replacing legendary slugger Ted Williams as manager of the Texas Rangers.

The 1973 Rangers were a miserable team. Just two pitchers, relievers Mike Paul (5–4) and Rick Henninger (1–0) posted winning records, and that era of Rangers baseball was immortalized in *Fort Worth Star Telegram* Mike Shropshire's book, *Seasons in Hell*. Rangers owner Bob Short brought Herzog in to build the franchise from the bottom up as he had done in New York. But that changed in September of 1973 when the Detroit Tigers fired Billy Martin. Suddenly, a top manager was available and Short wanted him.

"I thought the emphasis here was supposed to be more on development than winning right away," Herzog said later. "I guess I was wrong about that, and when you're wrong with a 47–91 record, you are not going to get very far."[8]

After a brief stint with the California Angels, Herzog landed in Kansas City, where he began to build a reputation as a top-flight manager. With a solid core of talent, led by third baseman George Brett, the Royals won the American League West in 1976, '77, and '78 but were knocked out of the postseason each year by the New York Yankees. After a second-place finish in 1979, Herzog was fired once again and entered the new decade without a job in baseball. That lasted until June when St. Louis Cardinals owner August Busch decided it was time to make a change on his ballclub. Herzog recalled:

> It started off simple. They offered me a one-year contract for $100,000. That was less money that I made the year the Royals canned me, but that wasn't the problem. It was the length. I said, "Mister Busch, I understand it's your policy to just offer one-year deals. But I won three straight titles in Kansas City, and the first time I finished 2nd, I was out on my ass. I won 88 games and got fired. Thanks for the offer, but I'm not signing any more one-year contracts." I shook his hand got up and started walking out. I made it halfway to the door.
>
> "Siddown!" he barked in that gravelly voice. "The damn players get five-year contracts; you can get a three-year sonofabitch." I signed that day, and like the man said in Casablanca, it was the beginning of a beautiful relationship.[9]

It did not take Herzog long to determine that major changes were needed if the Cardinals were to return to the glory of the late 1960s, when they appeared in back-to-back World Series.

"I was sitting in my office about a week after I had taken over, when Butch Yatkeman, our clubhouse guy, brought me a Budweiser," Herzog wrote. "I said, 'Dang it, Butch, it takes us four hits to get a run.' He said, 'Whitey, this is the slowest team and the worst base-running team I've ever seen, and I've been here 57 years.'"[10]

The Cardinals had talent, but it did not match their ballpark. Busch Stadium, with its Astroturf and spacious outfield, was a perfect ballpark for the type of team Herzog had in Kansas City; one that pitched well, hit balls in the gaps, and ran. The current iteration of the Cardinals did not fit the bill, and Herzog knew it. Once the 1980 season was over, he went to work on remaking the team. The moves began at the Winter Meetings 1980 when Herzog signed Darrell Porter, his former catcher with the Royals, as a free agent. From there, Herzog began moving players as if they were baseball cards rather than actual people. There was an eleven-player deal with the San Diego Padres, in which St. Louis acquired relief ace Rollie Fingers, followed by a four-player deal with the Cubs that brought another relief ace in Bruce Sutter. Suddenly, Herzog had two of baseball's best relief pitchers and could make another move, a big one. Herzog met with Dalton and put together a seven-player deal that sent Fingers, starting pitcher Pete Vuckovich, and catcher Ted Simmons, to Milwaukee in exchange for outfielders David Green and Sixto Lezcano, and pitchers Dave LaPoint and Lary Sorensen. At the time, Green was considered a superstar in the making. He was just twenty years old, had blazing speed, and, at six foot three and 170 pounds, had the potential to develop into a premier power hitter. Herzog was not the first person to ask about him in a trade, but no one else offered a return that included two future Hall of Famers (Fingers and Simmons), and Milwaukee agreed.

"When I [made that trade], you'd have thought I'd traded Abe Lincoln and George Washington," said Herzog. "People were calling the sports talk shows, saying, 'Whitey is giving away too much!' 'Who the hell is this guy running off Ted Simmons?' 'Handing over fourteen players and getting back eleven. Can't the son of a bitch count?'"[11]

Herzog's prediction nearly came true. Behind Fingers, Simmons, and Vuckovich, the 1981 Brewers reached the postseason for the first time since moving to Milwaukee. They fell short of winning the pennant, but the nucleus was in place.

In St. Louis, Herzog wasn't finished making moves. In June of 1981, he swung a deal with the Houston Astros for starting pitcher Joaquin Andujar, and, just after the season ended, he sent pitcher Bob Sykes to the Yankees for a minor league outfielder named Willie McGee. After that, he sent shortstop Garry Templeton to San Diego in exchange for Ozzie Smith. The last major move came at the 1981 Winter Meetings when Herzog acquired outfielder Lonnie Smith in a three-team deal with the Phillies and the Indians. All told, from the time he took over the team as manager and general manager in June of 1980 until opening day of the 1982 season, Herzog made twenty-nine moves involving more than sixty players. The moves culminated in a huge turnaround for the Cardinals. The 1980 team finished fourteen games under .500. By 1982 they were in the World Series. There was just one problem. In reshaping his own team, Herzog helped create the team he'd need to beat to win his first World Series. The 1982 Brewers were a powerhouse and, in many respects, the exact opposite of the Cardinals. The season culminated in a clash of styles. Two cities well known for both beer and baseball would play seven games to determine a champion. It would be a matchup of the speedy St. Louis Cardinals against the powerful Milwaukee Brewers.

1. THE OFF-SEASON

Am I Gonna Get to First Base?

> CLASSIFIEDS:
> **Drummer looking for other metal musicians to jam with Tygers of Pan Tang, Diamond Head, and Iron Maiden.**
> —1982 newspaper advertisement

The drummer who placed the ad in the Los Angeles newspaper *The Recycler* was Lars Ulrich, the son of a Danish tennis player named Torben Ulrich. Torben's father, Einer, was also a tennis pro, one good enough to play in Wimbledon twice. But Lars eschewed the family business in favor of the world of heavy metal music, and in the spring of 1981 a guitar player named James Hetfield answered his advertisement. On October 28, Ulrich and Hetfield recruited Ron McGovney and Dave Mustaine to join them. The only thing left was a name for their band. They chose Metallica. Their first album, *Kill 'Em All*, hit record stores in the summer of 1983, and the band has sold more than 100 million albums and counting worldwide. Their 1991 hit "Enter Sandman" would become synonymous with a relief pitcher from Panama named Mariano Rivera, who would win five World Series rings with the New York Yankees.

On the day Ulrich posted the ad in L.A., Metallica was a blip on the national radar. All eyes in the city were on the Dodgers, looking to win their first World Series since 1965. Their opponents were the hated New York Yankees. In nine head-to-head matchups in the Fall Classic, the Yankees had bested the Dodgers eight times. The two teams met in 1977 and 1978, and New York won both series, thanks in large part to the heroics of Reggie Jackson.

But 1981 was a different story. After winning the first two games of the Series, the Yankees lost three straight and faced elimination in the bottom of the ninth inning of Game Six at Yankee Stadium. With two outs and Jackson on first base, Dodgers reliever Steve Howe got Bob Watson to fly out to center field, and the Dodgers were World Series champions for the first time since 1965. As the visiting team celebrated on the Yankee Stadium turf, the press corps received a mimeographed statement from New York's owner, George Steinbrenner: "I want to sincerely apologize to the people of New York and to the fans of the New York Yankees everywhere for the performance of the Yankee team in the World Series. I'm disappointed. I expect more from some of our people. But that's life. We will be at work immediately to prepare for 1982."[1]

"Apologize . . . Apologize . . . I'll tell you what," said Jackson. "He can apologize all he wants. I have nothing to apologize for. We didn't lose, we got beat. There's a big difference. We were second best. There's nothing wrong with being second best. Avis makes money. Miller High Life makes money."[2]

The 1981 World Series was the culmination of one of the most interesting, and bizarre, seasons in major-league history. A fifty-one-day player strike that began on June 12 forced the cancelation of more than seven hundred regular season games. The agreement finally reached between the baseball owners and the Players Association on July 31 implemented a "split season" format. Teams leading their division at the time of the strike, the Yankees and A's in the American League and the Phillies and Dodgers in the National League, were declared winners of the first half. A "second season" would begin play in August, and new divisional races would ensue. The idea was to give teams who were buried in the standings a chance to salvage their seasons and to create additional interest with an extra round of playoffs. Division winners of each half of the season were set to play one another in a five-game series, with the winners of those series advancing to the League Championship Series. But the plan had its critics. One of the most vocal was Cincinnati Reds president Dick Wagner. A staunch baseball conservative, Wagner hated free agency and the increasing power enjoyed by Marvin Miller and the players association. He was opposed to the terms of the strike settlement and didn't care for the split-season format either, saying, "What's wrong with it? Only about 15 or 20 things. Beyond the 'integrity factor' since there's no bye, you also have the possibility that a first half winner could [by losing certain games] play a big role in deciding who its playoff opponent would be. . . . Certain managers think that way."[3] As it turned out, that would be the least of Wagner's complaints. His Reds finished the first half just a half game behind the Dodgers in the National League West, and then one and a half games behind Houston in the second half to miss the playoffs despite posting a combined win/loss mark of 66-42, the best overall record in baseball. Prior to the season finale, the Reds hoisted a flag that read, "Baseball's Best Record 1981," in recognition of their accomplishment and in protest of the system.

"If I wasn't a grown man, I think I'd go cry on a curb or in a park somewhere," said Cincinnati manager John McNamara. "I don't know how to explain it or how to explain myself. Still waters run deep—I'll never forget this."[4] Joining McNamara and the Reds in their disdain for the system was Whitey Herzog and the St. Louis Cardinals, who finished with the second-best overall record in the National League and, like Cincinnati, watched the postseason on TV. The two teams would have very different fortunes the following summer.

Preparations for the 1982 season began in earnest the day after the conclusion of the 1981 World Series when Bill Giles and a group of investors officially announced that they had purchased the Philadelphia Phillies for $30 million. Giles's entry to the game came in the 1950s at the heels of his father, Warren, who was then general manager of the Cincinnati Reds and would later become National League president. From Cincinnati, Bill moved south as part of the first executive team of the Houston Astros, beginning as traveling secretary and publicity director. In 1969 he joined the Phillies as vice president of business operations and eventually became vice president of the team. In the spring of 1981, then Phillies owner Ruly Carpenter III told Giles he was selling the team. The Carpenter family had owned the team since 1943, but the game had changed immensely since then, and family-owned teams were now a rarity. The advent of free agency meant teams needed to spend more money to compete, and Carpenter was unable to do so on his own. Philadelphia won a World Series in 1980 and made the playoffs in 1981, but the Montreal Expos were on the rise, and Herzog had completely reshaped the Cardinals. Competing in the National League East would take talent and money. Carpenter's talent was getting older, and his money was running out. It was time to move on.

Giles immediately went to work trying to find partners to buy the team and eventually raised enough capital to seal a deal, edging out, among others, Philadelphia native and host of *The Gong Show*, Chuck Barris. Jayson Stark of the *Philadelphia Inquirer* thought Giles was exactly the type of owner baseball needed in the new decade.

"The words 'free agent' don't send pains shooting up his spine," Stark wrote. "You mention something about cable, and he knows you're not talking about a telegram. He likes to see his name in the papers. But he won't storm into locker rooms, run through managers . . . or have his lip punched in an elevator to do it [a direct reference to George Steinbrenner, who was involved in a fight with some Dodger fans during the 1981 World Series]. He has been roaming around ballparks since he was five years old. . . . And he hopes still to be roaming around ballparks on his final day on earth."[5]

Once Giles took over, changes to the Phillies roster began quickly. The team he purchased was coming off a world championship in 1980 and a playoff appearance in 1981 but also had an aging core. Pete Rose would turn forty-one in April, Steve Carlton was thirty-seven, and Mike Schmidt, who won the National League MVP Award in both 1980 and 1981, was thirty-two. Not a single member of the regular starting lineup in 1981 was under the age of thirty. A team that was in danger of being broken up prior to their 1980 World Series championship now *needed* to be broken up, and one of the first things on the Giles agenda was to get better behind the plate.

After winning back-to-back Gold Gloves in 1978 and 1979, veteran catcher Bob Boone saw his production slip after a late-season knee injury in 1979. His caught stealing percentage fell by more than 50 percent, and his offensive production also dropped from a .286 batting average in 1979 with 9 homers and 58 RBI, to an anemic .211 average and a slugging percentage of less than .300 in 1981. Entering his age-thirty-four season and having lost the starting catcher position to Keith Moreland in the second half of 1981, the Phillies deemed Boone expendable.

Philadelphia general manager Paul Owens looked to Cleveland for Boone's replacement and sent outfielder Lonnie Smith to the Indians in exchange for Bo Diaz. Five years younger than Boone, Diaz was coming off a 1981 campaign in which he hit .313, made his first All-Star team, and threw out 40 percent of would-be base stealers. What the Phillies didn't know was that the Indians needed pitching more than they needed an outfielder and planned on flipping Smith to St. Louis. What began as a simple Smith-for-Diaz trade morphed into a three-team deal with the Indians sending Smith to the Cardinals in exchange for Lary Sorensen and Silvio Martinez. Not only was Smith gone, but he would remain in the National League's Eastern Division, where he had the potential to haunt Philadelphia for years.

"If you are among the million or so fans who figure the Phillies paid through the nose to solve what they considered a desperate catching problem, welcome to the club," wrote Bill Conlin in the *Philadelphia Daily News*. "The Phillies have become a used car lot for catchers."[6]

Adding Diaz gave the Phillies five catchers on the forty-man roster, but Owens promised fans he was not finished making moves. A few weeks later, he sold Boone to the California Angels, where manager Gene Mauch had long coveted Boone for his leadership capabilities. The Phillies were going with youth, but the Angels were a veteran team looking for a catcher who knew how to handle a pitching staff. Despite his recent struggles at the plate, Boone was a perfect fit. "He's not a .211 hitter. I know that," said Mauch. "I don't care what he hits, really, if he can move the ball around and catch for me."[7] Asked what he thought about Boone's defensive woes, Mauch replied, "What's the difference? Who's going to throw out [Oakland speedster] Rickey Henderson anyway? I just want [Henderson's teammate] Mickey Klutts thrown out."[8]

There was one other side effect of Giles's purchase: the loss of Dallas Green. Green had been a member of the Phillies for all but two seasons since 1955. After retiring as a player for the Phillies in 1967, Green managed in the Philadelphia system for more than a dozen years, leading Philadelphia to a World Series title in 1980. After nearly thirty years in the Phillies organization, he wasn't looking to leave. Green and his wife Sylvia owned a sixty-acre farm about an hour from Philadelphia. She was a teacher who loved her job, and the youngest of their four children was about to start high school. Uprooting all that would come at a price, but it was one the Chicago Cubs were willing to pay. The Tribune Company purchased the team in 1981 and went after Green enthusiastically. Chicago wanted him to be their general manager, a title Green had never held, and discussions began midway through the 1981 season. But Green continually turned down increasingly higher offers. At the end of the season, Green talked to Phillies GM Paul Owens, who assured him that Giles wanted him as the field manager. But Owens also told Green he couldn't make any guarantees beyond that. By contrast, the Cubs would make Dallas Green one of the highest paid general managers in the game, buy him a house, and give him stock options and opportunity to rebuild one of the most storied franchises in the game. Green still wanted to stay in Philadelphia, but Owens convinced him the offer was simply too good to walk away from.

"Dallas, you have to take it," Green recalled Owens telling him. "This is crazy. You're not going to get that kind of money here or anywhere else. I know you love everything about the Phillies and your farm, but Chicago is a great city and you'll love it. You've got to take it."[9]

Green took Owens's advice, and among his first orders of business was to ask the Phillies how many people he could take with him. At the top of his list was coach Lee Elia, whom Green wanted as his manager. Green's other target was John Vukovich. "Vuke" spent ten seasons in the big leagues as a player, but his main claim to fame may be that he was the person bumped out of the Cincinnati Reds lineup when Sparky Anderson moved Pete Rose to third base in 1975. Despite batting just .161 in his big-league career, he was a leader off the field, and Green credited him with keeping other players in line on the 1980 Phillies. "Whether reminding Greg Luzinski to watch his weight or telling Larry Bowa to shut his trap, Vuke got players to listen," Green said in his autobiography, *The Mouth That Roared*.[10]

Now that Green oversaw the Cubs, he pulled off a trade with his former boss to acquire catcher Keith Moreland and two others in exchange for pitcher Mike Krukow. Like Smith, Moreland played a key role as a rookie in the 1980 World Series championship. But with Diaz as the starting catcher, Moreland, too, was expendable, and the Phillies needed starting pitching, specifically someone to follow Steve Carlton in the rotation. Carlton (13) and Dick Ruthven (12) combined for twenty-five wins in 1981, but no other starting pitcher contributed more than four. Philadelphia needed pitching depth. Green knew it, and Krukow provided it.

"I'm psyched," said Krukow. "The prospect of going to what I think is the most talented organization everyday player wise in the National League . . . it's a tremendous challenge."[11] Shortly after the deal was announced, Krukow was on hold to talk to WWDB radio in Philadelphia when the caller ahead of him talked about how terrible he was and what a bad deal the Phillies had just made. Not surprisingly, the Philadelphia press wasn't happy either.

"If Paul Owens and . . . the rest . . . are right, the Phillies chances of regaining the National League pennant are better today than they were a week or so ago," wrote Frank Dolson in the *Philadelphia Inquirer*. "If they are wrong, the deal that made Smith and Moreland ex-Phillies will come back to haunt the organization, again and again, in the months and years ahead."[12]

Aside from Moreland, there was one player who was a key link between Giles and Green, and his legacy would impact both the Phillies and the Cubs franchises for the next fifteen years. When Green took over the Phillies in 1979, Larry Bowa was one of the top shortstops in the National League. He was a five-time All-Star, a Gold Glove winner, and finished third in the N.L. MVP balloting in 1978. He also had a temper and butted heads with Green on multiple occasions. In spring training of 1980, when Green posted signs reading "We, not I," Bowa mockingly asked reporters when the pom-pom girls would show up. Bowa ripped Green on a radio show late in the season when Green benched underperforming veterans. But all was forgiven when the Phillies won a world championship, and one enduring image of the postseason was that of a smiling Green with his arm around an emotional Bowa, champagne bottle in hand, in the Philadelphia clubhouse after the World Series-clinching Game Six.

"You're a winner," Green told Bowa that night. "You . . . are . . . a . . . winner. You play my game."[13]

Bowa claimed to have a verbal agreement with Ruly Carpenter for a new contract for the 1982 season. But once Giles purchased the team, the new owner felt no obligation to honor verbal agreements made by his predecessor. Things got ugly, especially when Giles was quoted as saying the team needed to build around its core players and left Bowa off a list including Mike Schmidt, Pete Rose, Steve Carlton, and Gary Matthews. The situation reached a breaking point before Christmas when Bowa ripped Giles in the *Philadelphia Inquirer*. "I've been with an organization that's always been dead honest with me," he said. "Now, . . . all I get is deceit, lies. To me, the class went out of this organization when Ruly Carpenter stepped down."[14]

Bowa wanted a contract that would take him through the 1984 season, but the Phillies had multiple middle infielders who were almost big-league ready and didn't want to impede their progress. Julio Franco was already being tabbed as the shortstop of the future, and that future appeared imminent. He hit above .300 at three different minor league levels and was just twenty-two years old. His bat was ready, but his glove was in question. Another prospect, Ryne Sandberg, hit .285 across four minor league levels, but there were doubts in the organization about what position he could play at the big-league level. The Phillies still needed pitching, and rumors were rampant that Sandberg might be headed to Toronto as part of a package that would send Dave

Stieb to Philadelphia, or to Milwaukee for Mike Caldwell. Meanwhile, the Cubs emerged as the leader for Bowa, and Dallas Green made a trip to Philadelphia to meet his former boss face-to-face and consummate a deal for his onetime nemesis. The deal was finally done in January, with Philadelphia sending Bowa and Sandberg to Chicago in exchange for shortstop Iván DeJesús. Again, the Philadelphia media wasn't happy.

"The finest shortstop in the town's history was traded along with rookie infielder Ryne Sandberg for a guy who hit .194 last season," wrote Conlin. "And, although DeJesus didn't hit very well, he didn't exactly field up a storm either."[15]

DeJesús was seven years younger than Bowa, but he had just come off the worst season of his career at the plate. Not only had he hit just .194, but he also mustered only 13 RBI in 106 games, along with 24 errors. A case could be made that the Phillies were "buying low," but many thought they simply got fleeced for the second time in two months by their former manager. For many, the twenty-two-year-old Sandberg was a "throw-in" to the deal. He had potential but not a clearly defined future in the organization. He was blocked by Franco at shortstop, and his other minor league position, third base, was occupied by future Hall of Famer Mike Schmidt. That gave Green an advantage in having him included in the deal.

Ryne Dee Sandberg was the youngest of four children born to Derwent and Elizabeth Sandberg of Spokane, Washington. His parents saw a hard throwing righty named Ryne Duren on television pitching for the Yankees against the Milwaukee Braves in the 1958 World Series and liked his name. Eleven months later, they decided to name their son after him. In addition to baseball, Sandberg was an outstanding football player, good enough to earn Parade All-American honors at quarterback. Following the football season, he earned All-City honors in basketball before playing baseball in the spring. He announced his intention to attend Washington State in the fall of 1978, but there was a question as to whether he would play football or baseball.

As the baseball draft approached, Spokane newspapers speculated it would take a lot of money to get Sandberg to walk away from Washington State, and when he slipped to the twentieth round of the draft, in part due to uncertainty about his future, it seemed he was heading for Pullman to be a Cougar. But the Phillies recognized what they had and offered Sandberg a contract he couldn't turn down. Instead of heading to Pullman, he was off to Helena, Montana, in the Pioneer

League. After four years in the Phillies system and a six-game stint with the major-league club at the end of 1981, Sandberg was driving home from Florida after playing a season of winter ball when he found out he was a member of the Chicago Cubs.

"I was disappointed because my goal was to play for the Phillies' big-league club," Sandberg wrote in his autobiography, *Second to Home.* "That's how Dallas and everyone in the minor-league system brought up the young players. I had been traded for the first time in my life and I knew nothing about the Cubs."[16]

Most people in Chicago knew nothing about Sandberg, either. Jerome Holtzman of the *Chicago Tribune* said the Cubs acquired "Larry Bowa, an aging but feisty veteran, and an untested minor leaguer from the Philadelphia Phillies in exchange for Ivan DeJesus. For the deal to work to the Cubs' advantage, Green must be correct in his assessment that Sandberg has the ability to win a starting spot within the next two years."[17]

In addition to their new additions from the Phillies, the Cubs also brought back pitcher Fergie Jenkins, who had spent the past four seasons with the Texas Rangers. Jenkins was another former Phillies prospect who was traded to Chicago after a brief look at the major-league level. All Jenkins did for the Cubs was win 147 games and a Cy Young Award. Now, thirty-nine years old, Jenkins's best days were behind him, but he could still win games at the major-league level and added legitimacy to a starting rotation that desperately needed it. The Cubs were the worst team in the National League in 1981 and hadn't had a winning record in a decade. The additions of Jenkins, Bowa, and Moreland and new leadership had Chicago fans hoping for a turnaround.

* * * * *

The turnover in Chicago was not as big as the transformation taking place in St. Louis. Since taking over the team in the middle of the 1980 season, Whitey Herzog had cleaned house, getting rid of players he considered dead weight and acquiring the kinds of players he thought could play winning baseball, especially on the speedy artificial turf of Busch Stadium. But there was one more move Herzog needed to make—one born of necessity.

On August 26, 1981, the Cardinals were hosting the San Francisco Giants on Ladies Day. It was a day game after a night game, one many regulars like to have off. But Herzog had most of his regulars in the lineup, including shortstop Garry Templeton, who had asked Herzog not to play him in such situations.

"This kid had already told me he hates playing in Montreal, he doesn't like playing in the rain, he don't like batting against certain pitchers, leave aside the fact that he's 22 years old and I've got guys in their thirties like George Hendrick playing every day and never saying a word about it," Herzog said in his autobiography, *You're Missin' a Great Game.* "I'm looking at a starting shortstop—a guy I'm paying $667,000 a year—who doesn't want to play half the damn games. I said, 'What's the matter with you? You're tired? Get your damn rest!'"[18]

Templeton had a reputation as a player that didn't always give his all, something that didn't sit well in St. Louis, whose fans are as knowledgeable as any in baseball. On that 1981 afternoon, he struck out in his first at-bat, and the fans started heckling him. According to Templeton, fans began shouting racial slurs[19] within earshot of Herzog and several Cardinals teammates, who did nothing about it. As Templeton headed back to the dugout, the taunts of the crowd got the best of him. "Garry turned to the fans, stuck his middle finger in the air, grabbed the family jewels and gave 'em a good hearty shake," wrote Herzog.[20]

Herzog grabbed Templeton and pulled him down the dugout steps, an incident captured on film by a *St. Louis Post Dispatch* photographer. The photo became infamous and it, along with Templeton's actions, spelled the end of his career in St. Louis. At that point, Garry Templeton was one of the top shortstops in baseball. A two-time All-Star, Templeton averaged 188 hits per season from 1977 through 1980. But Herzog valued defense at shortstop, and Templeton was lacking in that department. Over the same span he was averaging 188 hits, he was also among the league leaders in errors. Now, however, Herzog's problem was that the incident had made Templeton considerably more difficult to trade. Fortunately for Herzog, the San Diego Padres weren't happy with their current shortstop, or at least with his agent.

Ozzie Smith made the jump from the short-season Walla Walla Padres in the Northwest League in 1977 to the San Diego Padres starting shortstop in 1978, finishing second in the National League Rookie of the Year balloting behind Atlanta's Bob Horner. Smith was a premier defensive shortstop, but his bat left something to be desired. He hit just .211 in 1979 and followed that up with seasons of .230 in 1980 and .222 in 1981. He had incurred the wrath of Padres management by demanding, and getting, a no-trade clause in his contract and asking for a substantial

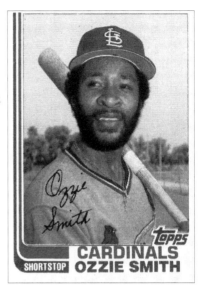

Figure 1: Shortstop Ozzie Smith was one of the keys to the Cardinals' season in 1982. He hit .248 and provided St. Louis with the kind of defense Whitey Herzog coveted. 1982 Topps® trading cards used courtesy of The Topps Company, Inc.

raise for 1982. At the 1981 winter meetings, a year after swinging the eleven-player deal with the Padres, Herzog struck up a conversation with San Diego general manager Jack McKeon.

"You still interested in Ozzie?" asked McKeon.

"What the hell, Jack," responded Herzog. "You told me he was untouchable."

"We still like Ozzie," replied McKeon. "It's his agent we are angry with. Everybody in the organization is pissed at him."[21]

Both teams made their starting shortstops the centerpiece of a six-player deal, but Smith invoked his no-trade clause and refused to go to St. Louis unless the Cardinals gave him a raise. The situation dragged on for more than a month before Herzog finally convinced Smith to accept the terms of the deal and offered an arbitration hearing to settle the contract situation.

"With the two Smiths (Lonnie and Ozzie) in the fold, I had completed what I'd set out to do 18 months earlier," wrote Herzog in his book *White Rat*. "Our starting lineup had only two players in it—George Hendrick and Keith Hernandez—who'd been there when I arrived. More importantly, we had 25 good guys on the club. It was a club that could win a pennant, and so I figured I'd end my career as a general manager. I had the team I wanted and if I couldn't win with it, I didn't want to have to fire myself."[22]

And so Herzog stepped down as general manager, allowing him to focus full-time on overtaking the new-look Phillies for supremacy in the National League East.

As the off-season wound down, there was still one big free-agent signing that everyone was anticipating. By 1982 Reggie Jackson was in the back half of his career, but it had been an amazing run. Jackson was the second overall selection in the 1966 draft and made his major-league debut the following season. From 1968 through 1975, he won an MVP, finished in the top five in MVP voting two other times, smashed 253 home runs, and helped the Oakland A's win three straight World Championships before being traded to the Baltimore Orioles prior to the 1976 season. *Sports Illustrated* once put Jackson's photo on the cover of their magazine under the tile "Superduperstar." The free-agent contract he signed prior to the 1977 season with the New York Yankees had expired, and his relationship with George Steinbrenner had soured to the point that George didn't want him back despite the tremendous numbers Jackson put up in New York. In five seasons in Yankee pin-stripes, he hit .280 with 183 homers and helped the Yankees win two World Series titles. Along the way Jackson provided one of the seminal moments in World Series history when he homered on three consecutive pitches in 1977 to bring New York their first World Series title since 1962. The performance earned him the moniker "Mr. October."

But it wasn't always a smooth ride. Jackson ruffled feathers immediately upon joining the Yankees when he was quoted in *Sport* magazine as saying that he, not All-Star catcher Thurman Munson, was "the straw that stirs the drink."[23] He had run-ins with teammates, the press, and with Steinbrenner. When Dave Winfield signed with the Yankees as a free agent prior to the 1981 season, Jackson offered some words of advice to his new teammate, saying New York "is the greatest place to play. It can be a lion's den, or it can be Disneyworld."[24] When asked if he and Winfield could coexist in the same city, Jackson replied, "I don't think it will be a problem. I'm sure they'll find a spot for both of us."[25]

The pair led New York to the World Series, where they lost to the Dodgers, but the Yankees outfield was getting crowded by January of 1982. Like Herzog in St. Louis, Steinbrenner wanted more team speed and brought in quick outfielders Dave Collins and Ken Griffey and the new emphasis on speed left Jackson in the dust. "We're not going to be the old put one out of the park big inning team anymore," said Steinbrenner. "It's not just the longball that puts them in the stands anymore. A running team is the toughest thing on an opposing pitcher, and it's exciting. I want the first five guys in our lineup to be burners."[26]

Reggie Jackson was a lot of things, but "burner" was not among them, and it became clear that he would not be returning to New York. He tested the free-agent waters, and three contenders quickly emerged: Atlanta, Baltimore, and California. Ever the showman, media mogul and Braves owner Ted Turner pulled out all the stops to entice Jackson, which included flying to New York to meet him on his home turf. Signing with the Braves was always a longshot, but Reggie couldn't pass up the opportunity to sit down with Turner, saying in his autobiography, "I basically wanted to see where the crazy ended, and the genius began."[27]

The pair met at Jim McMullen's, one of Jackson's favorite spots in Manhattan. Turner was already seated when Jackson arrived, and as the latter walked toward the table the chant started: "Reggie, Reggie, Reggie." But the chant was not coming from the other people in the restaurant. It was coming from Turner. When they were finished with dinner, Jackson said, "I don't know if I'm going to come work for you or not, but we've got to get together and do this more often. You're not a dull date."[28]

Press reports said Jackson was asking for a three-year deal worth about $2.4 million, but he insisted that money wasn't his primary concern, saying, "I don't have an asking price. I know what I want, but I still need to talk to each owner quite a bit. I just want what's commensurate with the upper crust."[29]

The upper crust at the time was somewhere in the neighborhood of Dave Winfield's annual $1.4 million 1981 contract and Mike Schmidt's $1.5 million 1982 contract, double what Jackson was asking. Jackson was no longer on that level, but he was still an elite player and, perhaps more importantly for the team that signed him, a box-office draw, which he summed up well in 1978 when he said, "There's no one who can put meat in the seats like I can."[30]

As negotiations progressed, Turner made Jackson a $100 million offer, but with a catch. "I told him I'd have to defer some of it," the Braves owner said. "I told him I'd give him a dollar a year for 100 million years. Or maybe $10 a year for 10 million years. But what the hell? He could still say he has the biggest contract in the history of sports. That's what everybody wants, right?"[31]

The $100 million offer was made in jest, but Turner was serious about his vision of a lineup with Jackson sandwiched between young sluggers Dale Murphy and Bob Horner. "It would be fun for the fans, for the TV viewers, for the writers, for our pitchers, for me, for management, for the ticket sellers, for the peanut vendors . . . I know Reggie hasn't had as much fun with any other owner as he's had with me. The other night when we met, we were laughing, giggling, singing, having cocktails, having a great time. It was like college recruiting."[32]

As enthusiastic as Turner was, the California Angels and Jackson's former team, the Baltimore Orioles, were the leaders in the Reggie sweepstakes. Staying in the American League East was appealing, especially the opportunity to play thirteen games against the Yankees. That was also something that George Steinbrenner was not thrilled about, and rumors swirled that he had talked to Jackson's agent to dissuade him from signing with Baltimore.

"I know George looks at us as his No. 1 enemy and chief rival," said Orioles general manager Hank Peters. "And I guess anything the Yankees can do to prevent us from strengthening ourselves, they would do."[33]

Jackson and his agent met with the Angels but couldn't get a deal done with general manager Buzzie Bavasi, so Reggie called team owner Gene Autry directly. "The Cowboy," as he was known, was one of the more respected owners in baseball *and* one of the most loved.

"Gene," Jackson recalled telling Autry, "I'm at a point in my life where I no longer care if I'm the highest-paid member of a team. I know you've got Fred Lynn and Rod Carew. I'm not here to put your salary structure through hoops."

"Reggie," said Autry, "that's music to these old ears."[34]

Jackson enjoyed the courting process, just as he had after becoming a free agent after 1976 and, ultimately, signing with the Yankees. But the prospect of returning to the state of California, where he enjoyed much of his early success with the A's, was enticing, and he ended up inking a four-year deal with the Angels worth just shy of $4 million plus incentives, including one based on the Angels reaching 2.4 million in home attendance. They drew just under 2.3 million in 1980,[35] but it seemed a safe bet that Mr. October's presence on the roster would more than make up the missing 100,000 paying customers, and not all to cheer the newest Angel. "A guy came in and bought 4 season tickets in the first row down in right field," said Bavasi. "We offered him better seats, but he didn't want them. He wanted to be in right field, to boo Reggie."[36]

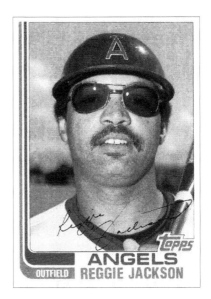

Figure 2: Reggie Jackson was one of the most sought-after free agents heading into 1982. His signing gave the Angels five former MVP winners in their everyday lineup. 1982 Topps® trading cards used courtesy of The Topps Company, Inc.

"From the standpoint of excitement and drawing power, Reggie and Pete Rose are in a class by themselves," said Autry when introducing Jackson. "I've long admired the way he hustles and handles himself, and while we already have a number of players who have been on championship teams, Reggie adds yet another dimension. His desire should rub off."[37]

The Los Angeles media wasn't convinced that Reggie's desire would make a difference on a team that had struggled for most of its existence and finished near the bottom of the American League in 1981. A *Los Angeles Times* headline under the story announcing Jackson's signing read, "Slugger Agrees to Four-Year Contract With Team That Doesn't Play in October."[38] *Times* columnist Bill Dwyre called the signing "the ultimate public relations gamble" and indicated that Jackson could either be the straw that stirs the drink or "the straw that breaks the camel's back."[39]

"At best, Jackson is an aging superstar who can generate enough new life and excitement . . . to keep the Angels interesting," he wrote. "At worst, Jackson is just plain aging, with . . . Bavasi and crew [giving] the public one more Packard at Mercedes prices."[40]

After Jackson signed with the Angels, *The Atlanta Constitution* ran a cartoon depicting Autry as a fisherman, a pouch of "Reggie Bait" on his hip, with a large fish attached to a fishing pole draped over his back, with the caption, "The One That Got Away." A forlorn Ted Turner stood in the background. But fans in Atlanta had something to take the sting out of losing Jackson when the National Baseball Hall of Fame announced their 1982 class. It contained just two members, but they were two of the best players in recent memory, Hank Aaron and Frank Robinson. Robinson began his career in Cincinnati, where he won Rookie of the Year honors in 1956 and an MVP award in 1962. Traded to Baltimore prior to the 1966 season, he won the MVP again and led the Orioles to World Series wins in 1966 and 1970. He capped his on-field career by being named the first African American manager in major-league history when he took over the Cleveland Indians as a player-manager in 1975.

Aaron spent nearly his entire career in a Braves uniform, first in Milwaukee and then in Atlanta. On April 8, 1974, Aaron passed Babe Ruth on the all-time home run list with 715 and ended his career back in Milwaukee with 755 career homers. Being the all-time home run king should ensure a slot in the Hall of Fame, but there were times when Aaron wasn't so sure.

"I kept reading where there were other things that went beyond what a person did on the field that were taken into consideration," Aaron said after the announcement. "When I heard that I got scared for the first time in my baseball career. If talking about records and what I accomplished between the lines, I don't see how anyone would not vote for me. I feel for the first time that what I did on the baseball field has been fully appreciated by the people I played against, the people I played with, and especially the sportswriters."[41]

One person who appreciated Aaron's accomplishments was a young comedian named David Letterman, who was about to begin a project that would define his career and change television. NBC was looking for someone to replace Tom Snyder as the host of the poorly rated *Tomorrow Show*, which aired immediately following *The Tonight Show Starring Johnny Carson*.

Letterman made multiple appearances on *The Tonight Show*, and Carson took a liking to the Indiana native whose TV career began as a local weatherman in Indianapolis. NBC had given Letterman an afternoon talk show in the summer of 1980, but it lasted just four months before being canceled. "David's got a certain flair, a certain style—a sly, offbeat approach to things that's really quite appealing," said Carson. "However, he wasn't right for daytime. I don't know, maybe it took too much attention on the part of the viewers to watch his show in the day-time but now that he's on late night I think he'll be successful."[42]

NBC was hoping Carson's intuition was correct, especially since they were paying Letterman a reported $1 million salary. On February 1, 1982, *Late Night with David Letterman* debuted with comedian Bill Murray as the first guest. Murray had established himself as one of Hollywood's biggest names, with hit comedies *Meatballs*, *Caddyshack*, and *Stripes* already on his résumé, but even those accomplishments paled in comparison to those of Hank Aaron, who made an appearance on the February 3 show. The nine-minute segment began with Letterman playing film of Aaron's record-breaking home run in 1974 and the baseball legend telling the story of getting a phone call from the White House during the game requesting he come to Washington to meet with President Richard Nixon. When Aaron asked Nixon when he should come to Washington, he was told as soon as possible.

"I didn't get there quick enough,"[43] Aaron said, alluding to Nixon's resignation four months later. Once Aaron finished his interview, and in a preview of the kind of comedy Letterman would offer viewers, NBC cameras followed him off set, where he ran a gauntlet of staffers offering congratulations, and through a set of doors where he was met by WNBC sports anchor Al Albert for a post-interview interview.

"Would you place him in the same league as a Carson and the others?"

"I've never been interviewed by Johnny Carson," replied Aaron. "But as far as I'm concerned David is on top."

"Never been interviewed," said Albert. "I guess that's why he's being called Scoop Letterman."[44]

Aaron's election to the Hall of Fame was the beginning of an amazing year for Braves fans and for baseball. An off-season that saw Whitey Herzog finish his reshaping of the Cardinals, Reggie Jackson join three other former MVP winners with the Angels, new ownership in Philadelphia, and big contracts handed out to big stars set the stage for an exciting regular season that would culminate in seven thrilling games come October.

2. SPRING TRAINING

Danger Is My Business

> I got some coke. Let's go back to the Marmont.
> —John Belushi

About ten hours after John Belushi asked Cathy Smith to go back to his hotel room in the early morning hours of March 5, 1982, he was found dead of a drug overdose in his bungalow at the Chateau Marmont, in Los Angeles. Coroners listed the official cause of death as "acute cocaine and heroin intoxication,"[1] the culmination of a days-long binge as the actor/comedian was battling depression and trying to revive his career. Belushi was born in Chicago in 1949 and was an original cast member of a new late-night NBC comedy show called *Saturday Night Live*, which first aired on October 11, 1975. The opening sketch of the series featured Belushi as an immigrant taking English lessons and repeating a series of bizarre sentences involving wolverines. The skit ends with the teacher grabbing his chest and dying of a heart attack. The good student Belushi then grabs his chest and dies as well. The show launched the careers of Chevy Chase, Dan Aykroyd, Gilda Radner, Jane Curtin, and others, but Belushi was the main attraction. During his four years on the show, he created memorable characters such as Samurai Futaba and Pete Dionisopoulos, the owner of the Greek restaurant that serves nothing but cheeseburgers, chips, fries, and Pepsi. His imitations of *Star Trek*'s Captain James T. Kirk, Henry Kissinger, and Ludwig van Beethoven were well received, but perhaps his most enduring character was Jake Blues, the ne'er-do-well half of the Blues Brothers. Teamed with Aykroyd, who played Jake's younger brother, Elwood, the Blues Brothers made their debut as a way to warm up the crowd before SNL shows. They were popular enough to make their way onto the show and eventually to the big screen as a follow-up to Belushi's smash box-office hit, *Animal House*. *The Blues Brothers* feature film debuted in the summer of 1980, and its success established Belushi as one of the biggest stars in Hollywood. But 1981 follow-up films *Continental Divide* and *Neighbors* flopped, leaving Belushi wondering if his career was over. The pressure of a failing movie career, coupled with his voracious appetites and the prevalence of drugs in Los Angeles, proved fatal for Belushi.

"The temptation may be to hold back on any extreme praise of Mr. Belushi considering the apparent brevity of his career," said the *Chicago Tribune*. "But if one were to total the hundreds of live appearances he made at Chicago's Second City comedy theater and add the dozens of *Saturday Night Live* television shows, it could be argued that John Belushi truly was a major comic actor of his time."[2]

In his third season on *Saturday Night Live*, Belushi appeared in a short film called "Don't Look Back in Anger," which, in retrospect, is both poignant and incredibly ironic. In it, he plays an elderly man, the sole survivor visiting the graves of all his former SNL colleagues. Belushi's character mentions that Garrett Morris died of a heroin overdose and that Bill Murray outlasted all of them, living to the age of 38. But one line stands above the rest. As Belushi enters the cemetery, walking with a cane, he turns to the camera and says, "They all thought I'd be the first to go. I was one of those live fast, die young, leave a good lookin' corpse types, ya' know?"[3]

Unfortunately, drug problems were not limited to the entertainment world in the early 1980s. By 1982, recreational drugs, especially cocaine, had made their way into major-league clubhouses, and the fallout would be far-reaching, culminating with the Pittsburgh drug trials in 1985, a scandal that ensnared some big names in major-league baseball, including stars like Keith Hernandez and Dave Parker, both of whom were suspended by then-commissioner Peter Ueberroth, although the suspensions were commuted in exchange for fines and community service.

Less than ten miles from the Chateau Marmont sat Dodger Stadium, home of the 1981 World Series champions, and, befitting their Hollywood roots, their training camp had plenty of drama beginning with their superstar pitcher, Fernando Valenzuela, who wanted a new contract. Valenzuela made his Dodgers debut in 1980 and secured a spot in the L.A. rotation out of spring training in 1981. By season's end he was the biggest attraction in baseball. Not since Mark Fidrych in 1976 had a rookie pitcher drawn so much attention. Valenzuela went 8–0 in his first eight starts with an ERA of just 0.50, and Fernandomania had begun, much to the delight of Dodgers management. Eleven of his twelve home starts were sellouts, and road attendance when he was on the mound grew by an average of more than fourteen thousand extra fans.[4]

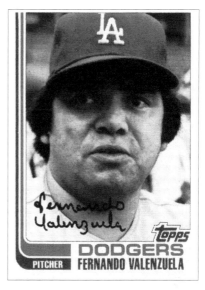

Figure 3: After having led the Dodgers to their first World Series title since 1965, Dodgers pitcher Fernando Valenzuela was looking for a raise in 1982, but the negotiations turned ugly. 1982 Topps® trading cards used courtesy of The Topps Company, Inc.

After finishing the year with a 13–7 record, Fernando went 3–1 in the postseason, helped Los Angeles win a World Series, and took home both the Rookie of the Year Award and the National League Cy Young Award. Now he and his agent, Tony DeMarco, wanted a contract befitting one of the game's top players. "I want Valenzuela to be associated with greatness," said DeMarco. "That's my mission. And the first thing associated with greatness is a lot of money, even if he doesn't need it."[5] The Dodgers offered a salary of $300,000, a sizable raise from the $42,000 he made the year before. But DeMarco insisted Valenzuela was worth more and advised his client not to report to Vero Beach when the Dodgers opened spring training. The stalemate dragged on until March 1, when the Dodgers, following MLB rules, renewed Valenzuela's contract for one year at $350,000. He had a contract, but he still wasn't in camp.

"We tried hard to sign Fernando, and we have made a number of very fair offers," said team owner Peter O'Malley. "Many proposals were exchanged and considered, but we were unable to persuade Fernando's representatives how unrealistic their contract demands are. Our only alternative is to renew Fernando's contract."[6]

While many of his Dodger teammates supported Valenzuela's efforts, media reaction varied. The *Los Angeles Times* published dueling columns from Scott Ostler and Jim Murray, with each taking a side. Ostler wrote:

> All he did was almost single-armedly pitch the Dodgers into the World Series, which the Dodgers won." He also generated a lot of positive publicity and millions of ticket sales for baseball. All in all, a swell season.
>
> Now this youngster is trying to hit up the Dodgers for $1,000,000, and you're steamed . . . because he didn't even have the decency to wait until the national unemployment rate hits zero again and everyone is eating well and paying their bills.
>
> But I guess you expect Fernando to defend what's left of baseball's fiscal sanity by taking the Dodgers first offer.[7]

Murray came out blazing against Fernando, saying:

> Unemployment is rising. Auto plants are going belly up. Stocks are taking nosedives. Financial institutions are failing. Welfare is being cut back. America is in big trouble.
>
> And a kid from Mexico with little or no formal education, a noncitizen who cannot speak the language, wants $1.4 million a year for a job where he works only every 4th day and then no more than an hour and a half. And he usually requires a backup to come in and finish the job for him.

But then Murray shifted his tone when he wrote, "I'll tell you who's at fault. We are. Particularly we press boxers who cover outfield flies for a living. We created this golem. . . . The Dodgers . . . had always dreamed of getting a good Spanish speaking ballplayer. Then, it came to a shuddering stop. They put the guitars away and the Fiesta was over when it was contract time. Fernando came to the table with no cards and few chips."[8]

Murray's assessment was dead-on. Despite his on-field success, Valenzuela had no leverage. According to Major League Baseball's rules, a first- or second-year player's contract could be renewed without the player's signature for one year. His choice was to sit out the season or report and earn a substantial raise.

While the Dodgers were preparing to defend their World Series title, their longtime rivals, the Cincinnati Reds, were still angry about not qualifying for the 1981 postseason, despite posting the best record in baseball. Like the Dodgers, the Reds were a team in transition. Entering spring training, just three of the starting eight players from the Big Red Machine, Johnny Bench, Dave Concepcion, and George Foster, remained, and Foster wanted out. From 1975 through 1981, no one in baseball drove in more runs than Foster's 749, and only Mike Schmidt had more home runs than Foster's 221. Foster was one of the top run producers in the game, and he wanted to be paid accordingly, something Cincinnati was not known for doing. Since winning back-to-back World Series titles in 1975 and 1976, the Reds had either traded many of their best (that is, most expensive) players, or simply let them walk away via free agency. Gone were future Hall of Famers Tony Pérez and Joe Morgan, as well as Pete Rose, César Gerónimo, and Ken Griffey.

Foster had one year left on a contract that paid him $800,000 per season, and he wanted a new deal. The Reds could either pay him, trade him, or let him play out his contract and receive a free-agent compensation pick, a system in which teams losing players via free agency could select a "replacement" from a pool of available players. None of the options were appealing and none, save making Foster one of baseball's highest-paid players, would make the Reds a better team. A trade seemed the logical solution, but the return was unlikely to match what they would give up.

"There is no player available on another team who can give the Reds what Foster gives them," said the *Cincinnati Enquirer*. "Foster and perhaps three or four other men are in a salary category of their own. It's a category that has been created by the market, not the players."[9] That market dictated that Foster would be a very rich man, so the Reds began shopping their slugging left fielder. Reds president Dick Wagner needed a catcher since Bench moved to third base to save wear and tear on his knees. Joe Nolan assumed the catching duties for the Reds, and, while he'd hit .309, that average came with just one home run and 26 RBI. On top of that, Nolan had thrown out just 15 percent of would-be base stealers. Wagner had been interested in a young Mets catcher named Alex Trevino since 1979, and the Mets had a new ownership group looking for a marquee player. They'd lost out to the cross-town Yankees for Dave Winfield and didn't want to come up short again. Foster provided the Reds a list of teams from which he was willing to accept a deal, and the Mets were on it. It was a perfect fit. Shortly before spring training began, the Reds agreed to send Foster to the Mets for Trevino and a pair of relief pitchers. The Mets gave Foster a new five-year contract worth $10 million, a price the Reds simply could not afford to pay.

"The wonderful world of $ports, with it$ $tellar athlete$, ju$t doe$n't have that old team $pirit when it comes to a$$isting Pre$ident Reagan $tem inflation," wrote David Condon in the *Chicago Tribune*.

> It'$ obvious$ that $tandout$ in $port have it much better than, $ay, the worker$ laid off by the automobile companie$, or the $enior citizen$ who have life $aving$ invested in the $tock of those automobile companie$. It'$ even a cinch bet that Tom Reich, the agent who negotiated Foster'$ contract with the Met$, ha$ a much better deal than the aforementioned $enior citizen$. Reich, a$ well a$ George Fo$ter, his client, al$o ha$ a better deal than you fan$ who will be the one$ really paying for the e$calated $alarie$.[10]

* * * * *

The Atlanta Braves also had a big-name player seeking a new contract. Bob Horner was one of the game's most-feared sluggers . . . when he was in the lineup. Unfortunately for him, and the Braves, it was not often enough. After missing nearly forty games in each of the last three years, the main goal for Horner for 1982 was to play a full season.

"In 1979, I broke my ankle in the first game of the season and missed six or seven weeks," Horner told *Baseball Digest*. "The year before last, I had a little problem with Ted [Turner] . . . I would like to stay healthy and play in 150 games."[11]

The "little problem with Ted" was an ugly incident at the beginning of 1980. Horner began the year by going 2-for-35 and, on April 20, Turner decided he should be sent to Triple-A Richmond. Horner had never spent a day in the minor leagues since the Braves drafted him first overall out of Arizona State in 1978, and the fact that he had hit .314 with 33 homers in 1979 was seemingly irrelevant. The move did not sit well with Horner, who refused to report to Richmond.

"If I felt there was any justification for being sent down to the minors, I would go," he said. "But when everyone calls me—fans, friends, teammates, high level people in the front office—and tells me that it's just Ted going a little wacko again, it confirms what I already know. Ted Turner's a jerk, an absolute jerk."[12]

"I don't want to punish him. That's ridiculous," said Turner. "I've even been thinking of offering to go with him to the minors. If I was vindictive, why did I give him a three-year, $1 million contract? I didn't have to do that. It's me and the Atlanta Braves who are being punished for Mr. Horner's terrible play."[13]

Horner battled slumps and injuries again in the 1981 season and asked for a trade, but his feelings toward the organization improved when new manager Joe Torre, who replaced Bobby Cox, made Horner just the third team captain in Atlanta Braves history, following in the footsteps of Hall of Famers Hank Aaron and Eddie Mathews.

"It might put him over the hump," said shortstop Jerry Royster, Horner's close friend. "It could be the one move that gets the best out of him. He's the kind of guy who needs a vote of confidence. And it's the only honor I know of that has come from management—for anybody—since I have been here."[14]

Coming off a strong finish to 1981, Horner was hoping to contribute to a winning team and set himself up for a new contract. His agent, Bucky Woy, felt Horner should be paid commensurate with other big names who got new deals in the off-season: "I don't think anyone would trade Horner for Foster or [Gary] Carter. [Mike] Schmidt, yeah, but not the other two. If Bob has a good year, we figure we can get seven figures in arbitration."[15]

The Braves' chances of re-signing Horner were not helped by the fact that, in addition to Turner's run-in with him, there was also bad blood between Turner and Woy. Atlanta general manager Bill Lucas passed away in 1979 while the Braves were negotiating Horner's last contract, and Turner had told the media that negotiating with Woy played a part in Lucas's death.

"I don't want Bucky Woy coming around my organization and killing anyone else," Turner said after Lucas died. "In my opinion Bucky Woy is guilty of manslaughter. If Horner doesn't fire Woy he'll get only the bare minimum from the Braves for five years."[16]

Woy had clients in baseball and football and was developing a reputation as a tough negotiator. That reputation no doubt led to Turner's comments, which then led to Woy filing a $17 million libel suit against the Braves owner. "He told the press that I killed Bill Lucas, who died an untimely death of an aneurysm right as we were going to arbitration," said Woy, "and that [new Braves general manager] John Mullen should take out insurance, and that if there was a pay scale for agents I wouldn't qualify."[17]

Such was the backdrop against which Horner's contract negotiations, and season, were set. But Horner was not the only Braves player with contract difficulties. Center fielder Dale Murphy seemed poised for a big year in 1981 after hitting .281 with 33 home runs in 1980. But the six-foot-four California native took a big step backward in 1981. His average slipped to .247, and his home run total fell to 13. Dale Murphy had something to prove in 1982.

"I'm upset with myself for last year," Murphy told the *Sporting News*. "Not for the year I had, but the way I had it. Not being selective, like the year before and the year before that. I know I struck out a lot last year and I remember taking a lot of pitches that were strikes."[18]

"Last year, Murph took a lot of pitches, and when he swung, it wasn't an aggressive swing," said teammate Claudell Washington. "He just sort of waved through the ball. I thought he was hurt last year. Maybe his hand, maybe his back, something."[19] Murphy wasn't injured, he was confused. At times he tried to pull every pitch to left field, and at others he tried to hit everything to the opposite field. The approach made him tentative at the plate, and the more he struggled, the more pressure he put on himself.

"We wouldn't be scoring," Murphy said. "It would be the seventh inning, and (I) would say 'I'd better hit a home run.' I get the feeling we're going to do a lot of things this year that take the pressure off to hit a home run."[20]

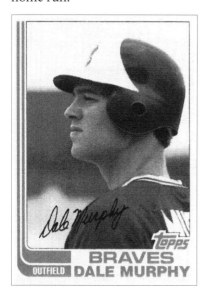

Figure 4: Dale Murphy entered 1982 with something to prove. He spent the next two seasons silencing his doubters. 1982 Topps® trading cards used courtesy of The Topps Company, Inc.

"Almost every prediction of progress by the 1982 Braves is based on the premise that Horner and Murphy will bounce back," wrote Tim Tucker in the *Atlanta Constitution*. "There are many keys to this team—the starting pitching, the shortstop, the leadoff batter, the bench—but the lock will not turn unless Horner and Murphy produce."[21]

In the National League East, despite the Mets and Braves stealing off-season headlines, the Montreal Expos were the team to beat. After being eliminated in heartbreaking fashion in the final weekend of the season in both 1979 and 1980, Montreal finally won a division title in 1981. But after taking the second half title and dispatching the defending champion Phillies in the first round of the playoffs, the Expos had their hearts broken again. Rick Monday's ninth-inning solo home run off Steve Rogers in Game Five of the National League Championship Series gave the Dodgers a 2–1 win and a berth in the World Series. Still, the Expos were loaded with talent and were picked by many to win a World Series title.[22]

"The Expos have a nucleus of Gary Carter, Andre Dawson, Tim Raines, and the most solid four-man pitching rotation in the division," write Rick Hummel in the *St. Louis Post Dispatch*. "All are 28 years old or under, with the exception of pitcher Steve Rogers, 32. Dawson, for one, may just be coming into his prime at 27."[23]

At six foot three and 195 pounds, Dawson was developing into one of the game's top players. The Miami native slipped to the eleventh round of the 1975 draft in part due to a knee injury, but he spent fewer than 200 games in the minor leagues before winning the Rookie of the Year Award in 1977. Over his next five full seasons, Dawson hit .282 and averaged 22 home runs, 76 RBI, and 29 stolen bases.

"Dawson has all the ingredients of the best players in the game today," said Pittsburgh Pirates manager Chuck Tanner. "There is no sense comparing him to anyone else because he's the best. You compare others to him."[24]

Flanking the All-Star center fielder was one of the most exciting young players in the game in Tim Raines. The twenty-two-year-old left fielder was named Minor League Player of the Year in 1980 by the *Sporting News*, and the Expos thought enough of him to let outfielder Ron LeFlore depart via free agency. LeFlore's 97 stolen bases in 1980 led the National League, but the production came with baggage. He angered manager Dick Williams by sometimes showing up to the stadium just before game time leveling accusations of racism against teammates and the city of Montreal. Upset by what he felt was the lack of support for himself and other Black players in All-Star balloting, LeFlore said, "This town is 80, 90% white. Regardless of how many Blacks are on the team, you still feel like you're a nigger here."[25]

But the final straw may have come when LeFlore offered an analysis of his teammates, saying, "Some of these guys are from the South and all southerners are rednecks. They've been brought up to hate niggers."[26]

"The nucleus of this team has been together for four years," said Rogers. "If suddenly there's any racial tension, consider the source."[27]

By the following spring training "the source" was gone, and the move immediately paid off, as Raines made an instant impact. In Montreal's first game of 1981, he drew a leadoff walk from Pirates starter Jim Bibby and stole second on the next pitch. Pittsburgh catcher Steve Nicosia's throw bounced and skipped into right field, allowing Raines to score. Raines never stopped running and finished second behind Valenzuela in the Rookie of the Year balloting on the strength of a .304 batting average and a National League-leading 71 stolen bases. His pace was enough for many to believe Raines had a legitimate shot at breaking Lou Brock's single-season record of 118 steals, set in 1974. Among the believers was Montreal first-base coach Steve Boros, who said Raines had "the fastest start from first base of any base stealer I've ever seen. That includes Lou Brock, Maury Wills, and Willie Wilson. Tim is very knowledgeable about pitchers. I watch them very closely, but he picks up on a lot of things I don't. His instincts are simply amazing."[28]

As potent as Dawson and Raines were, the heart of the Expos lay behind the plate. From 1977 through 1981, Gary Carter caught nearly 90 percent of the Expos games while batting .268 and averaging 24 homers and 80 RBI per season. The California native, who grew up dreaming of being a quarterback at UCLA, was now the best catcher in the majors. The Expos rewarded him with a new contract, extending his existing deal to eight years and $15 million. Carter's new salary was so shockingly large in the eyes of Expos team president John McHale that he refused to pose for photos with the starting catcher at the press conference. But business was business, and McHale knew it.

"The system is driving the clubs to do this," McHale said. "One question we had to ask ourselves was, 'Can we win a championship without him?' The answer is obviously no. So, we had to pay the price."[29]

Carter weighed the options of signing a long-term deal. He was smart enough to realize that the way salaries were exploding he'd likely be underpaid when his deal expired. But he also knew he was a catcher and that a home plate collision or other injury could limit, or even end, his future earning power if he signed a short-term deal. "The feeling of security is common on our club," Carter said. "In addition to probably having the best talent, that's another reason we expect to win everything this year. The media is predicting we will, and we believe we will. All of us are wrapped up in contracts. Now we can go out and play without worry.[30]

"The Expos appear to be interested in keeping the nucleus of a good club together," said staff ace Steve Rogers. "For the solidarity of that club, it will be a good thing to have Carter catching—and happy. It will be easier to win with him than without him, that's for sure."[31]

But while Carter and the Expos were heavy favorites to win the division, the Phillies and Pirates were still the class of the division. Philadelphia had arguably the game's best player in third baseman Mike Schmidt, coming off back-to-back MVP seasons, as well as Pete Rose and Steve Carlton. Rose was coming off a 1981 season in which he hit .325 and led the National League in hits. But he would also turn forty-one years old in April and was hampered in spring training by a back injury. Carlton was thirty-seven, as was closer Tug McGraw, who was also coming off elbow surgery and wouldn't be ready for the start of the season. The Phillies still had talent, but there were questions as to whether the window had closed on this group.

Across the Keystone State, the 1979 World Series Champion Pittsburgh Pirates still featured Willie Stargell and Dave Parker, but Stargell hadn't been a regular contributor since 1979 when he shared MVP honors with Keith Hernandez. Parker led the National League in batting average, hits, and doubles in 1977, followed that up with an MVP season in 1978, and helped lead Pittsburgh to a championship in 1979. But even then, Pirates fans did not seem to appreciate him. Things began to go south in 1980, a year after Parker signed a five-year $5 million contract. Injuries mounted, his weight ballooned, his production went down, and the Pirates fans turned on him. By the spring of 1982 Parker wanted out, and the Pirates were more than willing to accommodate him. The only question was where he would land, and the rumored destinations and deals were plentiful. Maybe he was headed to the Yankees along with Jason Thompson for a package including Bob Watson and Ken Griffey, or off to Montreal for Scott Sanderson, or to Texas in a package that would return Al Oliver to Pittsburgh. Houston was interested; so were Toronto and Philadelphia.

"I think it might be in the best interest of Dave Parker, the Pirates, and the fans in Pittsburgh that we trade Parker," general manager Pete

Peterson told the *Sporting News*. "I want to emphasize we won't give Parker away."[32]

When a deal failed to materialize, Tanner lashed out at Parker's agent, Tom Reich, saying he was a disruptive influence on the Pirates and the trade talk was a distraction. "I think Reich should do his job, get the players signed, then get the hell out of here," said Tanner.[33]

"I'm surprised and disappointed because Chuck Tanner is generally a class act," Reich fired back. "Dave Parker . . . has one career. Chuck Tanner doesn't have to worry about Dave Parker when his career is over. I can't understand why suddenly I'm the bad guy. In 1978, when Dave could have become a free agent, I used my influence to keep him in Pittsburgh."[34]

Despite all the rumors and all the angry rhetoric, Parker remained a Pirate throughout the spring. "I'd say it's 99.9 percent certain that we will not trade Dave Parker," Peterson told the *Sporting News* for their April 10 issue.[35] It was shaping up to be an uncomfortable summer at Three Rivers Stadium.

There was one other team in the NL East that seemed to be getting some attention, though not a lot of respect. "St. Louis' title hopes are shaky because the Cards have almost a one-man pitching staff in reliever Bruce Sutter," wrote George Cunningham in the *Atlanta Constitution*.[36] The Cardinals pitching staff certainly was a question mark with former twenty-game-winner Bob Forsch heading an unimpressive starting rotation. Just three of the projected members of that rotation, Forsch, Bob Shirley, and Joaquin Andújar, had ever won ten or more games in a season. Lary Sorensen, who led the team in starts with twenty-three in 1981, was gone in the Lonnie Smith deal, as was Silvio Martinez, who started sixteen games in 1981. But Whitey Herzog finally had the team he wanted, a team perfectly suited for his home ballpark.

"Everybody says we lead the league in hitting, but nothing else," Herzog said. "We won't lead the league in hitting this year. But we will lead it in stolen bases, saves, and wins."[37]

To boost the running game, Herzog brought in a former minor league teammate, Dick Tettelbach, as a baserunning instructor. Tettelbach went to Yale, where he played with then Vice President George Bush, before making his major-league debut with the Yankees in 1955. He was later dealt to the Washington Senators for the 1956 season, along with three others and a player to be named later, who turned out to be Herzog.

"He was a big guy, about 200 pounds, but he was a hell of a baserunner," said Herzog of Tettelbach, "a very intelligent person. He stole 77 bases at Joplin before base stealing was the 'in' thing."[38]

"We had too many guys last year—fast guys—who didn't score from second with two outs," Herzog said. "I want Dick to go around and watch each player and then take them aside and talk to them. I want him at all the games for a while to observe. We need to work on leads and moving instinctively. If we can win two or three games by doing that, we're that much better off."[39]

That aggressiveness was on full display in the Cardinals spring training opener against the Houston Astros. St. Louis stole six bases, including one by third-string catcher Glenn Brummer, in seven attempts, in a 5–4, 11-inning win. "They aren't going to learn to run if they don't run here," said Herzog.[40]

The other big story of the Cardinals spring opener was the performance of outfielder David Green, the centerpiece of the seven-player deal with the Brewers at the 1980 winter meetings. Green went 3-for-4, stole three bases, drove in a run, scored two, and stretched a single into a double. "He's just got it," said Tommy Thompson, Green's Triple-A manager in 1981. "I wouldn't say he's a superstar yet, but he's got the potential to be a superstar."[41]

Superstar or not, Green was ticketed for Triple-A. The St. Louis outfield was set with veteran George Hendrick in right field, Dane Iorg in left, and newcomer Lonnie Smith in center. Freed from Philadelphia, where he never felt he was appreciated, Smith welcomed the chance for a fresh start.

"I never felt like I was in their plans," Smith told reporters. "The only reason I played the last month [of the 1981 season] was because Dallas Green had gotten mad at Garry Maddox. I don't want to be used that way. I want to be used because I'm needed."[42]

The knock on Smith was his defense, specifically his arm strength and staying on his feet. He earned the nickname "Skates" because he frequently fell down in the outfield. Prior to trading for him, a Cardinals scout wrote Smith was "More than adequate defensively, but he slips once a game."[43]

If David Green impressed in the Cardinals' first spring game, Smith opened some eyes in the second contest when he fell four times in the outfield and almost had a fly ball hit him in the head. Herzog wasn't concerned. With speed at the top and the bottom of the lineup, he was excited to turns his guys loose on the basepaths. Whitey-Ball was ready to debut.

* * * * *

"We're very pleased with the court's decision," said Fleer president Don Peck. "We've felt from day one that Topps and the players association were in violation of antitrust laws."[44]

The ruling handed down by US district judge Clarence C. Newcomer in Philadelphia on July 1, 1980, ended the twenty-five-year stranglehold the Topps Chewing Gum Company had on the baseball card market. The company had held exclusive rights to produce baseball cards featuring player photos since 1966, when Fleer sold its existing contracts to Topps. The contract came with a noncompetition agreement, and, once it expired, Fleer, the maker of Double Bubble Chewing Gum, decided it wanted back into the game and sued. Topps argued that the cards were simply a marketing tool to entice consumers to purchase their gum rather than that of a competitor, but Newcomer disagreed, saying that concept was "outdated."[45] Kids didn't buy Topps gum over another brand because they came with baseball cards. They bought baseball cards that came with gum, and Newcomer recognized that in his decision. "For decades [baseball cards] have been an important and distinctive part of many childhoods," he wrote. "The permanence of those cardboard pictures is a market reality that the court must recognize. A baseball card consumer . . . knows if he has not yet found Dave Winfield, Keith Hernandez, Robin Yount, or Ron Guidry. Baseball cards are the only product on a typical candy rack to set forth baseball statistics. They are, in other words, an education in baseball."

Newcomer's ruling stated that Topps and the Major League Baseball Players Association had to grant at least one other card manufacturer publishing rights by 1981, and both Fleer and Donruss, the former manufacturer of Little Leaguer Chewing Tobacco Bubble Gum, quickly signed contracts. But the two companies were under a severe time crunch, and it showed in their initial offerings in 1981. Both the Fleer and Donruss cards were riddled with errors. Player names were misspelled, statistics were incorrect, and many of the photos were blurry or of otherwise poor quality, including a few Donruss bought from a young photographer named Keith Olbermann.[46] Topps appealed Newcomers' ruling in the summer of 1981 and won, but Fleer appealed and the case was eventually put in front of the Supreme Court, which ruled in Topps's favor. But the contract Topps signed with players had a loophole. The contracts restricted Major League Baseball players from appearing on any other card brand packaged alone or with candy. They did not, however, restrict players from appearing on cards packaged with other items, so Fleer and Donruss simply stopped including gum with their baseball cards. For 1982 Fleer included stickers while Donruss included puzzle pieces that, when collected and assembled, featured a painting of Babe Ruth done by noted baseball artist Dick Perez. But the puzzle wasn't Perez's only contribution to Donruss. Beginning in 1982, Perez painted a portrait of one player per team in a subset called "Diamond Kings" that were included in packs of cards. Perez had been working with the Phillies since 1972 and had also formed a relationship with the Baseball Hall of Fame with his business partner Frank Steele. Like most kids in the 1950s, Perez grew up collecting baseball cards, and the artwork on the early Topps offerings left an impression on him.

"Donruss was a division of Nestle and they got a license, but they knew nothing about baseball cards," said Perez. "They got (*New York Daily News* writer) Bill Madden to write the backs of the cards and Bill knew our work and suggested they call us because we might have design ideas. Frank and I started talking and we thought, 'Let's bring art back to baseball cards.'"[47]

The initial "Diamond Kings" set featured Pete Rose as card Number 1, but with only one player represented per team the choices were not always easy, particularly when factoring in the time it took to produce each piece. "By the middle of the [1981] season I had to get started painting to get them produced. Frank was looking at the stats, and we knew that we had to represent every team. There were times when there were . . . thin achievements, like John Mayberry for Toronto in 1981. It wasn't the best year anybody had [.218 with ten homers], but he had the best year on that team. I didn't hear anything from anybody at the time other than that Donruss noticed that it helped sales."[48]

Sales of baseball cards were brisk and Topps's fear of losing their monopoly was offset by the rise in popularity of card collecting. The hobby was exploding, with some estimating that card collectors numbered as many as 250,000 strong in the United States.[49] Publications like *Baseball Digest* and the *Sporting News* routinely featured ads hawking baseball cards, both old and new. "The business is as good or better than it was last year," said Larry Fritsch, a Wisconsin collector and owner of one of the largest card dealerships in the country. "With all the new sets out, there is a multitude of stuff available. People still set aside so many dollars out of their paycheck for recreation and obviously, baseball card collecting is included."[50]

With that explosion in popularity came an influx of people who collected not for the love of the hobby but as an investment, and there were multiple publications that featured updated prices on individual cards. Among them were *Baseball Hobby News* and *Card Prices Update*, run by Mark Lewis. "Some people buy our paper like the *Wall Street Journal* to see how much they made this month," said Lewis. "What you buy now—and I'd write this in blood—will triple or quadruple in the next ten years. It's a tremendous investment. I hate to use that word, but other people do."[51] Lewis's prediction would prove false as companies realized collectors were hoarding cards as an investment and kept printing more and more. By the middle of the 1980s, the increase in card production, and the increase in companies producing cards, gave collectors more options but less value.

* * * * *

Since taking over for Hank Bauer midway through the 1968 season, Baltimore Orioles manager Earl Weaver had won at least a hundred games in a season five times, along with three American League pennants and a World Series championship in 1970. As the Birds manager, Weaver utilized the platoon system with great success and was an early adopter of data rather than "gut feelings" in the decision-making process. Along the way, he had become famous for his on-field battles with umpires and off-field battles with pitcher Jim Palmer. Now, at age fifty-two, he was on his way out, though many thought he would be back.

"Earl has told us this is his last year," said Baltimore general manager Hank Peters. "We respect his decision and we're taking him at his word, but whether it will really be his last year remains to be seen. I think maybe he needs a sabbatical, not retirement. Sometimes, you need a year or two off to recharge the batteries. Earl's too young to talk about early retirement."[52]

The Baltimore lineup was mostly set entering Weaver's final season. Switch-hitting first baseman Eddie Murray was a bona-fide star and anchored the batting order. He won the Rookie of the Year in 1977 and in the following four years finished eleventh in the MVP balloting in his *worst* season, 1979, a year in which he hit .295 with 25 home runs and 99 RBI.

But under Weaver, the Orioles were best known for their pitching. He'd had at least one twenty-game winner in each of his twelve full seasons at the helm, highlighted by his 1971 staff, which featured four in Dave McNally, Mike Cuellar, Pat Dobson, and Palmer. Weaver's final season was no exception, as his projected rotation of Palmer, Dennis Martinez, Mike Flanagan, and Scott McGregor had a combined career record of 463–282 with four Cy Young Awards.

There was, however, one big change in the Baltimore lineup for 1982, and it was one Weaver wasn't happy about. Doug DeCinces had the unenviable task of taking over for Brooks Robinson at third base in 1976 and had performed well in his six seasons at the hot corner. But the Orioles felt they had a better option in the form of twenty-one-year-old Cal Ripken Jr., a second-round draft pick in 1978 and the son of Baltimore third-base coach Cal Ripken Sr. The plan was for Ripken to play third base and move DeCinces to left field or trade him, but Weaver was having none of it. He wanted DeCinces at third and Ripken at short. The idea of having three infielders, (DeCinces, Ripken, and Murray) with 20+ home run power was enticing for Weaver, and he insisted that was how it was going to go in 1982. There was only one person who could overrule Weaver, and that was team owner Edward Bennett Williams. Williams was a successful attorney in Washington, DC, whose client list included Frank Sinatra, Jimmy Hoffa, and would-be assassin John Hinckley Jr. Williams purchased controlling interest in the Orioles in August of 1979, which proved to be very bad timing. Less than two years into his tenure the Major League Baseball Players Association went on strike, and DeCinces was one of the union representatives.

"I had a good relationship with Williams," said DeCinces. "He thought (the strike) was crazy. He didn't agree with what management was pursuing in their effort to take away free agency and was constantly calling me for updates. He'd fly me down from New York to have dinner to bring him up to speed and then I'd end up going home in the evening and then taking a train the next morning to go back to New York."[53]

When the strike was settled, DeCinces said Williams stopped speaking to him. Union reps aren't the most popular players with team owners, especially after a work-stoppage, and, not coincidentally, two of the four lead player reps, Bob Boone and Mark Belanger, found themselves in a new uniform the following year. DeCinces soon joined them when he was sent to the Angels for outfielder Dan Ford.

"When the trade finally came through, I knew [it was] because I was the head of the Players Association and Williams didn't want me around anymore," said DeCinces. "Of the four league guys, the only one who didn't get traded was Steve Rogers because he was Cy Young. Three days [later] there was a conflict with Dan Ford and the Angels about their ability to trade him. Williams called me. It was the first time he'd called me since the strike. He said, 'Doug I just want you to know there's a lot of things going on and if this trade doesn't work out, you're my starting third baseman.'"

"You know, Mr. Williams, let's stop kidding each other," DeCinces responded. "I know for a fact why I got traded. I did nothing but speak honestly to you during the entire process. I'm here to tell you, you'd better make that trade go through because I'm never going to play for you."[54]

The deal was eventually consummated, and DeCinces joined Boone in California, with Ripken taking over third base duties in Baltimore. It was the end of a somewhat familial relationship between DeCinces and the Ripkens. In 1972, DeCinces was in Double-A Asheville, North Carolina, trying to reach the big leagues, and Ripken Sr. was his manager. Before a game one day, DeCinces and Cal Jr. were playing catch when shots rang out.

"There was some kid outside the stadium on a hill with a high-powered rifle," DeCinces said. "I heard this bam on his first shot and saw the bullet sail right by me. On the second shot, I saw the grass fly up right in front of us. I grabbed Cal and we both dove right into the dugout. Cal's dad has been my manager in the minors and my coach with the Orioles. You could say I know the family."[55]

"In one sense it's kind of hard to see Doug go," the younger Ripken said. "He was the one player above all others who paid attention to me in the minors, and I know how much he was part of Baltimore. I would rather replace someone else. On the other hand, I realized that if Doug didn't go, I don't play. Sometimes you've got to look out for yourself. I'm kind of happy because of the opportunity. I feel a lot more confident knowing it's [third base] really kind of my position."[56]

The stability of the Orioles roster was in stark contrast to that of the defending AL champion Yankees. After falling to the Dodgers in the World Series, Yankees owner George Steinbrenner promised changes, and they came in the form of a new offensive philosophy. The 1982 Yankees would abandon power and embrace the running game. Steinbrenner brought in Ken Griffey to replace Reggie Jackson in right field and acquired Griffey's Cincinnati teammate Dave Collins to play first base, bumping the slower Bob Watson to the bench. With a lineup that already had second baseman Willie Randolph and outfielder Jerry Mumphrey, the Go-Go Yankees were complete, and Randolph was excited to be part of it.

"Those are always tougher teams to beat," he said. "The ones who run a lot and force mistakes. We have four or five guys who can run and steal bases. We may steal 200 bases this year if we run a lot."[57]

But the question surrounding the team was not how many bases they could steal but if they could win without Jackson. The hope was the speedsters at the top of the lineup would provide added opportunities for the guys in the middle of the order, but Weaver wasn't so sure, saying, "I know one thing. There's a certain fella named George Herman, also known as Babe, turning over in his grave today."[58]

In addition to a new philosophy, the Yankees also had a new team captain, a position left vacant after the 1979 death of catcher Thurman Munson. Just before spring training began, Steinbrenner introduced third baseman Graig Nettles as his new captain. Like many Yankees, Nettles had his problems with Steinbrenner in the past, especially around contract negotiations. But Nettles was also the longest-tenured Yankee, having been with the club since 1973, and the two hoped a new title would help bury the hatchet.

"George and I have butted heads for a long time," Nettles said. "For him to name me captain shows he has respect for me. It's time we stopped having a feud. I'm going to try to work with him and be cooperative."[59]

There was one problem, though. Nettles admitted he was unsure what the position entailed. When asked what a captain did, he joked, saying, "I think it means I go out before the game for the flip of the coin." He then asked manager Bob Lemon if he should kick off or receive.[60]

"Take the ball, meat," replied Lemon. "We've got a running team."[61]

Between them, the Yankees and Orioles had won the last six AL East titles and five of the last six AL pennants. But there was a new team on the rise in the division. After ten years of futility, the Milwaukee Brewers finally reached the postseason in 1981, falling in five games to the Yankees in the American League Division Series. If the Yankees were built on speed in 1982 and the Orioles around pitching, the Brewers were counting on their high-powered offense. Milwaukee finished second in the AL in runs scored in 1981 and fourth in home runs. Outfielders Ben Oglivie and Gorman Thomas were both former home run champs, first baseman Cecil Cooper hit .352 in 1980, Robin Yount was a budding superstar, and Ted Simmons, part of the key Cardinals/

Brewers trade at the 1980 Winter Meetings, was still one of the best hitting catchers in the game. At the top of the order was Paul Molitor, the number three overall pick in the 1977 draft who made the jump from Single-A Burlington in 1977 to runner-up in the American League Rookie of the Year balloting in 1978. Molitor's bat was never in doubt, but the big question was where he would play. The twenty-five-year-old native of St. Paul, Minnesota, split his rookie season between second base and shortstop, but he'd also spent time in right field. The Brewers moved him to center field in 1981, displacing Gorman Thomas, who begrudgingly moved to right, and now Molitor was being asked to move again, this time to third base.

"The biggest adjustment I'm going through is mental," said Molitor. "Just preparing yourself for a new position and the frustrations that go with it. You've just got to tell yourself you're going to have bad days and you're going to have good ones. You've got to realize that it wasn't your choice to go there and just try to make the best of the decision."[62]

Molitor did have some experienced tutors in spring training in former Milwaukee third baseman Sal Bando, who moved to the front office, and veteran Don Money. Now in his fifteenth season, Money was the starting third baseman for the Philadelphia Phillies for four years but was dealt to Milwaukee after the 1972 season to make room for Mike Schmidt. Money moved to second base when Milwaukee signed Bando as a free agent in 1977, made the All-Star team, then moved back to third in 1978. Now he was being asked to step aside again. "Every time somebody in the lineup is moved, I'm moved too," he said. "This year whether I play third base or not depends on how Paulie makes out at the position this spring. The club is trying to find some place for him to play after his trial in the outfield last season and this year their thinking is that he should be at third."[63]

That thinking came from general manager Harry Dalton and manager Robert Leroy "Buck" Rodgers, who began his baseball career in the Detroit Tigers organization in 1956 as a catcher with the Jamestown Falcons. Rodgers made his big-league debut in 1961 after a trade to the California Angels and was a promising player but battled injuries and retired following the 1969 season. When Milwaukee hired Harry Dalton as their general manager prior to the 1978 season he brought Rodgers with him, and the latter took over as manager in 1981, leading the Brewers to the playoffs for the first time. Even still, Rodgers found himself on shaky ground. A September 1981 newspaper article contained quotes from anonymous Brewers players criticizing Rodgers for the way he handled players and accusing him of being out of touch. It was criticism he was not open to hearing.

"I'm sure there are people who are upset, but I'm not going to change the way I am," he said. "If I did that, I'd be a hypocrite. You can call me anything, but you can't call me a hypocrite. I don't expect people out there to like me. I just expect them to do what they're told."[64]

Tough-guy exterior aside, Rodgers knew 1982 was an important season for him and the Brewers. The team posted the most wins in the AL East in 1981 despite off years from Oglivie and Simmons. Molitor missed a month with an ankle injury, and Yount missed a month with a knee injury. In 1982, Milwaukee's management felt this team was good enough to make a run at the pennant.

"If we don't win, I'm gone," said Rodgers. "It's that simple."[65] To win, the Brewers needed the pitching staff to step up. Milwaukee could score as many runs as they wanted to, but without quality pitching they weren't going anywhere, and Rodgers knew it. "You can put some runs on the board and that will get you through a few games," he said. "But most of the games you're going to have to win 2–1 and 3–2. That's when pitching really becomes an important part. We've got to shut somebody out once in a while. We're not going to be able to beat everybody 10–2."[66]

A key part of the pitching staff was Rollie Fingers, acquired along with Simmons. Fingers had his best season in 1981, winning both the Cy Young Award and the American League MVP. He led the Major Leagues in saves with 28 and held opponents to a paltry .198 batting average. Perhaps the only blemish on his season came in the All-Star Game, when he surrendered what turned out to be the game-winning home run to Schmidt.

"It was one of those years where nothing went wrong," he said. "I could come in with the bases loaded and give up three line drives and they'd all be right at guys. It was one of those fantasy years. The guys made the plays behind me."[67]

Despite Fingers's dominance, the 1981 Milwaukee pitching staff was mediocre at best. They finished twelfth in the fourteen-team American League in team ERA and ahead of just four other teams in runs allowed. For the Brewers to have a real chance in 1982, multiple starting pitchers would have to step up, and Fingers would need to consistently shut the door in the late innings. In short, the fate of the team rested on his shoulders. And then, Rollie Fingers hurt his shoulder.

Heavy rain saw practice called off one day in spring training, but some of the pitchers stuck around to get their work in, and it did not take long for the work to turn into a mud battle. Fingers snuck up behind Randy Lerch to dump mud on his head. But Lerch saw Fingers coming, wheeled around, and tossed him to the ground. Fingers landed hard on his left shoulder and stayed down. He knew something was wrong. Lerch thought his teammate was kidding initially but soon realized the gravity of the situation. Fingers wasn't screwing around: he had separated his shoulder. Luckily, the injury was to his nonthrowing shoulder, but both pitchers understood there would be hell to pay, so they made up a story.

One of the teams' favorite activities was a game they called, "flip," in which players would flip a baseball off their glove toward a teammate. Whoever let the ball hit the ground was out of the game. It was the perfect cover for the injury, as the Brewers flip games were known to get a bit rowdy. Bloody lips were common, but separated shoulders were another matter.

"After that they wouldn't let us play flip until finally, we told them what had really happened," said Lerch. "I was later told by a couple of investigators on the team that if I even looked at Rollie strange again, I'd be gone. We were just having fun, but this was the Cy Young Award winner and MVP we're talking about."[68]

Fingers predicted a quick return but also wanted to be cautious. He had been hit in the face with a line drive in the minor leagues and knew that coming back too soon could result in alterations in his delivery that could have disastrous results in the long term. Fortunately, Fingers was ready to go on Opening Day.

While the Brewers hoped to get past Baltimore and New York in the American League East, the AL West had been dominated by the Oakland A's and, more recently, the Kansas City Royals. From the first year of divisional play in 1969 through 1980, Kansas City or Oakland won all but three division titles.

Billy Martin's A's were the consensus choice to win the division in 1982, and the turnaround under his direction had been remarkable. The 1979 Oakland A's lost 108 games and drew a paltry 306,763 paying fans.[69] Then Martin took over in 1980 and got them back to the postseason in just two years with his aggressive and pugnacious style. His forte was taking over moribund franchises, turning them around, and wearing out his welcome in the process. He did it in Detroit and Texas before bringing the Yankees back to prominence in the late seventies.

But run-ins with media, players, fans, ownership, or some combination of the four always seemed to lead to his downfall.

Martin took over the Yankees for a second time in June of 1979 and was slated to return in 1980 before a much-publicized fight with a marshmallow salesman in a Minneapolis bar forced Steinbrenner to cut Martin loose. Oakland's owner Charlie Finley hired Martin right before spring training in 1980, and the colorful manager took a team that had won 38 percent of its games over the last three seasons and immediately turned into a winner. Oakland went 83–79 in 1980, and their 64 wins in 1981 were the most in the American League. The secret to the A's new-found success was something that became known as "Billy-Ball." Martin emphasized a strong starting pitching staff and an aggressive running game on his way to victory. Oakland pitchers threw 94 complete games in 1980, more than twice as many as the second-place Brewers, and another 60 in the strike-shortened 1981 season. On the basepaths, the A's stole 273 bases in 271 games under Martin, second only to Kansas City in the American League.

The third aspect of Martin's style was the one that had gotten him in trouble over and over: his willingness to fight at seemingly any slight, real, or imagined. The A's were scheduled to open the season against the California Angels, and the two teams did not like each other. In April of 1981, then Angels outfielder Dan Ford homered off Oakland starter Mike Norris. A's catcher Mike Heath grabbed Ford's bat as he was rounding the bases and asked the home plate umpire to inspect it for signs of tampering. When Ford finished his home run trot, he went after Heath, and the benches emptied. A second altercation took place after the game when Angels pitching coach, and former Martin teammate, Tom Morgan began jawing with some Oakland players. Martin pinned Morgan against the wall before the two were separated, but the bad blood persisted.

"I'm putting the Angels on notice: we won't tolerate their petty intimidation," said Martin in spring training of 1982. "If they start something, I'll tell my players to go and punch everybody's lights out. No rasslin' anymore. We're going to kick some ass. This 54-year-old manager is going to turn his guns loose, too. I've stopped a lot of fights as a manager. But against California, I'm not. I'm participating. They can punch me. But there are going to be some broken jaws."[70]

The comments caused some controversy, and Martin called Angels general manager Buzzie Bavasi to clear the air. Ever the businessman,

Bavasi told Martin not to retract his comments, knowing the chance of renewed fisticuffs between the two teams could lead to increased ticket sales.

Kansas City's George Brett was fighting a different battle in the spring of 1982, one of public perception. After captivating the baseball world with his chase for a .400 batting average in 1980, Brett struggled through 1981, batting what for him was a pedestrian .314 with just nine home runs and 43 RBI. On top of that, his wholesome image took a hit. The onetime 7-Up pitchman, who once took hitting advice from a youngster on a television commercial, was now unhappy with his contract, a deal he had signed just a year earlier, which paid him $900,000 per season. And that wasn't all.

"Brett, in one depressing season, destroyed a bathroom at the stadium in Bloomington, Minnesota, swatted a photographer with a crutch, slapped a female reporter and fell out with his best friend," wrote Gerry Fraley.[71]

"[My image] got tarnished a little bit," Brett said. "No, it's ruined. I thought the public had a good image of me. They'd say, 'There's a nice guy.' They don't do that anymore. It doesn't bother me now. It did for a while."[72]

Brett was the Royals second-round draft pick in 1971, hit .282 in 1974, his first full season at the major league level, and followed that up by leading the American League in hits for the next two seasons. By 1980, he was a star. In his breakout season, Brett hit .390, won the American League MVP Award, and got the Royals to the World Series.

But 1981 was a disaster. Brett broke two toilets and a sink in a bathroom near the visitor's dugout in May in Minnesota after grounding out with multiple runners on base. He began the second half of the season in a 1-for-23 slump and rounded out the year with an ugly incident in a hotel bar in Anaheim. Brett was upset with *Kansas City Star* reporter Janis Carr, who criticized him for the incident in Minneapolis.

"Here's a player whose ability has put him in the limelight," Carr said. "He has to be able to deal with everything that goes with it. That was the essence of what I said to him and that was all I said to him. He put his finger in my face, I pushed his hand away and he shoved my face. I'm surprised he'd do that to anyone, let alone a female."[73]

"She came at me [verbally] pretty hard," replied Brett. "I took as much crap from a girl who doesn't know me as I'm going to take. I've had to deal with a lot of crap, on and off the field, and I wasn't in a mood for anymore, particularly when she wasn't even there [in Minnesota]."[74]

Mike Fish, a colleague of Carr's, came to her defense at the bar, and Anaheim police were summoned, but no charges were filed. The two cleared the air the next day in a meeting set up by the Royals. Bathroom and barroom drama aside, George Brett was one of the best players in the game, and the Royals needed him to bounce back if they wanted to compete in 1982.

To win the division, Brett and the Royals would have to get past Martin's A's and a retooled California Angels roster. The addition of Reggie Jackson had the Angels thinking 1982 could be the year they finally played in a World Series. Reggie was many things; brash, controversial, outspoken, gruff at times, but he was also a proven winner. In fourteen full seasons, Jackson had been to the playoffs nine times and won five World Series championships, Now, it was "Mr. October's" job to do the same for the Angels.

"If any of us ever hoped to play in a World Series," said new teammate Don Baylor, "this is it. This is our chance. You may boo him, or you may cheer him, but the bottom line on Reggie is that he's a winner."[75]

Jackson and Baylor joined center fielder Fred Lynn and first baseman Rod Carew as Angels starters who had won American League MVP awards. The roster also included slugging left fielder Brian Downing and the newly acquired Bob Boone and Doug DeCinces. Like the Brewers, the Angels would score their share of runs, but the question was whether they could prevent them. California's pitching staff had ranked next to last in team ERA in the AL in 1980. The numbers improved in 1981 to league average, but, while a batting order with four former MVPs could intimidate opponents, a starting rotation headed by Geoff Zahn and Ken Forsch, who posted a combined record of 21–18 in 1981, could not.

"I'd like to think our pitching staff is OK the way it is," said Angels manager Gene Mauch. "I don't know that it is, but I'd like to think so."[76]

One AL West manager who was thrilled with his pitching staff was Texas's Don Zimmer. The fifty-one-year-old Zimmer was in his second season as the Rangers' skipper after stints with the Boston Red Sox and San Diego Padres.

"I think I'm going to be managing the best pitching staff I've ever managed," he said. "If [Frank] Tanana can do the job like I think he can and [Charlie] Hough pitches anywhere similar to what he did for us in his five starts last September, we're going to be stronger in the starting rotation. That's allowed us to take [Danny] Darwin and put him in the bullpen with [Steve] Comer and that certainly strengthens us there."[77]

The addition of Tanana, who signed as a free agent after a down year in Boston, certainly looked to improve the Texas pitching staff. But it, along with the signing of first baseman Lamar Johnson, also ruffled some feathers. Texas owner Eddie Chiles was spending lavishly on new players, which had existing players wondering where their share was. To soothe hurt feelings, Chiles gave $50,000 bonuses to designated hitter Al Oliver, third baseman Buddy Bell, and catcher Jim Sundberg. All that did was anger players like Doc Medich, Bill Stein, and Leon Roberts, who wondered why they didn't get a bonus.

If California's Gene Autry, the former movie cowboy, was one of baseball's most beloved owners and New York's George Steinbrenner one of its most hated, Texas's Eddie Chiles was one of its most eccentric. Chiles made his money in oil and purchased the team in 1980. Zimmer was one of his first hires, but there were warning signs from the beginning, at least for Zimmer. Shortly after accepting the job at the 1980 winter meetings, Zimmer was sitting in Rangers general manager Eddie Robinson's hotel room when Chiles entered, introduced himself to his new manager, and then dressed down his general manager for nearly ten minutes. Chiles then turned to Zimmer and told him he would have to move to Texas. Zimmer had worn a baseball uniform since 1949 as a player, coach, or manager, and he knew that moving each time you got a new job was a recipe for misery. He had also been a longtime resident of Treasure Island, Florida, and he informed Chiles that he wasn't about to move his family to Texas, no matter how much he was being paid. Chiles relented, but it was not a great way for Zimmer's tenure in Texas to begin.

The Rangers finished a game and a half behind Oakland in the first half of the 1981 season but slipped to third in the second half, and Chiles wanted changes. He brought in Tanana and signed Johnson to replace Pat Putnam at first base. He also acquired second baseman Doug Flynn from the Mets, something that did not sit well with incumbent second baseman Bump Wills.

Zimmer installed Wills at the top of the batting order at the beginning of 1981 and told him to steal as many bases as he could. But Wills said he wouldn't run because he claimed Al Oliver, who hit behind him, told him not to. When Zimmer asked Oliver why, the thirteen-year veteran, who had amassed more than 2,000 hits to that point, said, to the contrary, that he wanted Wills to run because it opened holes for him to hit through. Zimmer later found out that the reason Wills did not want to run was because he was in the last year of his contract and didn't want to get hurt.

As spring training wound down, the Rangers traded Wills to the Chicago Cubs, but they were far from finished. A few days later, they sent Oliver to the Montreal Expos in exchange for Larry Parrish and Dave Hostetler. Then Robinson approached Zimmer with another possible deal.

Lee Mazzilli was no longer a fit with the New York Mets. A youngster named Mookie Wilson had taken his job in center field and New York had acquired Ellis Valentine to play right field and George Foster to play left. Mazzilli was twenty-seven years old, could hit for average and power, *and* steal bases, and all the Rangers had to do to get him was to surrender two minor league pitchers named Walt Terrell and Ron Darling.

In his book, *Zim: A Baseball Life*, Zimmer said he was apprehensive about the deal. Terrell was a thirty-third-round draft pick, and there was some question as to whether he'd ever pitch in the major leagues. The same could not be said for Darling, the Rangers' first-round pick in 1981 who had impressed at Double-A Tulsa in thirteen starts. Part of Zimmer's reluctance was self-preservation. He was an American League guy, and because he had not seen Mazzilli play, he was hesitant to vouch for the team trading away the number nine overall pick in last year's draft to get him. But the deal went through, and the Rangers media saw it as another example of shortsightedness. Texas had a habit of trading away young pitchers who then went on to bigger and better things in other markets.

"In the beginning, there was Brad Corbett," wrote Gil Lebretton in the *Fort Worth Star-Telegram*. "And then there were . . . Len Barker, Jim Clancy, Dave Righetti . . . Rick Waits, and Gene Nelson. Soon there were none of them. Now no more Darling. No more Walt Terrell. *Et, tu*, Eddie Robinson?"[78]

"Listen," said Robinson. "I was not the author of those deals. This is the first minor league player of any consequence I've traded. I'm one of those ones that hate to give up a young prospect."[79]

Lebreton wasn't the only one displeased with the deal. Despite the opportunity of seeing more playing time, Mazzilli was not happy either.

But the Mets were moving in a new direction, and there did not seem to be a place for him.

"There is more behind this, though," Mazzilli said. "I'm part of the old regime. I've been here the longest of the regulars. I'm a little too big in New York, too."[80]

"I think I was a commodity to the Mets," Mazzilli said. "But I don't think Frank Cashen is going to keep me here because I'm Lee Mazzilli to the fans. I could not have survived here not playing regularly. And I might become a better player outside New York. But New York is New York. No place like it. Even when I was getting booed last year, people on the street would shout to me, 'We're behind you, Maz!'"[81]

Mazzilli would not enjoy the same support in Texas that he received in New York. He also may have overestimated his worth.

3. APRIL

This Could Be the Best Year of My Life

It's a mental challenge and you also get an emotional high from playing it that's hard to describe. We got into a $20 a day habit. We were real junkies.
—Jerry Buckner

The habit Jerry Buckner and Gary Garcia slipped into began when they walked into an Atlanta bar after a recording session in the fall of 1981. The native Ohioans, veterans of the Akron music scene that produced Devo and Chrissie Hynde, were in town to record some commercial jingles and were looking to unwind.

In just a few hours, the two men were hooked on Pac-Man. The yellow, dot-eating video game character became such a powerful force in their lives that they wrote a song about him called "Pac-Man Fever," which eventually reached the Billboard Top 10 and spawned an entire album of video-game-related songs.

By April of 1982 Pac-Man Fever, the malady as opposed to the song, had taken hold in the United States. The video game sold more than 100,000 units in its first year in the United States and the effects were felt across the country, including institutions of higher learning. Profits from Pac-Man machines made up the bulk of a $500,000 renovation of the student center at the University of Pennsylvania, while Temple University used Pac-Man profits to lessen their annual tuition increase. Studies showed that a single Pac-Man machine, placed strategically in a student union, could bring in more income than an actual student.[1]

One of the biggest days in the game's history was April 3, 1982, when Atari released a version of the game that was compatible with their home system. Suddenly college students could save their quarters and play Pac-Man for hours at a time from the comfort of their dorm rooms. Atari hosted official National Pac-Man Day events in twenty-seven cities across the country, featuring human beings dressed up as the man himself. They conducted contests, handed out T-shirts, and gave away game cartridges.

"The truth is," said the *Philadelphia Inquirer*, ". . . Pac-Man is nothing short of addictive. It is variously challenging, amusing, frustrating, mentally and even physically exhausting, arguably sexually suggestive and—though it is hard to say exactly why—strangely rewarding. In short, it is a complete waste of time in which millions of people love to indulge."[2]

But not everyone was happy with the new fad. The *Baltimore Sun* ran an article titled "Video Games: Suburban Menace?"[3] in which local leaders claimed the games were magnets for drug use and gangs and threatened the very safety of the communities in which they were placed. The health and safety issues even spread to major league clubhouses; Brewers reliever Rollie Fingers suffered blisters from playing the game, thereby sustaining his second unusual injury of the spring.

Two days after Pac-Man Day, Major League Baseball kicked off the 1982 season in Cincinnati. Astronauts Joe Engle and Richard H. Truly provided a baseball for the ceremonial first pitch, one that had accompanied them in orbit on the Space Shuttle *Columbia* the previous November. When the ceremonies concluded, Dallas Green's new look Chicago Cubs, dubbed "Phillies West" due to the number of former Phillies players and coaches Green had brought to Chicago with him, defeated Mario Soto and the Reds 3–2 in a weather-shortened game in front of more than 51,000 people at Riverfront Stadium.

Cubs catcher Keith Moreland went 3-for-4 with a homer and 2 RBI to lead the "Phormer Phillies," who included shortstop Larry Bowa and third baseman Ryne Sandberg, while first baseman Bill Buckner went 3-for-4 and new second baseman Bump Wills homered to pace Chicago.

"You can't beat winning early," said Cubs Manager Lee Elia. "A game like today, the first one, it's important to win it."[4]

The first game in the junior circuit featured Earl Weaver's Orioles hosting the Kansas City Royals at Memorial Stadium, where another rookie third baseman was in the spotlight. For years, Baltimore manager Earl Weaver was a proponent of good pitching and big power. Weaver was famous for his affection for the three-run homer and, on Opening Day, he got that and more when the Orioles homered for the cycle against the Royals. Eddie Murray hit a grand slam, Dan Ford provided the three-run shot, and Gary Roenicke hit a solo homer. But it was the two-run homer in the second inning that was perhaps the most special.

Ken Singleton led off the inning with a walk-off Royals starter, Dennis Leonard. Murray popped out to third base to bring up Cal Ripken Jr., who sent a Leonard pitch over the wall in center field for his first career home run, one of three hits on the day for the rookie. "As soon as I hit it, I knew it was going out," said Ripken after the game. "I was so excited I couldn't stop running the bases. I almost passed Kenny. I could have jumped up and down all the way home."[5]

The one person who did not show much emotion when the ball cleared the fence was the man who should have been most excited. Cal Ripken Sr. was a baseball lifer and, more specifically, an Orioles lifer. He began his baseball career as a minor league outfielder for the Phoenix Stars in 1957 and had been an Oriole ever since. He spent thirteen years managing in the minor leagues and finally reached the big leagues as a coach in 1976. Now, twenty-five years after his baseball career began, he was Baltimore's third base coach and the first to congratulate his son after he hit his first major league home run. He did so stoically. "I said, 'Nice going.' The same thing I would have said to anybody," said the elder Ripken. "I don't get keyed up over things like that."[6]

His son was still keyed up after the game, which Baltimore won 13–5. Still a rookie by Major League Baseball rules, Cal Jr. made his debut in 1981, and it did not go well. In twenty-three games, Ripken managed just five hits, all of them singles, and he was eager to prove he belonged at the major league level. "I feel like I have something to prove," said Ripken. "I wanted to show people I wasn't a .128 ball player. Shoot, .128, 5-for-39. I'll never forget those numbers. Now I can settle down and play the way I'm used to."[7]

The following day's Major League Baseball schedule called for eleven games, but a massive snowstorm postponed games in six different cities. Accumulation ranged from six inches in Philadelphia and New York to close to a foot in Chicago and forced the postponement not only of games but of entire series, including Detroit's home series against the Blue Jays. The Tigers flew directly to Kansas City in advance of their matchup with the Royals, but things went awry. At some point in the early evening of April 7, three police cars and two ambulances arrived at Kansas City's Alameda Plaza due to a report of a fight with injuries. There was no fight, but there was an injury. The Detroit Tigers were in town, and they had time to kill so a group of players decided to spend the evening in the restaurant district of Kansas City.

"There were seven of us," said Detroit shortstop Alan Trammell. "We were standing by this railing watching people dance. Rozey [pitcher Dave Rozema] was standing next to me."[8]

Rozema playfully pressed Trammell's head down toward the bar, and Trammell instinctively tried to evade his teammates grasp. He was successful in not banging his head on the bar, but only because a bar patron's glass was in the way. Blood began pouring from a wound just above Trammell's left eyebrow. "My head just banged into the top of [the glass] and it broke all over," said Trammell.[9]

The result was a trip to Kansas City's St. Luke's Hospital for forty stitches and a lot of explaining for Trammell, Rozema, and the rest of the Tiger entourage, who met with manager Sparky Anderson to discuss the incident. "We worked out a little deal for the kids," said Rozema.[10] He and Trammell would visit sick children at a Detroit hospital and host a party for them later in the year. Anderson declined to discuss specifics of the conversation with his pitcher and shortstop, but Trammell offered a summary, saying Sparky "wasn't too pleased."[11]

Fortunately, the injury wasn't serious enough to keep Trammell out of the lineup when his team faced the Royals the following evening, but Amos Otis's first inning grand slam off Tigers starter Jack Morris gave the Royals the win. Forty stitches and a 4–2 loss was likely not what Sparky Anderson had in mind when he brought his team north from Lakeland, Florida, to begin the season.

While the Royals were hosting Detroit, the Boston Red Sox were visiting Chicago to play the White Sox. Boston had been scheduled to open the season at Comiskey Park, but snow in the Chicago area postponed the series. It did not, however, delay the Red Sox from getting into town. On the way to the Windy City, the team discovered that their plane was in a lengthy holding pattern due to the weather. But one member of the Red Sox had some influence. Rookie infielder Wade Boggs made his way to the cockpit and got on the radio. A few minutes later the team plane was bumped to the front of the line thanks to Boggs's brother Wayne, who was an air traffic controller at O'Hare airport.

Wade Anthony Boggs was a seventh-round draft pick of the Red Sox in 1976. He hit .485 as a senior at Plant High School in Tampa, Florida, and once he signed with Boston he kept hitting. He amassed a .320 batting average over six minor league seasons, but there were questions about whether he could contribute at the major league level. He did not have a natural position, he didn't hit for power, his fielding was suspect, and he couldn't run. "My brother-in-law is a writer in Tampa and asked [then Red Sox Manager Don] Zimmer about me a year ago," Boggs said in 1981. "Zimmer answered, 'Who?' What I have to get is a shot somewhere. I can put the raps aside if I hit. And I always have."[12]

Boggs finally got his shot in 1982 when he made the team out of spring training. In his second start of the year, he stepped in against Chicago's Richard Dotson to lead off the top of the eighth inning and singled to left field for his first big league hit. He would play sparingly during the first half of the season but would begin to assert himself as a bona fide major league hitter as the year progressed.

Opening Day temperatures in Minneapolis were in the low 30s, but the Twins home opener against the Seattle Mariners went on as scheduled, thanks to the Twins new indoor home. Since Calvin Griffith moved the Washington Senators northwest for the 1961 season, fans in Minnesota had endured a lot of bad baseball in some really bad weather. The 1965 Twins took the Los Angeles Dodgers to the seventh game of the World Series before succumbing to Sandy Koufax, and there were division titles in 1969 and 1970 as well. But aside from that, winning baseball in the Twin Cities was something of an anomaly, and fans showed their displeasure by not showing up in foul weather to watch a bad team.

The 1981 home opener drew a crowd of 42,648 to Metropolitan Stadium, but it was downhill from there, with the Twins finishing last in baseball in attendance by nearly 50,000 spectators on the season. The team was optimistic that their new home, the Hubert H. Humphrey Metrodome, would draw fans and bring winning baseball back to Minnesota, but it was a tough sell.

On April 6, as more than 52,000 people packed the new ballpark, a small group of fans played softball in the parking lot of Metropolitan Stadium in protest. Their photo appeared on the front page of the following day's *Minneapolis Star Tribune*, just below a photo of Pearl Bailey singing the national anthem at the new ballpark. Section A articles in the paper focused on parking and traffic rather than the wonders of the team's new home.

Once the game began, the differences between "The Met" and "The Dome" became evident immediately. Balls took high hops on the spongy artificial surface, and players complained about the stickiness of the outfield turf. "It doesn't look like we'll be able to dive on that stuff," said right fielder Dave Engle, referring to a ball he failed to reach in the third inning. "Normally, on a play like that I'll slide. But as soon as I hit the ground, I stuck and stopped. On grass, I'm sliding, and I get that ball easy."[13]

A few innings later a similar play cost the Twins a few runs and almost cost them their left fielder. With the bases loaded, Seattle first baseman Jim Maler blooped a ball in front of Mickey Hatcher in left that fell for a bases-clearing double.

"I had it. I had it in my glove," said Hatcher. "But my glove stuck to the turf. I thought I broke my wrist. Maybe I'll put Vaseline on my glove next time."[14]

Maler's double capped a 5-RBI day as the Mariners beat Minnesota 11–7, an inauspicious debut for the new ballpark summed up concisely by manager Billy Gardner, who said, "We played lousy."[15] Things would only get worse for Gardner. Less than a week after opening their new $55 million stadium, the Twins began shedding their best players.

Long considered one of the (if not the) cheapest owners in the game, Calvin Griffith further solidified his status when he dealt shortstop Roy Smalley to the Yankees for relief pitcher Ron Davis, minor leaguers Paul Boris and Greg Gagne, and $400,000. Smalley was one of the highest-paid players on the team, and one of the best. The California native emerged in the late 1970s as one of the top offensive shortstops in the American League, hitting 24 homers and driving in 95 runs in 1979 while playing in every game. A back injury slowed him down, but he was seemingly healthy again and ready to lead the Twins into a new era. None of that mattered to Griffith, and the fallout was predictable.

"Why would they do that?" asked Smalley's double-play partner Rob Wilfong. "I think the rest of the guys are searching for a reason. He's a team leader. I've played as long as he has, but I still look up to him and we've got nobody who can take his place."[16]

"I've got comments, but you can't print them," said pitcher Pete Redfern.[17] *Minneapolis Star Tribune* columnist Joe Soucheray was able to print his comments, and he pulled no punches when assessing Griffith's latest move. "Calvin Griffith must now be considered beyond redemption in the hearts and minds of local baseball fans," he wrote. "The jowly one traded Roy Smalley to the Yankees yesterday, an act that was so astonishing as it was stupid, but then, Calvin is the proprietor of his very own Hall of Stupidity."[18]

Some 1,100 miles to the southeast was another team with a fan base that was used to mediocrity. Since moving to Atlanta in 1966, the Braves had finished higher than third place exactly one time. That year was 1969, when they won the National League West and were swept three games to none by the Miracle Mets in the first-ever National League Championship Series. But the 1982 version of the Braves showed promise. Expectations were high in Atlanta, and they began with owner Ted Turner. "The experts are picking us in the middle of the division, but I'm picking us first. First!" he said. "I'm very, very pleased with what's happening. Ecstatic. Enthusiastic. Tickled pink. We're going to finish first . . . Atlanta will go berserk."[19]

The Atlanta media was less optimistic but still realized the importance of the 1982 season. "This will be a season of truth for Braves management which, in recent years, has made relatively few deals and justified it by claiming the talent is here," said the *Atlanta Constitution*. "The relatively young team needs only development and experience, management says. It's put up or shut up time."[20]

Atlanta began the "Put up or Shut Up campaign" of 1982 on the road in San Diego and did so without their scheduled Opening Day starter. Phil Niekro was in his nineteenth season in a Braves uniform. He had won twenty games three different times and lost twenty games twice, including an improbable 1979 season in which he went 21–20 and threw 342 innings. He was in line for his eighth Opening Day start until he was felled by a line drive in batting practice. It was also the second time in his career he had been hit by an errant batting-practice line drive. Just two years earlier, Niekro spent the night in the hospital after being struck by a shot in BP. In 1980 he pitched again two days later and threw a two-hit shutout. This time, the injury was more serious, and the forty-three-year-old pitcher began the season on the disabled list. He still offered words of encouragement via telegram, which manager Joe Torre read at a team meeting. "Good luck to you, the coaches and all the players for a great season," he wrote. "Bring back two wins. I wish I could be there with you."[21]

Ironically, the man who took Niekro's spot on Opening Day, Rick Mahler, was also the one who had hit the line drive that knocked him out of action. Perhaps feeling the weight of his batting practice mishap, Mahler allowed just two hits while striking out seven and threw the first complete game shutout of his career in beating the San Diego Padres 1–0.

"You can't pitch them any better than that," said Torre, who picked up his first win as Atlanta's skipper. "You can't use enough superlatives for the type of game Rick pitched."[22]

Atlanta beat the Padres again the next day, then came home and swept the Astros in a three-game series before heading to Cincinnati and Houston, where they went 6–0. More than 3,500 giddy fans packed Gate B-21 at Atlanta's Hartsfield Airport as an Eastern Airlines flight brought the 11–0 Braves back home. The streak tied the major league mark for consecutive wins to start a season, but, more important, it signified hope to a fan base that badly needed it. Ted Turner predicted the city would go berserk if the Braves won their division, and his prognostication seemed dead-on in the early going. As flight 865 began to disembark, a chant of "Torre, Torre, Torre!" began to rise in the terminal.[23] In four-plus seasons managing the New York Mets, Joe Torre lost nearly six out of every ten games his team played. Now, he was undefeated. "Torre is gutsy. That's what it takes to win. That's what we've needed," said Sandy Bowlin, who was among the crowd cheering for the new skipper.[24] She was also holding a sign that read, "Torre, Torre, Torre—162–0."

Thoughts of an undefeated season may have been a bit optimistic, as was the question from a fan about when he could buy World Series tickets after the team's eighth win, but the Braves were impressing many around the baseball world, including themselves. "This team hasn't felt this good since we won the division in 1969 and, even then, we didn't feel like winners until three-quarters of the way through the season," said Niekro. "These kids don't care what time of the year it is. They're beautiful to watch."[25]

There were others who thought the furor over Atlanta's start was premature. "Two years ago, we won 11 of our first 12 games, but we didn't win the pennant," said Cincinnati Reds shortstop and two-time World Series champion Dave Concepcion after Atlanta beat his team on April 13. "The Braves have more than 150 games to go. I think they're good, but I don't think they'll even win the division title."[26]

Now the Braves were gunning for their twelfth straight win to start the season, and Concepcion's Reds provided the opposition. The two teams squared off in Atlanta on the evening of Tuesday, April 20, with Cincinnati jumping out to a 2–0 lead in the top of the second. But Atlanta scored a single run in the bottom of the frame, added three more in the bottom of the third and held on for a 4–2 win. Fans poured out onto the field when Dale Murphy recorded the final out, a symbol of how much the streak meant to the city. The Braves hadn't won this many games in a row since 1897, when the then Boston Braves reeled off 17 straight.

"We had an October-type crowd at the airport to meet us on Sunday," said Torre. "Tonight was sort of like that, and we want to keep the fans excited. It was very emotional tonight. It's nice to break the record, but we won't relax now."[27]

The streak stretched to 13-straight the following night before finally ending on April 22 when the Reds beat Atlanta 2–1. Atlanta had their chances but went 0-for-13 with runners in scoring position and stranded ten in the game. The remarkable run was over, but the Braves were still a confident bunch. "We're still in first place and we'll be there all year," said pitcher Rick Camp, who went 2–0 with three saves during the streak.[28] "I told them I was proud as hell of them and to go out tomorrow and start another one," said Torre.[29]

During the 13-game winning streak the team batted a remarkable .270 with runners in scoring position while also posting a team ERA of just 2.01. The numbers obviously were not sustainable, but they showed that Atlanta would be a factor in the NL West race, despite what Dave Concepcion, or anyone else, thought.

The St. Louis Cardinals were also off to a great start. They wasted no time jumping all over Astros starter Nolan Ryan on Opening Day, scoring five runs in a twenty-minute first inning and cruising to a 14–3 win. Darrell Porter's three-run first-inning homer set the tone, and Cardinals starter Bob Forsch allowed seven hits over eight innings to pick up the win.

"It's going to be tough to play any better than that," said second baseman Tom Herr, who went 2-for-6 with two doubles.[30] After knocking Ryan around, St. Louis lost three straight, but then won twelve games in a row, including five against the Phillies. That fact stung a bit more, considering former Phillie Lonnie Smith went 10-for-22 against his old team in the five wins, and the Philadelphia media didn't let it slip by unnoted. "Already, the magnitude of the Phillies' blunder in getting rid of Lonnie Smith is becoming embarrassingly evident," wrote *Philadelphia Inquirer* sports editor Frank Dolson. "He is more than just another good, young, ballplayer. He has the look, the feel, the drive of a right-handed Lou Brock, another young outfielder the Cardinals stole."[31]

The San Diego Padres were another team asserting themselves after years of mediocrity. Dick Williams's team began the season with a 1–4 record but then reeled off eight wins in a row, including a four-game sweep of the defending World Series champion Los Angeles Dodgers. The Padres were winning and having a good time, which angered some members of the Dodgers. During the series San Diego second baseman Juan Bonilla did an excellent job of getting under L.A.'s skin by committing such atrocities as laughing and high-fiving teammates. The Dodgers responded by throwing at him multiple times. "I would understand it if it was the last week of the season and they were going after the pennant," said outfielder Dusty Baker of Bonilla's enthusiasm. "But this is the second week of the season."[32]

The irony of the Dodgers complaining about the exuberance of other teams was not lost on Williams, who shot back, "All I know is the fellow who claimed to invent the high five is on the Dodgers, Dusty Baker. Evidently their patent ran out because we're using it. And if we offend some people in the process, that's tough cookies."[33]

"I was seeing Dodger Blue on TV before I ever got to the big leagues," added Bonilla. "They were high fiving, low fiving. I saw Tommy Lasorda hugging Fernando Valenzuela, almost kissing him on national TV. That's not showing the other club up?"[34]

Lasorda denied his team tried to hit Bonilla, firing back at reporters, "You accusing the club of having a vendetta against Bonilla? I don't think anybody's trying to throw at him."[35] When asked if it was just a coincidence that Bonilla had drawn the ire of Dodgers pitchers, and that Baker had pointed directly at the Padres second baseman while rounding the bases after a home run, Lasorda replied, "I don't think anybody was trying to throw at him. That's my opinion."[36]

The Dodgers manager could be forgiven for his grumpiness since his team was experiencing a World Series hangover. The defending world champs were a .500 ballclub for most of April, and they also had to deal with a personnel mistake. Dave Goltz was the team's major free agent acquisition heading into 1980, leaving the Minnesota Twins to sign a six-year deal worth $3 million. But by midseason Goltz was 3–6 with a 5.68 ERA and went to manager Tommy Lasorda offering to be removed from the starting rotation. He finished his first season in Dodger blue with a disappointing 7–11 record, including a poor performance against the Astros in a tie-breaking game 163 loss that would have sent L.A. to the playoffs. He followed that up with a 2–7 record in 1981 and lasted just 3⅔ innings in his 1982 debut before the Dodgers ended the experiment, eating more than $1.5 million on his contract. It was the second big contract doled out to a free agent pitcher that did not work out. L.A. bought out the contract of Don Stanhouse the year before, meaning they were paying the pair more than $3 million to go away.

"I think he was embarrassed by the money," said Goltz's former manager Gene Mauch. "He didn't know how to accept the fact that he might be worth it. He's the nicest kid there is, but he's also very sensitive. You may not believe it, but every time I took him out of a game, he apologized to me."[37]

Toronto Blue Jays fans could have used an apology after sitting through five years of last-place finishes, but new manager Bobby Cox hoped to change the atmosphere surrounding the hapless team. That optimism lasted twenty-six pitches into the top of the first inning of the season, which was all it took for the Milwaukee Brewers to knock Toronto starter Mark Bomback out of the game. Singles by Paul Molitor and Charlie Moore were followed by a two-run double from Cecil Cooper and a two-run homer off the bat of Ben Oglivie. Four batters later, Milwaukee had a 6–0 lead and Bomback's day was over. Milwaukee added seven more in the top of the sixth inning and rolled to a 15–4 win. The beating Milwaukee handed Toronto was so thorough that every Brewers starter save second baseman Jim Gantner had at least one hit *and* one RBI, prompting Gantner to quip that he took one for the team. "Somebody had to make the outs, or we'd still be out there,"[38] he said. But, like Ted Turner and the Braves, the Brewers felt they were in a good position.

"Maybe this is an omen," said Paul Molitor, who reached base five times and scored two runs in the win. "We know we have the type of lineup that's going to hit and drive in runs from top to bottom. I just hope it's an indication of what we can do for the rest of the season."[39]

Canada's other team, the Montreal Expos, opened the 1982 season by renewing their rivalry with the Philadelphia Phillies at Veterans Stadium. Montreal opened the year by beating Philadelphia 2–0 behind Steve Rogers and sent Bill Gullickson to the mound for Game Two. Game-time temperatures were in the forties and dropping, which may have been a factor in a historic performance by Gullickson.

Gullickson was the second overall pick in the 1977 draft and set a single-game rookie strikeout record in 1980 when he fanned eighteen Cubs in a September 10 start in the heat of a pennant race. He finished 1981 with a subpar 7–9 record but a solid 2.80 ERA and capped his season by beating the Phillies in Game Two of the National League East Division Series. The twenty-three-year-old was on the road to establishing himself as a top-tier pitcher, which made his 1982 season-opening start all the more bizarre. Gullickson retired the first six Philadelphia hitters in order before allowing a solo home run to Bo Diaz to lead off the third inning. Over the next five innings, Gullickson threw a record-tying six wild pitches, two of which allowed runs to score. Even more amazing was the fact that despite his wild night he allowed only three runs over seven innings and got the win as Montreal came out on top, 11–3.

"For a while there, I felt a little like Pete Peeters," said Montreal catcher Gary Carter, referring to the Philadelphia Flyers goaltender who allowed four goals to the New York Rangers earlier in the day in a Stanley Cup Playoff game that Carter attended. "I was making saves on those pitches, not catching them."[40] The performance tied a major league record, but it could have been worse. By Gullickson's count, Carter may have saved an additional nine pitches in the dirt from going to the backstop. "Carter never said anything to me," the pitcher said, "But he did throw the ball back harder sometimes. You've got to get in the record books somehow."[41]

The Phillies/Expos rivalry got a bit more heated when Jayson Stark printed some incendiary comments from Mike Schmidt in a *Philadelphia Inquirer* column. When asked what he thought of Montreal, Schmidt, who was out with a cracked rib, responded that his team was still the class of the National League. "Man for man I don't think there's a better team than us," the two-time defending MVP told Stark. "Montreal can't hit with us, and they can't play defense with us."[42] Schmidt admitted that Montreal's starting rotation may be better than Philadelphia's, but that was about it. "I don't think they've got much of a bullpen at all. [Jeff] Reardon just comes in and throws that fastball. It's a good one but what's he ever done?"[43]

The comments didn't sit well in the visiting clubhouse at Veterans Stadium, especially with Reardon. "I had two saves in the playoffs and both times I popped [Schmidt] up with men on base," he fired back. "What have I done? I have a 2.30 E.R.A. for 2½ years. He hasn't had a hit against me."[44]

The key to the Phillies rotation was Steve Carlton, who got off to an abysmal start. The man known simply as "Lefty" began his career with the Cardinals in 1965 and soon established himself as an elite pitcher. But coming off a 20–9 season in 1971, Carlton felt he deserved more money, and Cardinals owner August Busch disagreed. Coincidentally, Phillies pitcher Rick Wise also felt underpaid. On February 25, 1972, Wise heard a knock on the door of his apartment in Clearwater, Florida, where the Phillies held spring training. The visitor was Philadelphia general manager Bob Quinn. Wise initially thought Quinn was there to negotiate a new contract, but the real purpose of his visit was to inform Wise that he had been dealt to the Cardinals in a straight-up deal for Carlton.

Wise grew frustrated playing for the Phillies, a team that hadn't seen the postseason since 1950. "To win on this club, you have to pitch a shutout and hit a homer,"[45] he said. Wise did just that when he no-hit the Reds and homered not once but twice on June 23, 1971. Now he was headed to the Cardinals, a team with a history of winning.

Carlton's new manager, Frank Lucchesi, was ecstatic, proclaiming the trade "the best deal we've made in years,"[46] and he was proven right. On a miserable 1972 Phillies team that won just 59 games, Carlton recorded 27 wins on his own, running away with the Cy Young Award. He won it again in 1977, and again in 1980 while leading the Phillies to the first World Series title in team history. But now, at age thirty-seven, there were signs that he might be slowing down. Through his first four starts, Carlton was 0–4 for the first time in his career and sported an uncharacteristic 6.85 ERA. "I was talking with a couple of guys about this," said Gary Carter after his Expos beat Carlton 5–2 on April 21. "It didn't seem like his fastball had as much pop."[47]

The Phillies entered the final days of April mired in last place in the NL East, a disappointing 7½ games behind St. Louis. They began a West Coast road trip in Los Angeles against the Dodgers, sans Goltz, who were already five games behind the Braves in the NL West. Both of the last two World Series champions were struggling, and one of them would come out of the three-game set at Dodger Stadium in even worse shape.

L.A. took the first game of the series 3–0, thanks to a masterful performance from Jerry Reuss, who limited the Phillies to just four hits. The Dodgers carried a 3–0 lead into the eighth inning of the second game when the Phillies exploded for nine runs in the final two frames and won the game 9–4. Pete Rose, who was in his twentieth major league season and seemingly set a record every time he stepped on the field, paced Philadelphia by going 5-for-5. It was the ninth time in Rose's career he'd had at least five hits in a game, which tied a National League record. "I hit the ball hard in batting practice, so I had a feeling I was going to have a good game," Rose said. "But it looked like the kid [Dodgers pitcher Bob Welch] was gonna shut us out because I was the only one hitting the ball until the end."[48]

The Phillies hot streak lasted exactly two innings as they were shut out again in the series finale. Philadelphia needed someone to step up, and Carlton did just that by beating the Padres 3–1 the following day. The 6–13 record was the worst April in team history, but help was on the way. Carlton showed signs of turning things around, and Mike Schmidt was set to rejoin the lineup on May 1. Still, after winning the division in 1981, the hole the Phillies found themselves in in the spring of 1982 was a deep one.

* * * * *

"I have given him my word," said Yankees owner George Steinbrenner of manager Bob Lemon at the 1981 winter meetings. "He will manage the team all of next season. Even if we're 20 games out of first place, Lemon will stay as manager."[49]

Steinbrenner's word lasted nearly until the end of the season's first month before he replaced Lemon with Gene Michael, who, coincidentally, had been the Yankees skipper until he was fired and replaced by Bob Lemon in September of 1981. Lemon's firing brought the average tenure of a Yankees manager since 1977 down to 77 games and unleashed the New York press on the petulant Steinbrenner. "Anyone could plainly see there was cause for alarm," wrote Phil Pepe, tongue planted firmly in cheek. "The Tigers . . . had raced to a commanding lead, three and a half games ahead of the Yankees and only 148 games left to catch them. Obviously, something had to be done."[50]

Rumors had been swirling since spring training about Lemon's status. He had to be talked out of quitting in March after Steinbrenner publicly criticized him over a lineup decision. When a crowd gathered in Lemon's office after the Yankees win over Detroit on April 25, Lemon was initially surprised but quickly caught on when reporters began asking him about his job security. Shortly after the line of questioning began, the phone in Lemon's office rang, summoning him to meet with Steinbrenner.

"Jeez," Lemon said into the phone, "I feel honored. I'm the only one invited?" After hanging up, Lemon quipped, "I wonder what that's all about, probably a contract extension."[51]

Lemon was out after just 14 games, and Michael was in. The very same Gene Michael who was fired for insubordination seven months earlier when he told Steinbrenner to either fire him or let him manage after growing tired of Steinbrenner's constant phone calls. Michael wouldn't last the season either. Lemon's firing also lined up with the beginning of a three-game series against the California Angels at Yankee Stadium, and there were some who thought that was more than mere coincidence. The series marked the return of Reggie Jackson to New York, and there was speculation that Steinbrenner wanted to do something, anything, to take the spotlight away from the former Yankee slugger.

Mr. October was back in town for the first time since 1976 wearing something other than pinstripes, and his primary goal was to quietly play three games and leave town. But that was the problem with being Reggie Jackson: you can't do anything quietly. Go 0-for-4? It's a story, Go 4-for-4? It's a story. The man who once spoke of "The magnitude of being me"[52] simply could not be incognito, especially in New York. "If it was just a matter of playing them, of playing again in Yankee Stadium, I'd be excited," Jackson said. "But with everything else that's going to be going on, I'm just looking forward to getting in and getting out."[53]

He didn't have that luxury. Jackson walked a "red carpet" of white towels laid on the dugout steps by teammate Rod Carew prior to the first game of the series, then proceeded to hit ball after ball into the seats during batting practice, to the delight of the crowd. Just as they had in the 1977 World Series, fans began chanting Reggie's name when he came up with two outs in the bottom of the second inning against Ron Guidry. Jackson grounded out to end the inning, but upon returning to his position in right field, he was greeted by a fan wearing a T-shirt that read "Bring Back Reggie," who then bowed in front of the former Yankee and delivered a bouquet of flowers.

In his final at bat of the game, with his team up 2–1, Jackson hammered a Guidry slider off the façade of the third deck in right field. The solo shot was his first as a member of the Angels and drew a standing ovation from the Yankee Stadium crowd, one that did not subside until Reggie emerged from the visitor's dugout and tipped his cap. It was then that the crowd began a new cheer; this one simpler and straight to the point.

"Steinbrenner sucks! Steinbrenner sucks!"

It was at precisely that time when Steinbrenner opted to leave his private box and make himself unavailable for questioning after the game, but Jackson was more than happy to speak with the media, saying of the fans' chant, "Some people have a way of saying the right thing at the right time. The fans in New York can be very direct. They have a way of reading people's minds. It's a nice feeling being able to go to the park to do my job rather than worrying about who's going to say what and who's going to be on my case. It's a lot more conducive to fun baseball."[54] Guidry told reporters it was the only fun he had all night and added, "I had to put my glove in front of my face to keep from laughing."[55]

STANDINGS AS OF APRIL 30

Table 3.1. American League East and West

AL East				AL West			
Team	Wins	Losses	GB	Team	Wins	Losses	GB
Boston	13	7	-	California	15	7	-
Detroit	13	8	0.5	Chicago	11	8	2.5
Milwaukee	9	8	2.5	Kansas City	11	8	2.5
Cleveland	8	10	4.0	Oakland	11	11	4.0
Toronto	8	12	5.0	Seattle	11	12	4.5
New York	7	11	5.0	Minnesota	9	13	6.0
Baltimore	6	12	6.0	Texas	6	11	6.5

Table 3.2. National League East and West

NL East				NL West			
Team	Wins	Losses	GB	Team	Wins	Losses	GB
St. Louis	14	7	-	Atlanta	17	5	-
Montreal	10	7	2.0	San Diego	13	6	2.0
New York	10	10	3.5	L. A. Dodgers	10	11	6.0
Pittsburgh	8	10	4.5	San Francisco	9	11	6.5
Philadelphia	6	13	7.0	Cincinnati	8	12	7.5
Chicago	7	14	7.0	Houston	9	14	8.0

4. MAY

The Ultimate Set of Tools

There's room for something like this in America.
—John Murphy,
President and CEO of Miller Brewing, 1971

John Murphy was on a business trip in Germany in the early 1970s when a waiter offered him a "Diat beer."[1] Murphy was dining with George Weissman, the chairman of Phillip Morris, Inc., which had recently purchased Milwaukee's Miller Brewing company, and was intrigued. The two men discussed the possibility of bringing a similar, lower-calorie beer to America. The result was Miller Lite, the first light beer sold by a national brewery in the United States. Launched in 1973, Miller Lite quickly soared in popularity. A 1975 *Business Week* article quoted a distributor saying he could sell thousands more cases if he could get them. It was also in 1975 that Miller and their advertising agency, McCann-Erickson, changed beer advertising by launching a $10 million campaign that would become a staple of sports television broadcasts for years to come.[2] The problem was obvious: How do you sell a low-calorie beer and make it "manly"?

Phillip Morris had success with their Marlboro Man character and applied the same concept when they took over Miller. Their early advertisements didn't tout the beer but rather the men who drank it. At the end of a hard day, it was "Miller Time." But that concept was a tougher sell when you're marketing a low-calorie beverage. The solution: Get tough guys to do the commercials. Early advertisements featured former NFL stars Dick Butkus and Bubba Smith, and if Miller Lite was tough enough for them, it was tough enough for you. The campaign helped boost Miller past Coors, Pabst, and Schiltz, making them the second largest brewer in the US (behind Anheuser-Busch) by 1977.[3]

Ads also featured former baseball players like Mickey Mantle, Whitey Ford, and Billy Martin. One popular ad had former Baltimore Orioles players Frank and Brooks Robinson sitting at a table in a bar talking about how similar they were. The two were teammates who were referred to as "The Robinson Brothers" despite the fact they weren't related, the biggest hint being that Frank was an African American man from Texas while Brooks was a white man from Arkansas. A hallmark of the Miller Lite commercials was humor and the punchline to the Robinson Brothers ad was that despite their similarities they weren't identical twins. "I'm at least two inches taller than him," said Frank Robinson at the end of the spot, unable to control his laughter.[4]

By May of 1982 Baltimore manager Earl Weaver could have been forgiven had he contacted Brooks or Frank in an effort to coax them out of retirement. After their big Opening Day win, Weaver's club dropped 13 of their next 18 games and found themselves at the bottom of the AL East standings. Slow starts had become somewhat of a tradition in Baltimore. The team began 1978 by losing their first five games and started 1979 with a 3–9 mark before winning 102 games and a pennant. The following season, they started off 28–30 and then won 100 games. The culprit in 1982, however, was the pitching staff, long a strength of Weaver's teams. When the Angels came to town at the end of April, Baltimore pitchers were allowing nearly six and a half runs per game, and, aside from Eddie Murray, the hitters were not making up the difference. Among those struggling was Cal Ripken Jr. Since his three-hit performance on Opening Day, Ripken was able to muster just four hits in his next fifty-two at bats, dropping his batting average to .123 at the end of April. The frustration was building, both for Ripken and Orioles fans. "I'm upset about the Orioles playing Cal Ripken Jr. as a full-time third baseman," said a letter to the *Baltimore Sun*. "He didn't hit well in the major leagues last year and is not hitting well this year. . . . [The Orioles] have, in their organization, John Stefero, who is very talented, and I think if Stefero's dad was coaching third base, he would be playing for the Orioles this season."[5]

Weaver expressed confidence in Ripken and told his third baseman to focus on defense. He had seen the talent and knew it would prevail, but lots of other people offered advice. So many, in fact, that it became overwhelming for the rookie. He could not escape the slump because so many people were trying to help him get out of it. Then he got some help from an unexpected source. On the final day of April, with Ripken riding a 1-for-26 streak, Reggie Jackson led off the top of the sixth inning for the Angels with a base hit off Jim Palmer and advanced to second on a single. First base umpire Al Clark called a balk on Palmer, which brought Weaver out of the dugout to argue. The break in play afforded Reggie, now standing on third base, the chance to offer Ripken some advice. "Don't let anyone else tell you how to hit," Jackson said. "You could hit before you got here. Just be yourself and hit the way you want to hit. They traded Doug DeCinces to make room for you, didn't they? They think you can play. They *know* you can."[6] The words were not all that different from those of others at the time, but, coming from a future Hall of Famer, they stuck.

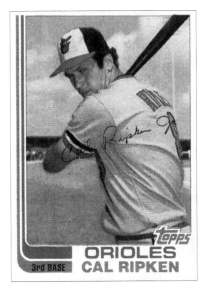

Figure 5: Cal Ripken Jr. took home American League Rookie of the Year honors in 1982 and went on to a Hall of Fame career. 1982 Topps® trading cards used courtesy of The Topps Company, Inc.

After going 0-for-3 on May 1, Ripken went 2-for-4 to close out the Angels series. The following day, a more relaxed Ripken faced the Seattle Mariners and caught a Mike Moore fastball in the back of the head. After a few days off, Ripken hit .406 in his next nine games and raised his batting average by more than 100 points. Jackson's advice, Weaver's confidence, and Moore's wake-up call had brought him around. "In the last few days, I told myself to simply go back to things that got me here," Ripken told reporters. "There was nobody in the minors telling me how to hit, and all the advice I'd been getting lately had totally confused me."[7]

Gaylord Perry had spent his entire career confusing people. The forty-three-year-old was in his twenty-first year in the major leagues and had two Cy Young Awards to his credit, but he had trouble finding a home for the 1982 season. Few were convinced that he could still pitch effectively, but the Mariners took a chance, signing him right before spring training. He entered camp with 297 career wins, which just happened to be seven more than the Mariners had as a franchise. How many of Perry's wins were obtained by throwing illegal pitches was open for debate. Nearly two decades earlier, Perry had just six career wins spread over three seasons when he entered the second half of a doubleheader against the New York Mets in the bottom of the thirteenth inning at Shea Stadium. Perry's catcher, Tom Haller, told him it might be time to break out the "new pitch" he'd been working on.[8] With the aid of a spitball, Perry threw ten scoreless innings in the game and got the win. He'd won 291 games since that day.

Throwing a spitball had its downsides, like when his daughter would come home from school in tears because boys were spitting on her, or when he embarrassed his wife by asking her OB/GYN for K-Y Jelly. But for Perry, the end justified the means. It was all part of the psychological warfare of baseball. The fact that he *could* throw a spitball at any time was just as valuable as actually throwing it. Perry would stand on the mound, look to the catcher for a sign, and touch the bill of his cap, the back of his neck, his pants, his eyebrows, behind his ear, anything to give the hitter the idea that the next pitch may be "loaded up." "When he was in Cleveland there were days when he beat us with nothing but fastballs," said Earl Weaver. "We never saw that Staten Island sinker of his. But we were always waiting on it."[9]

After starting the 1982 season 0–2, Perry won two of his next three starts, bringing him to 299 entering his May 6 appearance against the Yankees. The game was scoreless through two innings, but Seattle scored 5 in the bottom of the third inning off Doyle Alexander and Perry cruised to a complete game, 7–3 win, the three hundredth of his career. Ever since he signed with Seattle, the chase for three hundred wins had captured the attention of the national media. Now that he had reached the plateau, Perry did not want them to leave. "I hope you guys don't run away after this," said Perry after the game to the assembled media. "I want to see you tomorrow and the next day. I was just beginning to like you guys."[10]

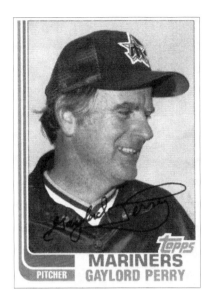

Figure 6: Gaylord Perry beat the Yankees for his three hundredth career win. 1982 Topps® trading cards used courtesy of The Topps Company, Inc.

The following day, Friday, May 7, the St. Louis Cardinals suffered a blow that threatened to derail their promising season. In the bottom of the eighth inning of their game against Atlanta, center fielder David Green hit a ground ball to the right side of the infield but tore his right hamstring on the way to first base. The Cardinals placed Green, who was batting .321 at the time of the injury, on the fifteen-day disabled list, but the prognosis was not good, and the team feared he would be out longer than just fifteen days. "I just stopped," said Green. "I saw [Braves pitcher Steve Bedrosian] was close to me and I didn't want to hit him. I have to learn. Next time I'll just kill him [run into Bedrosian] before I get hurt."[11]

The injury was ill-timed for St. Louis, which was also without right fielder George Hendrick, who was battling an elbow injury. With Hendrick in the lineup, the Cardinals were 16–2. Without him, they were 2–7. Green's injury meant Whitey Herzog was now without two of his three starting outfielders. But the injuries did not stop there. A week after Green's torn hamstring, Darrell Porter suffered a broken finger, and his replacement, Gene Tenace, broke a finger five days later. Then second baseman Tommy Herr went down with a leg injury that limited him to just six games over the next three weeks. The hot start the Cardinals enjoyed was suddenly in danger of being wiped out due to injury, and other teams in the National League East were ready to take advantage. "The Phillies had their ordeal by fire when Mike Schmidt missed two weeks with a rib injury," wrote Bill Conlin in the *Sporting News*. "Now, let's see how the Cardinals get along without catchers Darrell Porter and Gene Tenace for the next month."[12]

Fortunately for Herzog and the Cardinals, they had depth and a little magic sitting on their Triple-A Louisville team. To replace Green and add catching depth, St. Louis summoned outfielder Willie McGee and catcher Glenn Brummer from Triple-A Louisville. Both would contribute in important ways as the season progressed.

* * * * *

By early May, it was obvious something wasn't quite right with Twins outfielder Jim Eisenreich. The St. Cloud, Minnesota, native was a sixteenth-round draft pick in 1980 and spent the 1981 season in Single-A, where he hit .311 in 134 games. Despite his lack of seasoning, a strong spring training allowed Eisenreich to make the Opening Day roster of the major league club, and he was batting .299 at the end of April. But it was in that final game in April when the problems began. Eisenreich began twitching and hyperventilating and had to be removed from a game against the Brewers. "I just get nervous," Eisenreich said. "When I think about it and try to correct it, I make it worse. The more I do it, the madder I get it myself. When I forget about it and have fun, I'm OK."[13]

The problems worsened when the Twins went to Boston on May 3. Eisenreich led off the game with a double and scored on a ground out. But by the bottom of the fourth, he was hyperventilating again and left the game. The scene repeated itself the following night, a problem made worse by the taunts of Red Sox fans who mocked him from the outfield stands. "It was obvious that Jimmy's problems are uncontrollable and, as far as I'm concerned, the fans' conduct was lousy," said teammate Gary Ward. "I can usually talk to Jim in the dugout and settle him down. But I can't yell over them and settle him down."[14] Twins doctors put him on a sedative to help him relax, but that made the problem worse, and he returned to Minnesota for treatment. "Jimmy wants to stay and battle it himself," said manager Billy Gardner. "You have to admire him for that, but I'd like to see him go back and get it taken care of. When he's played, he's played well."[15]

That was the cruel part. During a stretch in which he began hyperventilating and had to be removed from five straight games, Eisenreich hit

.400. He took the situation, and the taunts, in stride and looked inward, telling the *Boston Globe*, "Fans are like that everywhere. That doesn't bother me. I'm just bothering myself right now. It's up to me, you know? It's a thing I've got to do myself."[16]

Eisenreich's struggles were just the beginning of an eventful month for the Twins. After trading Roy Smalley to the Yankees in April, the team pulled off two more deals in May. Minnesota sent catcher Butch Wynegar and pitcher Roger Erickson to the Yankees for three players and cash. On the same day, they traded closer Doug Corbett and Opening Day second baseman Rob Wilfong to the Angels for prospect Tom Brunansky, one other player, and cash. By mid-May, the Twins had opened a new ballpark and traded three Opening Day position player starters, their number two starting pitcher, and their closer. The moves left the Minnesota payroll at $1.95 million, less than the Mets were paying George Foster, and was not popular in the press or in the clubhouse. "I throw the ball up there, and if they don't hit it, fine. I'm not going to worry about it," said relief pitcher Ron Davis. "If Calvin [Griffith] doesn't care about winning why should I? This is sickening. I wouldn't pay $2 to watch this team play."[17]

The moves led to speculation that Griffith was trying to strip the team down and sell, speculation he denied. *Boston Globe* columnist Peter Gammons took Griffith to task in a May column, writing, "It wasn't the Corbett and Wynegar deals, per se, but the fact that these were the guys who were 'the future' when the [Larry] Hisles, (Bert) Blylevens . . . et al. fled. The majority of Minnesota fans feel the situation is hopeless, that no matter how good Kent Hrbek, Greg Gagne, (and others) turned out to be, they, too will be dumped for another group of tomorrows when they reach their peaks."[18]

The lone bright spot for the Twins seemed to be the play of rookie first baseman Hrbek, who went to high school a few miles away from Minnesota's former home, Metropolitan Stadium. Hrbek attended Kennedy High in Bloomington and did not receive much attention, but a concessions worker at the stadium recommended him to Twins management and they drafted Hrbek in the seventeenth-round in 1978. After hitting .239 in twenty-four games in 1981, Hrbek began 1982 on a tear. He hit five homers in the Twins' season-opening homestand, and by the middle of May was batting .315 with 10 homers and 26 RBI. The young slugger had Minnesota fans thinking he was the second coming of Harmon Killebrew.

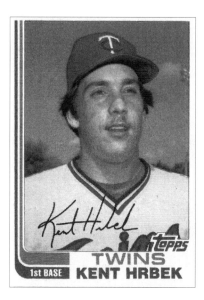

Figure 7: Local boy Kent Hrbek was perhaps the lone bright spot on a dismal 1982 Twins team, but they would win a World Series before the decade was over. 1982 Topps® trading cards used courtesy of The Topps Company, Inc.

"I hear the fans when I come up to the plate, and it definitely gets me pumped up," said Hrbek. "But it becomes a problem if I get too home run conscious. That's something I have to guard against. My dad told me many years ago that the important thing is to hit the ball hard someplace. That's why my hitting hero with the Twins was always Tony Oliva, not Harmon Killebrew. But when you've hit a couple into the upper deck, it's tough not to think home run."[19]

The six-foot-four, 200-pound Hrbek hit from the left side, and the early-season plan called for him to sit against many left-handed pitchers. But once Minnesota traded Smalley, Hrbek became an everyday player and he responded. The success meant even more to him because of the fact his dad was battling amyotrophic lateral sclerosis, also known as Lou Gehrig's disease. "The way my dad has handled it has given the rest of us in the family the strength to deal with it," said Hrbek. "I think by being able to be playing the major leagues, I've helped out my dad. It's been exciting for him."[20]

There was a lot of excitement when the Twins and Tigers faced each other in Detroit on May 14, and it began in the fourth inning, when Minnesota pitcher Pete Redfern hit Tigers center fielder Chet Lemon on the wrist. Lemon charged the mound and tackled Redfern, inciting a benches-clearing brawl that lasted nearly five minutes. The game was tied in the bottom of the eleventh when Ron Davis came up and in on

Detroit's Enos Cabell, who also charged the mound. The fight got ugly, with Tigers outfielder Larry Herndon, a victim of a Davis brushback earlier in the game, throwing wild punches in front of the pitcher's mound at anyone wearing a powder blue uniform. Davis and Cabell resumed their battle near first base, with each player throwing multiple punches. But the biggest casualty was Detroit pitcher Dave Rozema, who tore cartilage and three ligaments in his left knee and suffered a broken kneecap. "I was angry when I ran out there," Rozema said. "But it all happened so fast. I went for the first person I saw and tried to jump on him. It felt like I twisted the knee right off. I wasn't trying to cheap shot (anybody). I just wanted to knock somebody down and get in a fight. I'll be back though. I'm too much of an airhead to stay out of baseball."[21] Rozema did return but not until 1983. It took surgeons more than five hours to rebuild his knee, and he was lost for the season. After winning fifteen games as a rookie in 1977, he managed just eighteen more and was out of baseball after 1986 at age twenty-nine.

As was the case in Minneapolis and Detroit, in Montreal, things were not going as planned. The Expos went 9–5 in their first fourteen games, but the winning record masked a woefully deficient offense and not even a visit from Ron Howard could get them on track. The former *Happy Days* star turned director suited up prior to an Expos/Dodgers game in Los Angeles and took batting practice with the team. The plan was for him to be a batboy during the game, but once photographers got wind of the stunt, they turned their focus to the Montreal dugout, which drew the attention of the umpiring crew, who ejected Howard from the dugout for being a distraction.

Through early May, Expos starters Ray Burris, Scott Sanderson, and Steve Rogers were first, second, and third in ERA in the National League. Burris posted a 1.17 ERA in his first three starts, and his teammates showed their appreciation by scoring a total of one run for him. With players like Tim Raines, Andre Dawson, and Gary Carter, the offensive talent was there, but the production was not. Expos management turned their attention to second base, which had been a problem spot. They asked Tim Raines to move from left field to second base, a position he had played in the minor leagues, but Raines wanted to stay put, so the position became a revolving door. Four players saw time at the position in the team's first twenty-two games, and none of them provided any offense. On May 8 Montreal had seen enough and released second baseman Rodney Scott. Montreal acquired Scott prior to the 1979 season, and while he was a solid defender, he'd seen his batting average drop each year. The move infuriated pitcher Bill Lee, who felt Scott was vital to the team's success.

"Rodney was the key to our infield," Lee wrote in his autobiography, *The Wrong Stuff*. "At bat he only hit .230, but he walked a lot and stole a ton of bases. As a groundball pitcher, I thought he was indispensable on a team that never emphasized defense. I loved the way Rodney played behind me."[22]

Before Montreal's May 8 game against the Dodgers, Lee ripped off his uniform and put it in manager Jim Fanning's office along with a branch of pear blossoms and a note that read, "I can't put up with this bullshit. I'm going to be at the bar in Brasserie 77. If you want me, come and get me."[23] True to his word, Lee made his way to a nearby bar where he drank beer, played pool, and watched the game on TV before returning to the ballpark in case he was needed to pitch. The following morning, Expos president John McHale opened his office door to find Lee sitting on the floor eating a peanut butter sandwich. McHale fined Lee five thousand dollars and released him. "The most serious breach of a player's contract is for the player to make himself unavailable during a game," said McHale. "There's no telling what one game can mean, what one game might have meant during any of these past three seasons. One game simply can't be dismissed. This is not fair to the franchise, the fans, everyone."[24]

Dubbed "The Spaceman," Bill Lee was perhaps baseball's biggest free spirit. He incurred the wrath of commissioner Bowie Kuhn when he told reporters he sprinkled marijuana on his buckwheat pancakes, missed time in 1980 after injuring himself while climbing down a trellis to escape the husband of a woman he was in bed with, and once went AWOL from the Red Sox after they traded Bernie Carbo. Sure, he spent part of the afternoon in a bar, but he felt he was ready to pitch if the Expos had needed him.

"Guys have had a few drinks and played since Christy Mathewson," he said. "I was not drunk. I was able to pitch. Fanning always wants us to leave notes when we're going to be late. I left him a note letting him know that I didn't appreciate the manner in which he buried Rodney. They treated Rodney like a dog. They kicked him and they wondered why he snarled. They badmouthed him around the league. That's not right."[25]

Releasing Scott and Lee cost the Expos more than $400,000 in salary, but McHale was in win-now mode and couldn't afford to have bad clubhouse chemistry be the downfall of his team. Unfortunately for him, there were more problems to come.

There were plenty of problems in New York, too. George Steinbrenner had already fired his manager, so the next step was to make a trade. The Go-Go Yankees experiment ended when New York dealt first baseman Dave Revering and two others to Toronto for slugging first baseman John Mayberry. Revering had been a Yankee for just one year, but he had seen enough and welcomed the chance for a new start with the Blue Jays. "The trade isn't the answer," said Revering. "The attitude here has to change. George Steinbrenner has these guys in a state of confusion. Everybody is worried about going 0-for-4 because that means getting benched, so nobody is trying to advance runners or anything like that. It's a mess here and this little move isn't going to change things."[26]

On Revering's final day in pinstripes, the Yankees dropped an extra-inning affair to the Oakland A's, 9–7, in 13 innings. The following day was a scheduled day off before the team flew across the country to begin a 14-game road trip. But Steinbrenner was so incensed at his team's 9–13 record that he ordered them to report to Yankee Stadium for an 11 A.M. workout, which brought a predictable reaction from his players. "This workout stinks!" said Oscar Gamble. "They tell us in spring training they're going to give us days off. It's all a bunch of lies. It's ridiculous. We play 13 innings the night before, we got no time to pack and no sleep because we gotta be here. Ernie Banks is the only person who would have been happy to be here if he was on this team."[27]

The comments did little to mend bridges between Gamble and Steinbrenner, who earlier in the week threw the blame for the Yankees' slow start squarely at the feet of Gamble, saying, "There is no doubt in my mind that this team would be in first place if Oscar hadn't vetoed a trade to Texas for Al Oliver. Oscar promised me he'd be the best left-handed designated hitter in baseball, and he's batting .130."[28] Once he finished with Gamble, Steinbrenner turned his attention to Dave Winfield, who was off to a slow start. After a 0-for-4 day in which Winfield struck out twice and ground out twice, Steinbrenner publicly ripped his superstar. "I need Winfield to hit the ball in the air, not to dribble the ball through the infield . . . you don't pay $1.4 million a year for a guy to hit the ball through the infield. He's been a disappointment so far."[29] The bad blood between the two would only escalate as the season progressed.

The troubles in the Bronx were nothing compared to the disaster taking place in Arlington, Texas, where the trade for Lee Mazzilli was not working out. Mazzilli made two errors in the early going before being moved to designated hitter, and then further endeared himself to nearly everyone in baseball with his assessment of his new position. "Left field is an idiot's position," he said. "It's for catchers and first basemen, guys who can't play defense. I've seen teams use pitchers out there."[30]

"Tell him I know left fielders who were millionaires," said Boston left fielder Jim Rice. "I don't think I'd consider any of us idiots . . . Yaz, Willie Wilson, Dave Winfield, myself. Left fielders win batting titles and Most Valuable Player awards. I'd like to see him call me an idiot. If he doesn't like it, he can go carry a lunch pail."[31]

Dallas Morning News columnist Randy Galloway summed up the feeling of many when he wrote, "If Lee Mazzilli's right, he can't even meet idiot standards."[32]

"We didn't get Mazzilli just to play left field," said general manager Eddie Robinson, trying to smooth over Mazzilli's comments. "We also got him as insurance in centerfield. At the time of the trade, we couldn't be sure that George Wright was for real, and Mickey Rivers was going on the disabled list with a knee injury. We needed someone else capable of playing center."[33]

In Mazzilli, the Rangers had someone capable of playing center, but he was not as good as the guy who was already there (George Wright). He expressed a desire to play first base, but Texas already had Pat Putnam and Lamar Johnson there. When reporters asked Rangers manager Don Zimmer if he had plans to play Mazzilli at first, his answer was a quick no. It was obviously a bad fit, and Mazzilli, a Brooklyn native, missed New York. "The people in Texas have all been nice," he told a New York reporter, "But it's not New York. It's not the same. And I ain't wearing no cowboy hat."[34]

After opening with a 6–4 record, the Rangers lost fifteen of their next sixteen, and then players started going down. Mazzilli finally got a start in center field and injured himself making a diving catch. Left fielder Billy Sample hurt his wrist in an outfield collision, and Rivers came off the disabled list and reinjured his knee in his first pinch-hitting assignment. Relief pitcher Steve Comer was hit by a ricochet during batting practice and cracked a few teeth. That evening, while waiting for the team flight, Comer ordered a flaming shot from the airport bar only to have the liquid drip out of his mouth and catch his beard on fire. By mid-May, the Rangers were the only team in baseball who had yet to reach ten wins, and a Texas radio station introduced what they called the Rangers diet, which only permitted people to eat on days the Rangers won. Zimmer also received a letter from a fan advising him that second baseman Doug Flynn's biorhythms indicated he should not play in an early-May game against the Tigers. Zimmer ignored the advice only to see Flynn make an eight-inning error that cost Texas the game. A rookie sports reporter named Tim Kirkjian told Zimmer the situation was too much for him to take. "Too much for you?" replied Zimmer. "You're young. You've got your whole life ahead of you. I'm old, I'm fat, I've got metal in my head and I've got this team."[35]

The question became how much longer the team would belong to Zimmer and general manager Eddie Robinson. On May 24, a scheduled off day after returning from a 1–5 road trip, Rangers brass huddled for more than twelve hours of meetings at Arlington Stadium. Players, coaches, and front office staff came and went, but there were no announcements, and everyone was very tight-lipped about what was said during the marathon sessions. "Never have so many gone to so much trouble to say so little," wrote beat reporter Gil LeBreton. "Heads didn't roll Monday, just as Ranger owner (Eddie) Chiles promised. Robinson, who has nine lives and no left fielder, lived to order Steak Diane, and Zimmer, too, was invited to the supper table without having to wash the boss' feet."[36]

Chiles preached calm and patience, saying,

> It's never been my style to rant and rave and fire people. I'm well aware of the fact that the standard operating procedure when a baseball team is not performing well is to walk in and fire somebody. . . . Well, in industry that's not true. Probably the poor guy that got you into trouble has to get you out of trouble. I found out how these people talk, how they think, what their backgrounds are. There's no magic formula, like replacing Mr. X or Mr. Y or firing a manager or cutting somebody's head off. We're going to dig ourselves out of this hole but we're not going to jump out.[37]

Chiles's patience was in contrast to the lack of it coming from some of his board members, notably minority owner Mark Rankin, who said, "I'm about ready to call up the whole [Triple-A] Denver team and swap out with this one. Everybody's extremely disappointed with this team. It's the worst one I've seen here. I think we've seen enough. We've been more than patient. It's time to do something. It's time to change faces on the playing field and if we don't have a general manager and a manager capable of doing that, then we'll have to find another general manager and manager."[38]

Replacing Robinson and Zimmer was an option, but, as *Fort Worth Star-Telegram* writer Steve Pate pointed out, there was an overarching issue with the Rangers. "Chiles can rant, and he can rave," wrote Pate, "but until he buys a more talented team, or dumps more money out to get more talented players, he's going to have to live with what he's got . . . the bottom line remains this: Texas, 11 wins, 25 losses."[39]

The meeting so inspired the Rangers that they lost 10–2 to Baltimore the following evening to drop to 14.5 games behind the first-place California Angels, who were enjoying a fast start thanks to great pitching and solid defense. The offense hadn't kicked in yet, but the Angels pitching staff had allowed the fewest runs in the American League. "People keep saying our pitching can't be real," said manager Gene Mauch, "but look at our staff. Geoff Zahn, Bruce Kison, Ken Forsch, Doug Corbett, they're guys who put the ball in play and need defense."[40] He continued: "[Brian] Downing has made himself a far better than average left fielder. Doug DeCinces has made plays I can't believe. And the most important guy is Bob Boone. I don't think, with the possible exception of Carlton Fisk, there's a catcher who can quarterback a game better than Boone."[41]

One surprise in the rotation was the performance of veteran Steve Renko, who began the season in the bullpen but moved into the rotation after youngsters Mike Witt and Angel Moreno underperformed. The thirty-seven-year-old Renko was a multisport star as a youth, and his athletic success continued at the University of Kansas, where he started on the baseball, football, and basketball teams. On the gridiron, Renko played quarterback, where his primary responsibility was to turn around and hand the ball to a running back named Gale Sayers. But he showed enough promise to catch the eye of Oakland Raiders owner Al Davis, who selected him in the fifteenth round of the 1966 AFL draft. By that time Renko already had a year of minor league baseball in the Mets organization as a pitcher-first baseman under his belt and decided to turn Davis down. He made the switch to pitching full time in 1967 and was dealt to Montreal two years later where he won six games for the Expos. Since then he'd bounced around, playing for the Cubs, White Sox, A's, and Red Sox before landing in California, where he was reunited with Mauch, who was his manager in Montreal. Over the course of his career, he'd compiled a record of 117–129. Once installed into the Angels rotation in early May he went 3–0 with a 1.72 ERA in his first four starts.

Another bright spot was Zahn, who earned American League Pitcher of the Month honors for April. Zahn battled a knee injury in 1981 that left him with a 10–11 record as well as the league lead in earned runs (78) and home runs allowed (18). But off-season surgery stabilized his left knee, bringing strength to his "drive leg" and extra hop to his fastball.

He also added a slider and a changeup to his repertoire, and the result was a 5–2 record in his first nine starts along with a 2.35 ERA.

The strength of the Angels pitching helped keep them atop the standings in the AL West, but Oakland outfielder Rickey Henderson was doing all he could to keep his team in the race while establishing himself as perhaps the best leadoff man in baseball. Henderson didn't hit for much power at this stage of his career, but he was on base constantly. Through Oakland's first 49 games Henderson collected 48 hits and 57 walks, and once he got on, he ran. Four stolen bases in a doubleheader split with Detroit gave Henderson 49 swipes in Oakland's first 49 games. When former Cardinals outfielder Lou Brock set the modern record of 118 stolen bases in 1974, he had 14 at the end of April. Henderson stole 22 bases in April of 1982 and showed no signs of slowing down. "He's going to get that record this season," said A's manager Billy Martin. "He's going to get the record, but legitimately, not when we're eight runs ahead or eight runs behind."[42]

"I know I can get Brock's record if I stay healthy," Henderson said. "I'm not saying I'm going to steal 162, but it's possible. That's what I'm concentrating on—stealing a base a game. I was hoping to have a good first half. The second half is when I usually steal a lot of bases."[43]

The thought that Henderson could improve on his first-half pace was a terrifying one for the rest of the American League, but it was not without merit. In 1980, his first full season in the big leagues, Henderson stole 66 bases in the second half of the season en route to a Major League-leading 100. Oakland's addition of second-baseman Davey Lopes from the Dodgers not only gave Henderson a kindred spirit in the stolen base department, it also gave him a mentor. Lopes had the highest stolen base percentage in major league baseball history entering the 1982 season, and he worked with Henderson during spring training on reading pitchers' rhythms and moves. "Everybody knows he's going to run," said Martin. "The pitchers are throwing over to first more and pitching out more. But he's smarter. I didn't see [Maury] Wills or Brock, but Rickey's the best base stealer I've ever seen in our league."[44]

Unfortunately for Martin, Henderson's performance was one of the only bright spots for the A's. Rickey may have been stealing a base per game, but Oakland pitchers were allowing more than one home run per game, and the injuries were mounting. Outfielders Tony Armas and Dwayne Murphy both went down and were followed by starters Steve McCatty and Mike Norris. Norris was the runner-up in the 1980 AL Cy Young race while McCatty finished second in 1981. It was the kind of production that was impossible to replace. Still, there was no panic in Oakland.

"Everything is a little out of focus," said team president Roy Eisenhardt. "You keep watching it, it's like a television picture slightly out of focus. You just wait for the whole thing to come together. You can't panic by trading bodies and moving bodies around."[45]

* * * * *

While Henderson and the A's were dropping in the standings, Rocky Balboa was rocketing up the box-office list as *Rocky III* hit theaters at the end of the month. The film featured Sylvester Stallone's title character battling self-doubt, a professional wrestler named "Thunderlips" played by Hulk Hogan, and the formidable Clubber Lang, played by Mr. T, before ultimately prevailing. Born Lawrence Tureaud, Mr. T was a bouncer and a bodyguard for Steve McQueen, Diana Ross, and Muhammad Ali before venturing into acting. He was an extra in *The Blues Brothers*, which was shot in his hometown of Chicago, but playing Rocky's nemesis, Clubber Lang, was his big break. The film made him a household name and helped him land a spot on *The A Team*, which debuted on NBC in 1983. But even stardom didn't please his mother. At the premiere of *Rocky III,* when Mr. T's mother heard him make lewd remarks in the film to Talia Shire, who played Balboa's wife, she told him she didn't raise him to talk to a lady like that and walked out of the theater.

In addition to launching Hogan and Mr. T into prominence, the film also proved a boon for the careers of the band Survivor, who performed the film's theme song, "Eye of the Tiger." The band's second album, *Premonition,* hit record stores in 1981 and produced their first Top 40 single, "Poor Man's Son." Stallone liked the song and asked the band to write something similar for his next Rocky movie. It was the break Survivor founder Jim Peterik needed. He was living with a friend at the time and barely had enough money for rent. "The guitar I played on ["Eye of the Tiger"] had a broken headstock," he recalled. "I couldn't afford to get another one, so I glued it back together. A week after the film came out, I was driving on the freeway and I heard it on the radio. I switched over and heard it on another station. I switched again and heard it on a third station, and I pulled over because it was one of those moments I never wanted to forget."[46]

"Eye of the Tiger" became a huge hit, reaching Number 1 on the Billboard charts and staying there for six weeks while also winning a Grammy and receiving an Academy Award nomination. Survivor lead singer David Bickler would provide lead vocals to another project, a Budweiser campaign called Real Men of Genius that ran in the late 1990s and early 2000s. In 1999, during the Real Men of Genius campaign, Robin Yount, by then retired and elected to the Hall of Fame, starred in a Miller Lite commercial with George Brett, his fellow inductee. In the spot, Brett ribbed Yount about receiving a higher percentage of the Hall of Fame vote while Yount countered that he won two MVP Awards to Brett's one. The two of them racked up more than six thousand hits over the course of their careers, but, by the end of May 1982, what Yount and fans of the Brewers had hoped would be a hugely successful season had taken a bad turn. There was something seriously wrong with the team, both on and off the field.

Milwaukee began the season with a 16–10 record and were just two games off the pace in the American League East when things began to go sour. On May 3, Milwaukee trailed Kansas City 3–0 in the bottom of the seventh when Larry Hisle pinch-hit for Jim Gantner and delivered a long two-run homer. It was a big moment for Hisle, who had missed the previous two weeks due to a recurrence of the shoulder injury that had plagued him since 1979. Hisle established himself as a star with the Minnesota Twins in the 1970s, but, like many other young players, he fell victim to Calvin Griffith's tight-fisted ways. Contract negotiations became acrimonious, and he left via free agency after batting .302 and leading the AL with 119 RBI in 1977. He signed with Milwaukee and continued to be an offensive force, batting .290 with 34 homers and 115 RBI and finishing third in the AL MVP balloting in 1978. But everything changed in April of 1979 when he suffered a severe rotator cuff tear in his right shoulder while making a throw from the outfield. "It felt like someone stuck a knife in my shoulder," he said. "You think it's going to stop and the pain is going to go away. But it didn't."[47]

Hisle tried strengthening exercises to battle through the injury, but a second tear in 1980 necessitated surgery to repair the damage. He came back in 1981 but developed a bone spur that required a second surgical procedure. "After the second surgery, the doctor recommended I never play again or risk losing use of the shoulder," he said. "My dream was to play even after the two surgeries. I knew there would be a lot of difficulties and complications. I hoped the shoulder would allow me to get enough at bats to make a contribution to my team."[48]

Unfortunately, it did not. The pinch-hit home run was the last of his career. He played just three more games before his shoulder flared up again. His career was over. Four days after Hisle's injury, the Brewers pitching staff saw a recurrence of another sort: the dreaded Pac-Man injury. On the heels of Rollie Fingers developing a blister from playing too much Pac-Man, starter Pete Vuckovich injured his ankle . . . somehow. One report said he was injured when a Pac-Man machine fell on him, but Dan Okrent claimed in his 1983 book, *Nine Innings*, that Vuke injured his ankle when he became frustrated while playing Pac-Man and kicked the machine. At the time, Vuckovich claimed he twisted his ankle while walking down a hill on the way to the ballpark. Whatever the origins of the injury, the result was that Vuckovich missed his start on May 11 against the Royals, and things did not go well for his replacement, Jerry Augustine. Injuries and fatigue limited the Milwaukee bullpen to just three healthy arms, and the Royals scored seven runs in the first two innings against Augustine. Not wanting to tax an already depleted bullpen, manager Buck Rodgers sent Augustine back out, and he allowed five more runs in the fifth inning, an exquisite display of taking one for the team. "I am not out to show anybody up," said Rodgers. "I just wanted to get through this dammed thing with a pitching staff for tomorrow."[49]

"We were wondering if he missed curfew or something," said Kansas City catcher John Wathan of Rodgers leaving his pitcher in the game so long.[50]

On May 31, Augustine was again the center of a Brewers controversy, thanks to Rodgers. The Brewers led Seattle 3–2 in the bottom of the ninth inning with a runner on second and the left-handed hitting Bruce Bochte at the plate. Rather than summon Fingers, Rodgers called on Mike Caldwell, who gave up a game-tying single before being replaced by Fingers. Milwaukee took a 4–3 lead in the eleventh on a Robin Yount homer, but Augustine replaced Fingers and allowed a two-run walk-off home run in the bottom of the inning to lose the game and drop Milwaukee's record to 25–26. "That's probably the last nail in the coffin," said Fingers. "Does he [Rodgers] think I can't get a left-hander out? I'm getting paid good money to do that. That's my job. To come in and save situations like that. That sums it up. I can't think of anything else to say."[51] Rodgers defended the move, saying he went with the left-handed Caldwell to try to end the game in the ninth inning and that Fingers had thrown three innings a few days earlier.

"We're in serious trouble now," said first baseman Cecil Cooper. "Were in serious trouble if we can't beat these guys (Seattle), especially when you take the lead 3 times and can't hold it. We've lost three games on this trip and we should have won every one of them."[52]

"You can't fire 25 players," said second baseman Jim Gantner. "Sometimes the manager's in the wrong place at the wrong time. That's really too bad. We're going to have to do something to shake up this club. I'm not saying fire the manager, but something has to be done to shake up the club. Make some decisions somehow. That's not my decision, though. That's the front office."[53]

It wouldn't take long for the front office to decide.

STANDINGS AS OF MAY 31

Table 4.1. American League East and West

AL East				AL West			
Team	Wins	Losses	GB	Team	Wins	Losses	GB
Boston	30	17	-	California	31	18	-
Detroit	29	17	0.5	Chicago	28	18	1.5
New York	24	21	5.0	Kansas City	25	21	4.5
Cleveland	23	23	6.5	Seattle	25	26	7.0
Baltimore	23	24	7.0	Oakland	23	27	8.5
Milwaukee	22	24	7.5	Texas	14	29	14.0
Toronto	21	26	9.0	Minnesota	12	39	20

Table 4.2. National League East and West

NL East				NL West			
Team	Wins	Losses	GB	Team	Wins	Losses	GB
St. Louis	31	18	-	Atlanta	27	20	-
New York	27	21	3.5	San Diego	25	2	1.5
Montreal	25	20	4.0	L. A. Dodgers	25	24	3.0
Philadelphia	21	28	4.5	Houston	21	28	7.0
Chicago	21	28	10.0	San Francisco	21	29	7.5
Pittsburgh	18	27	11.0	Cincinnati	19	28	8.0

5. JUNE

Whatever Happens, Your Toes Are Still Tappin'

"*Still Life*, the Rolling Stones' fourth live album, opens with an absolutely savage version of 'Under My Thumb,'" wrote reviewer Christopher Connelly in *Rolling Stone* magazine. "Keith Richards starts it off, hammering out that killer riff as if it were 1965 again, while Charlie Watts slams away with equal fervor. And Mick Jagger tears into the unbridled misogyny of the lyrics like a man rabid for revenge."[1] The Stones released their *Still Life* LP on June 1, a live album recorded during the previous summer's American tour, and just in time to prime fans for their 1982 European tour. Connelly, who would go on to work for ESPN, wrote a somewhat tempered review despite the introduction. But he wrapped it up with the perspective that would become a hallmark later in his career by stepping back and putting himself in the shoes of the average rock-and-roll fan.

> For all its strengths, *Still Life* finally comes across as the aural equivalent of a Stones T-shirt, the final item of tour merchandise. But so what? People who get to see the Stones a lot—rock critics, for example—tend to forget that a lot of people don't get to see them at all. That kid who told one reporter in Los Angeles, "*Some Girls* . . . man, that brings back some memories," spoke, I think, for a lot of people. They are going to love this record.[2]

Stones fans may have loved the *Still Life* record, but Texas Rangers owner Eddie Chiles was not a fan of his team's record. The team went 7–8 after Eddie Chiles's heavily armed organizational meeting, and the disgruntled owner decided it was time to make a move. Thursday, June 10, was an off-day for the Rangers, so Don Zimmer and his wife, Soot, along with *Dallas Morning News* writer Randy Galloway and his wife, went to a horse track in New Orleans. On the way, Zimmer mentioned to Galloway he thought he would be fired before the day was over. As soon as they pulled up to the valet window, a police officer approached.

"Are you Mr. Zimmer?" the officer asked. "You have a very important call."[3]

Zimmer looked at Galloway and winked.

When he picked up the phone, Zimmer heard the voice of one of Chiles's executive assistants telling him, "We've decided to make a change. We need you to get back here right away. Mr. Chiles' private plane will take you back."[4]

"What's going on?"[5] Zimmer asked, though he was pretty sure he knew exactly what was happening.

"We've fired [general manager] Eddie Robinson."[6]

Zimmer was stunned. Not only did he think *he* was the odd man out, but firing the general manager of a struggling team less than a week before the trade deadline was a curious move, to say the least, especially when there was no one to take his place.

"I'll be acting GM," Chiles told the media after he announced Robinson's dismissal. "I hope not too long but it may be until the end of the year. We have no one in mind, have not talked to anyone, have not even thought about it."[7]

Two days later, Zimmer was in his office when he got a call from Chiles saying he was on his way down for a meeting. Upon arrival, he got straight to the point. "As of today, I'm the general manager of this ballclub," said Chiles, "and I will be until the end of the season. Starting today there will be nobody brought up from the minors unless you OK it. There will be no trades unless you OK them. You got that?"[8]

While Chiles officially held the interim title of general manager, it was Zimmer who was really in charge of the organization. "Then," Chiles continued, "when we start next year, you will be responsible for this team. Is that fair enough?"[9]

"That's fine with me," said Zimmer.[10] His tenure as de facto general manager would not last long.

The evening after Zimmer's meeting with Chiles, Cincinnati Reds outfielder Eddie Milner led off the top of the first inning at Dodger Stadium with a double to left-center field off Los Angeles starter Jerry Reuss, who proceeded to retire the next twenty-seven men he faced and cruised to an 11–1 win. It was Reuss's second one-hitter of the season and stopped a personal six-game skid in which he went 1–4 with a 7.31

ERA. "I'm just glad to win the damn thing," Reuss said after the game. "I think somebody else's been wearing my uniform the last four weeks."[11]

Reuss's struggles mirrored that of his team. Not only did his win snap a personal losing streak, it also snapped a four-game Dodger skid, which left them eight games out of first place in the National League West. Among the culprits in the Dodgers' struggles was first baseman Steve Garvey, who saw his batting average dip into the .220s the last week of May. A twelve-game hot streak brought his average to a more respectable number and included him playing in his one thousandth consecutive game. But the joy of his personal accomplishment was tempered by ongoing questions about his contract status. Dodger fans wanted him back, and, with a salary of about $330,000, he now qualified as underpaid. But he would also be thirty-four years old by Opening Day of 1983, and two of L.A.'s top minor league prospects, Mike Marshall and Greg Brock, were both first basemen.

Garvey's 3-for-4 night on the day of Reuss's gem brought his batting average to .257 with six homers, but Brock, ten years Garvey's junior, had already hit 20 home runs in Triple-A, while Marshall had 11. Still, the night of his one thousandth straight game was one to cherish, and Garvey was not interested in talking about the future. "Nothing will alter tonight," he said. "I don't want to think about it. It's something I want to share with the fans. I'm here tonight and the fans are here."[12]

Garvey's teammates did not let the day go by without having some fun at his expense. When he arrived at the ballpark before the game, he checked the lineup to see his name scratched out and replaced by Rick Monday. "For a second, I was wondering what was going on," he said.[13]

On the same evening Dodger fans were enjoying Reuss's performance, moviegoers were falling in love with an alien. *E.T. the Extra-Terrestrial*, the story of an alien stranded on earth and befriended by a ten-year-old boy, opened nationwide on June 11 and was an immediate success. Producer/director Steven Spielberg created the E.T. character as an homage to the imaginary alien friend he invented as a child to help him cope with his parents' divorce. Twenty-two years later, E.T. won the hearts, and money, of thousands. The film grossed more than $11 million in its first weekend[14] and stayed at number one in the box office rankings for six weeks en route to becoming the highest-grossing film of all time before another Spielberg film, *Jurassic Park,* surpassed it in 1993.[15]

"Steven Spielberg's '*The Extra-Terrestrial*' has been dubbed a masterpiece by Time and Newsweek," wrote John Stark in the *San Francisco*

Examiner. "It received an eight-minute standing ovation at Cannes. Preview audiences have been moved to tears. Can it really be this good? Yes, it really is. It's one of the most magical, entertaining and emotionally moving films ever made."[16]

Even more magical for Spielberg was the fact that *E.T.* was released just a week after *Poltergeist,* the story of a suburban family whose daughter is abducted by ghosts, which he also produced. It became the highest-grossing horror film of 1982.[17]

* * * * *

By June, the Phillies had put the horror of their 6–13 April behind them. An early-season injury to Mike Schmidt and a struggling Steve Carlton were partially to blame. But Schmidt's return meant opponents could no longer afford to pitch around Gary Matthews. With better pitches to hit, Matthews went on a tear, including a nine-game stretch in which he went 15-for-31 with three homers and eleven RBI. But the Phillies fortunes really began to turn around after manager Pat Corrales inserted Bob Dernier into the lineup on a regular basis. The twenty-five-year-old Dernier was signed as an undrafted free agent and stole 250 bases over four minor league seasons before finally cracking the everyday lineup at the big-league level. He responded by batting .333 in May, stealing 21 bases in 25 attempts, and acquiring the nickname "White Lightning."

"I think a large part of my success was that I was new on the scene and the pitchers didn't know me," said Dernier. "Maybe there wasn't as much attention paid to me as there should have been, but that was a way for me to let it be known that I'm here, and if you don't pay attention to me, I'm going to run every chance I get. It's the reason I'm in the major leagues, I have to make things happen."[18]

The Phillies were starting to get production from their veterans as well. After beginning the season 0–4, Carlton went 7–2 over his next ten starts, including a 16-strikeout performance against the Cubs. Even at thirty-seven years old, Carlton showed the Cubs, many of them former teammates, he could still dominate. His fastball still had life, and his signature pitch, the slider, which broke down-and-in to right-handed batters, was as sharp as ever.

"I'm just glad I played with the guy that long," said Cubs shortstop and former teammate Larry Bowa. "His breaking ball is so tight that it explodes at the end. When I used to play behind him, I always wondered how so many guys could swing at a ball down and in. Now I know why."[19]

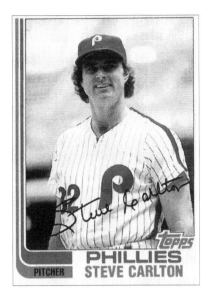

Figure 8: Steve Carlton overcame a slow start to win twenty-three games and his fourth Cy Young Award. 1982 Topps® trading cards used courtesy of The Topps Company, Inc.

"That's the Steve Carlton I've seen in the past. Wow!" said manager Pat Corrales. "In the case of Pete Rose and Lefty, there's a different mold. They made the mold and threw it away."[20]

In June, Rose became just the fourth player in major league history to play in three thousand games, joining Ty Cobb, Stan Musial, Hank Aaron, and Carl Yastrzemski. Later in the month, a double off Cardinals starter John Stuper moved him into sole possession of second place on the all-time hits list. Hit number 3,772 left him just 419 shy of passing Cobb to become the all-time leader.

"I don't look at it as if I'm chasing him," Rose said. "I'm going to catch him. It's not a chase. It's fun to go out there every night and face these good pitchers and try to get base hits."[21]

"I thought about it a lot today, thought about stopping him" said Stuper, who was making just his fourth career start. "But what I think about Pete Rose is, how could anyone boo him? He's what baseball is all about."[22]

The team most thought would run away with the division, the Montreal Expos, were also playing well, despite the issues with Bill Lee and Rodney Scott. The pitching staff was still on a roll, led by Charlie Lea, who threw 26 straight scoreless innings in May and into early June. The spring training trade of Larry Parrish for Al Oliver opened third base for Tim Wallach, and he responded by batting .367 in May with 23 RBI to earn Player-of-the-Month honors.

While Wallach, the Expos 1979 first-round draft pick, was a graduate of Cal State Fullerton and a former *Sporting News* College Player of the Year, Scott's departure in May opened a spot for another standout college player, Terry Francona. Terry's father, Tito, played in the big leagues for nine different teams over his fifteen-year career. Tito was a member of the Tigers when his wife, Birdie, became pregnant with Terry, and the elder Francona called the team to ask for a $1,000 raise due to the impending arrival of his son. But Tito called collect, and Detroit's general manager refused the call. Once he got through, the answer was a quick no. Tito wrapped up his career in 1970 as a member of the Milwaukee Brewers, and on one occasion he sent his son over to the batting cage to meet Ted Williams, then the manager of the Washington Senators. Williams rarely got along with newspaper writers, but children were a different story, and The Splendid Splinter welcomed the younger Francona, saying, "Well you are a great looking kid and your Dad is one helluva ballplayer. I just want to know one thing, young man, can you hit?"[23]

As it turned out, he could. Terry hit .550 and threw a no-hitter as a sophomore at New Brighton High School in Pennsylvania. He hit .769 as a junior, but a shoulder injury scuttled his senior season after just ten at bats. Undeterred, the Cubs drafted him in the second round in 1977 but offered him only $18,000 to sign, so he went to the University of Arizona, where he won a College World Series title and the Golden Spikes Award as the top collegiate player in the nation. The performance made him a first-round pick of the Expos. When it came time to negotiate a contract for his son, Tito called Montreal general manager John McHale and asked, "John, how good is your memory? Remember when my wife was pregnant and you wouldn't give me the extra $1,000? Well, you're going to have to pay now because this is the baby."[24]

Terry signed for $100,000, made his big-league debut a year later, and became a regular in May of 1982 when McHale released Rodney Scott. Francona hit .339 over his next 34 games, but his season came to an end in St. Louis on June 16 when he suffered a devastating injury while chasing a fly ball off the bat of Julio González. "I went back on the ball and went to jump and planted on the warning track and it gave way and I felt my right knee explode," wrote Francona in his 2013 autobiography, *Francona: The Red Sox Years*. "My momentum took me into the base of the wall. When I hit that wall, I thought my life was over. It looked like a cartoon. They had to peel me off. I'd never felt pain like that. It was completely torn."[25]

With Francona out, the Expos shifted Tim Raines from second base back to left field, where he felt more comfortable, but it meant the revolving door at second base continued to turn. Unfortunately for Raines, there was another issue looming, and it came to a head a few days later. Raines was twenty-two years old, making $200,000 a year, and hanging out with cocaine users, some of whom were teammates. He had lots of free time and lots of money. Before he knew it, he had developed a $1,000-a-week habit.[26]

"I learned that summer that when the exhilarating high of a drug wears off, a crippling low sets in," he wrote in his 2017 autobiography, *Rock Solid*. "Your body and brain crave more. So, you either give them more or you become a physical and mental mess."[27]

In his 1990 book, *No More Mr. Nice Guy*, former Expos manager Dick Williams discussed the growing problem in Montreal, saying, "By the end of my second year there [1978] I knew my biggest opponent wasn't the Philadelphia Phillies or the Pittsburgh Pirates, but the drugs."[28]

Olympic Stadium in Montreal hosted some good baseball, but it also hosted an area under the stands that Expos players called "The Launching Pad," where they would go to smoke marijuana.[29] According to Williams, there were also drug deals going down in the parking lot involving players from the Expos and opposing teams. By 1982, Williams was in San Diego, but the drug problems in Montreal remained. Toward the end of June, Raines was hitting .289, and the Expos were just a game out of first place when he went 3-for-3 against the Pirates with two walks and three SBs. The performance was even more impressive considering he had been out all night partying. After the game, Raines decided to keep the good times rolling.

"The next 48 hours were a blur," he said in his autobiography. "As I crisscrossed Montreal, snorting line after line, my mind started playing tricks on me. I saw objects and heard voices that weren't there. By the end of my 48-hour binge, I was drained of all energy and emotion . . . lying on the floor of my apartment . . . and feeling like I was going to die."[30]

Raines hadn't slept for days, but he was afraid that if he went to bed he might not wake up. A phone call brought him back to reality, but the voice on the other end was not comforting. It was someone from the Expos wondering where he was because their game with the Mets was about to start. Raines lied and said he had food poisoning. The team sent a doctor to his apartment to check him out, and it did not take long to figure out that food poisoning wasn't the issue.

Rather than continue the lie, Raines confessed to the doctor and to McHale the next day. McHale listened with compassion and offered to help his young star. Eventually, he did more than that. On multiple occasions, McHale drove Raines to his biweekly therapy sessions. Once the season was over, Raines went to a rehab facility in California and got clean.

While the Expos were a young team who had their first taste of winning the year before, the Angels were loaded with veterans for whom winning was routine. All nine of their regular starters had played in at least one League Championship Series, and Reggie Jackson, Bob Boone, and shortstop Tim Foli, who took over for the injured Rick Burleson, had seven World Series rings between them. The Angels won their first division title in 1979 but slipped to sixth place in the American League West in 1980 and only improved to fifth in 1981.

"I don't think last year's team felt good about itself," said manager Gene Mauch. "There were too many holes, and players aren't stupid. They can figure it out."[31]

General manager Buzzie Bavasi filled some of those holes by bringing in Doug DeCinces, Jackson, Boone, and Foli. *Sporting News* writer John Strege said the 1981 California Angels were a team that lacked personality and went through the motions, but that could not be said about a team with Reggie Jackson on the roster.

"The Angels had a lot of millionaires and egos to match the dollars," wrote Don Baylor in his book, *Nothing but the Truth: A Baseball Life.* "You couldn't take a swing without hitting an MVP, batting champ, or home run king. There were personality clashes. I can't count how many of them revolved around Reggie. And I can't count the number of times I wound up in the middle, trying to keep everybody from killing each other."[32]

One such incident involved Jackson and second baseman Bobby Grich. The two went out one evening and ended up vying for the affections of the same young woman, who left the bar with Grich. The next day in the clubhouse, Jackson was giving Grich a lot of grief. Grich knew what it was about, even if no one else did, and told Jackson he'd had enough. After batting practice Reggie started back up again. Grich again told Reggie to knock it off, but he kept it going.

"The next thing you know, Bobby stands up and his chair flies back," said DeCinces. "Don Baylor had the locker between Grich and Reggie and thank God for Donnie. He grabbed Bobby, turned to Reggie and said, 'you apologize by the count of three or I'm gonna let him go and he's gonna kick your ass.'"

Baylor started counting: "One . . . Two . . ." Jackson apologized.

But if the opportunity arose, Jackson could switch from instigator to team leader. When the Angels lost seven straight games, Mauch called a team meeting and asked if anyone wanted to talk; Jackson stepped up.

"I felt the time was right," he said. "I'd like to see this club have a nastier personality, tougher, lots of fiber. It's going to be tougher with this team because adversity comes quicker. That's part of the California Angels history. Charlie Finley said that during a storm you have to keep the windshield wipers going."[33]

Following the team meeting, the Angels won nine of their next 13 games to build a four-game lead in the American League West. Away from the scrutiny of New York, Reggie was having fun again. He hit just .188 in April with only one home run but bounced back with a .271 average in May, and his signature power was returning. "When a guy like him gets off to a slow start, you know he's going to have a lot of fun getting back to normal," said Mauch.[34]

Adding Jackson gave the Angels swagger and charisma, but the addition of Bob Boone gave the Angels a steadying influence. Boone seemed to be rejuvenated, both at the plate and behind it. "I don't see how he could play much better," said Foli, who had faced Boone often as a member of the Pittsburgh Pirates. "He never had a chance to throw anybody out over there (in Philadelphia). We'd steal off Steve Carlton and everyone else because the Phillies pitchers weren't holding runners on base. Right now, our pitchers are giving him a chance, and it shows."[35]

The other area in which Boone's effectiveness showed was in the success of the pitching staff, which was considered the Angels' Achilles heel heading into the season. By late June, Angels pitchers had the best earned run average in the American League. "At the start of the season we had something described as 'an alleged pitching staff,' said Bavasi. "And do you know who said our pitching staff was alleged? Alleged writers."[36]

On the other coast, the Boston Red Sox were perched atop the American League East, and among their leaders was Carl Yastrzemski, who at the tender age of forty-two was enjoying a renaissance season. Like DeCinces, Carl Yastrzemski had the unenviable task of replacing a legend when he assumed left field duties in Boston after Ted Williams retired following the 1960 season. Since then, he had appeared in sixteen All-Star games, amassed more than 3,000 hits, and won an MVP, three batting titles, and the undying love of Red Sox fans, a notoriously tough lot.

Yaz hit .246 in 1981, the worst batting average of his career. That, coupled with a poor performance in spring training, led to whispers that he might be finished. Undeterred, Yaz hit .348 in April and just kept going. "Nobody will have to tell me when I can't do it anymore. I'll be the first to know. When I can't hit, I'll retire," he told the *Sporting News*.[37]

Boston manager Ralph Houk came into spring training with six starting pitchers for five rotation spots. Which ones stayed in the rotation depended on how well they pitched, and Houk indicated that any starter who failed three or four times in a row would be relegated to the bullpen. Chuck Rainey, Bob Ojeda, and Mike Torrez were all banished to the bullpen at different times, but the pitching staff still had the fourth best earned run average in the American League through mid-June. One man who held onto his spot was Dennis Eckersley, who went 6–3 in his first ten starts, including four complete games in May. "Ojeda, Mike Torrez, and Chuck Rainey will come on before the season is over," said Houk. "I've said from the start that except for Eckersley we may not have a bona fide 20 game winner. But we have more quality starting pitching than anyone in the league and that'll show come July and August."[38]

"What Houk has done with the rest of us," said pitcher John Tudor, "is say 'let's see what we can do with what you have.' In so many places, as soon as you come up and experience rough times, all you hear is, 'he can't pitch' or 'he's got no guts.' There's more talent here than people thought, but sometimes (Fenway Park) convinces you otherwise."[39]

The fourth best ERA in the league, coupled with the second best team batting average, helped the Red Sox build a 5½-game lead in the AL East by June 23. Led by Yastrzemski, Carney Lansford, and Jim Rice, Boston was establishing itself as the team to beat in the division. The Red Sox could always hit, but a solid pitching staff made all the difference. "It's a different game when you're not behind 4–0 in the second inning every other day," said Rice.[40]

In New York, the problems continued for the Yankees, who were off to their worst start since 1971. The ill-fated speed experiment did not work, and some veterans weren't playing up to their abilities, but the

Yankees were also racked with injuries. Doyle Alexander punched the dugout wall in Seattle on May 6 and hadn't pitched since. Third baseman Graig Nettles suffered a broken thumb, as did catcher Rick Cerone and outfielder Jerry Mumphrey. As the injuries mounted, George Steinbrenner engaged in some proactive public relations in each day's press notes. "This Yankee team is *his* team," wrote Peter Gammons in the *Boston Globe*. "So, George Steinbrenner, to excuse why it is struggling around the .500 mark, has a new statistics sheet passed out every night detailing the team's injuries as 'incapacitations' and 'games missed.'"[41]

"I don't care if it sounds like an excuse," said manager Gene Michael. "If we had been healthy, we'd be right at the top. And when we have everybody back, we'll show how good we are."[42]

For outfielder Lou Piniella, the answer was simpler than that. "We haven't been winning because we haven't been playing well," he said. "Sure, injuries have hurt us. But injuries are part of the game. Other teams have injuries."[43]

At thirty-eight years old, Lou Piniella had seen a lot in his baseball career. He was signed out of the University of Tampa in 1962 and spent time with multiple organizations before winning Rookie of the Year with the Royals in 1969. Since then, he'd won two World Series rings and had countless run-ins with umpires, opposing players, and Steinbrenner. By this point, the man they called "Sweet Lou" knew exactly what was wrong with his team. "All the changes that we've made might have slowed us down a little. But the changes shouldn't be such a disruption. To me, it's clear why we haven't been winning. We haven't been playing the way we should be playing. At times we've really stunk."[44]

The poor play even got to public address announcer Bob Sheppard, who had been behind the mic for nearly 2,500 games at Yankee Stadium over the course of his career. His concise baritone delivery had become a staple of Yankees baseball for more than a generation, so much so that he had been given the nickname "The Voice of God" by Reggie Jackson.[45] "You're not in the big leagues until Bob Sheppard announces your name," said Yastrzemski.[46] So it was quite a gaffe when Sheppard left his mic open in a June game against the Indians after Yankees reliever Shane Rawley allowed a run-scoring single to Cleveland's Jack Perconte in the ninth inning. "That's relief pitching for you. Boy!" said Sheppard to a friend with him in the booth.[47] With the mic open, Sheppard's wisecrack went over the PA system for all 23,449 fans in attendance, and both teams, to hear. An embarrassed Sheppard apologized to Rawley the following day. But it would take more than apologies for the Yankees to get back into the race in the American League East.

"We will be a good team before the summer's out," said Piniella. "I just hope it's not too late. One thing that might be a problem is that in the past we've always relied heavily on certain veterans to pull us through, but it's not like 1978. We're older now."[48]

In 1978, the Yankees had rallied from fourteen games back at the All-Star break to tie Boston for the division title and win a one-game playoff en route to winning their second-straight World Series title. In 1982, they found themselves chasing Boston again, but they also had to leap-frog the Milwaukee Brewers, who had come to life after replacing manager Buck Rodgers with Harvey Kuenn at the beginning of the month.

"I think Buck's a good baseball man," said general manager Harry Dalton in announcing the decision. "The chemistry went sour. We haven't been getting what we had the right to expect with the talent we have. I recognized everything that happened wasn't Buck's fault. I wanted to give Buck every opportunity to right the ship."[49]

Poor play was one thing, but the "chemistry" issue likely played a much larger role in Rodgers's dismissal. Feuds with catcher Ted Simmons and pitcher Mike Caldwell became public, and the comments from Fingers after the loss in Seattle didn't help Rodgers's case either. In a *Sporting News* column, Peter Gammons noted that at least nineteen Brewers players had a problem with him. "It wasn't exactly unexpected," Rogers said. "I've had my mind made up for the last two weeks it might happen. It started to bother me, so I [decided] I wasn't going to let it eat me up. If I went out, I was going to go out with my chin up."[50]

Rodgers's replacement, Harvey Kuenn, was born in West-Allis, Wisconsin, in 1930, just a few miles from the stadium in which he was now managing. As a youth he attended a tryout for the minor-league Milwaukee Brewers but wasn't signed. That turned out to be a mistake on the part of the Milwaukee club. He eventually signed with the Detroit Tigers and won Rookie of the Year honors in 1953 before enjoying a fifteen-year big-league career in which he amassed more than 2,000 hits for the Tigers, Indians, Giants, Cubs, and Phillies. Upon his retirement after the 1966 season, Kuenn returned home and worked in television. It was also during this time that he began frequenting a local bar and boardinghouse called Ceasar's Inn on the city's west side. Over time, he developed a friendship with the owner's daughter, Audrey, and the two were eventually married in 1974. Harvey Kuenn the ex-ballplayer was now also Harvey Kuenn the tavern owner. Audrey handled the business side while Harvey hung out at the bar and told stories. The couple lived in the apartment at the back of the bar.

Kuenn had served as Milwaukee's hitting coach for the last eleven years when he was named interim manager. There was speculation that his time in the dugout could be brief, in part due to lingering health issues. Just fifty-one years old, Kuenn had already endured stomach surgery and a heart bypass operation. He also had his right leg amputated below the knee just before Spring Training in 1980. In a clubhouse full of pranksters, he sometimes emerged from the shower to discover someone had "borrowed" his artificial leg.

Under former skipper George Bamberger the Brewers had the nickname of "Bambi's Bombers." With Kuenn in place, they needed a new one. Among the suggestions was "Harvey's Ballbangers," but first baseman Cecil Cooper had a better idea. "Naw," he said. "Just like the drink. Harvey's Wallbangers. We bang them off the wall."[51]

Cooper's idea stuck. A few days after Kuenn took over, the Brewers pounded five home runs on the road against Oakland, including three consecutive seventh-inning blasts from Robin Yount, Cooper, and Ben Oglivie. Eight days later, Harvey's Wallbangers were home and again hammered out five homers in a 13–5 win over the Tigers. After beginning the season 23–24, the Brewers went 17–6 in their next 23 games to pull within two games of Boston in the division. "Our ballclub is in a good frame of mind right now," said Ogilvie. "We know we can win. We've been doing a lot of hitting."[52]

Oglivie in particular had been doing a lot of hitting. After going through a 1-for-17 slump, Kuenn pulled him from a game against Detroit and told him to relax. That night, Oglivie had a long talk with Cooper, who echoed Kuenn's advice. Gorman Thomas and several other teammates said the same thing, and it sank in. Over his next seven games, Oglivie hit .462 with 7 homers and 12 RBI. "I just told him that he was thinking too much," said Kuenn. "Hot? I haven't seen anyone hot as Benjy in a long time. He's been hitting everything—fastball, curveball, and changeup."[53]

"He became really depressed, thinking he wasn't helping the club," said Gorman Thomas. "All we wanted him to do was relax. Once he did, he became the Benjy of old. When I hit behind him, I'm not going to get many extra RBI's, but I hope he stays hot all year."[54]

Under Kuenn the pitching staff got hot as well. Starters Pete Vuckovich and Bob McClure both went 3–0 immediately after Kuenn took over, while closer Rollie Fingers went 2–0 with five saves. "The change in atmosphere has a lot to do with that," said Gorman Thomas. "Everybody's loose. Just go out and have a good time. Maybe things will be like this all year. Sure, we'll lose one every now and then. You can't help that. But I don't think we'll go through any more long losing streaks."[55]

* * * * *

After exploding out of the gate to a 13–0 record, the Atlanta Braves had turned into essentially a .500 ball club, and a pattern was beginning to emerge. In any given week, fans in Atlanta could expect their team to go 6–0, but they also would not have been surprised if the team went 1–5. Including their great start, the Braves put together four different streaks that added up to an amazing 32-4 record. Yet, they also suffered through three cold spells in which they went 6–19. Two factors seemed to be in play to determine the fate of the team: pitching, and the hitting of Dale Murphy.

In the hot streaks, Atlanta pitchers posted a 2.86 ERA, while Murphy hit 15 home runs and drove in 40. During the dark days, the team ERA swelled to 4.93, while Murphy homered just 4 times and drove in 14. Still, Murphy was batting .293 with 57 RBI and an NL leading 21 home runs after a 3-for-5 night against the Reds on June 25. "He never makes a mental mistake, and, in my opinion, he plays left field as good as anyone ever has," said manager Joe Torre. "Defense, stolen bases, great arm, he just does everything. I don't think you could find a more ideal candidate for MVP."[56]

"I'm not concerned about that," said Murphy. "Individual things don't mean much when you don't win. Naturally, I want to have a good year, but it won't mean much if we don't win the pennant. I've been with the Braves four complete seasons now and it's about time I start doing what people have been saying I'm capable of doing."[57]

Along with Murphy, third-baseman Bob Horner was also living up to his capabilities, batting .310 with 11 homers and 39 RBI through Atlanta's first 63 games. But Atlanta's erratic performance was cause for concern, especially for a young team, and questions lingered as to how they would hold up in the heat of a pennant race. It took the Montreal

Expos two heartbreaking second-place finishes before they finally qualified for the postseason, and Montreal had a far more talented roster. But Atlanta owner Ted Turner was not concerned in the least. "We will still run away with the pennant," he said. "We just wanted to let people in other cities have some interesting baseball, too."[58]

Pitcher Bob Walk echoed those sentiments after shutting out the Houston Astros. When asked about perennial also-rans Atlanta and San Diego being atop the National League West while teams like Cincinnati and Houston were bringing up the rear, Walk quipped, "I guess it does look kind of backward to people, but they better get used to it. It's going to stay that way."[59]

Whether Atlanta could hold on was up for debate, but what was certain was that the glory days of the Cincinnati Reds were over. During the 1970s, the Reds won six division titles, four National League pennants, and two World Series championships. During that stretch, Cincinnati players won MVP honors in 1970 and 1972 (Johnny Bench), 1973 (Pete Rose), 1975 and 1976 (Joe Morgan), and 1977 (George Foster). In 1981, Cincinnati posted the best overall record in baseball but failed to qualify for the postseason due to the split-season format. Then, just like that, it was over. By 1982, only Bench, shortstop Dave Concepcion, and first baseman Dan Driessen remained from the championship years. "At the end of April everyone was saying it's still early," said Bench. "Everyone was still saying the same thing at the end of May. Now we're into June. Such talk is getting old. Everywhere I go people keep asking, 'What's wrong with the Big Red Machine?' They don't understand there isn't any Big Red Machine anymore. It's gone."[60]

Lack of offense was a glaring deficiency in the lineup constructed by general manager Dick Wagner, which was understandable to a certain extent. No franchise could lose players the caliber of Rose, Morgan, Foster, Tony Pérez, and Ken Griffey, and not miss a beat. But it was the depths to which the Reds had fallen that were amazing to behold. Foster hit 52 home runs in his MVP season of 1977. In mid-May of 1982, the Reds were on pace to hit 52 as a team. The power came around in June, but the Reds were still floundering. They fell ten games under .500 for the first time since 1971, and, as the month wound down and the losses mounted, so did the level of frustration at Riverfront Stadium, especially among those who had been around for the heyday of the Big Red Machine.

"Do you realize how difficult it is to walk from the dugout to the clubhouse without being able to smile night after night?" asked Dave Concepcion, an eight-time All-Star and a Red since 1970. "I just sit here and wonder what's going on, wondering why we can't get it together. When we score runs, we don't get good pitching. And when we get good pitching, we don't score runs."[61]

"Getting your tail kicked every night is no fun," said Dan Driessen, who had been in Cincinnati since 1973. "I've never played on a loser in the majors or the minors. Maybe I've been spoiled. But it just doesn't seem like we can do anything right. It's a sad, sickening feeling."[62]

The losing took a toll on the fans as well, and they weren't shy about expressing their displeasure with both Wagner and manager John McNamara. In a letter to the *Sporting News*, one fan wrote, "I have seen [McNamara] and Wagner tear up the organization and turn the Big Red Machine into the Big Dead Machine. A manager must be able to organize his team in such a manner that runs can be scored, and McNamara has shown that he is void of that talent."[63]

Others were quick to exonerate McNamara, who could only work with the talent he was given, and lay the blame at the feet of Wagner. As another fan wrote in a letter to the *Sporting News*, "I can at this point only hope that the Reds continue to lose, that the fans continue to stay away from the park and that . . . ownership finally has the good sense to either fire Dick Wagner or sell the team to someone who cares about the fans and the Reds."[64]

In St. Louis, the Cardinals suddenly found themselves struggling and, as was the case in Cincinnati, the problem was a lack of offense. Whitey Herzog's team had a 33–19 record and held a 5½ game lead in the National League East early in June but then proceeded to lose 14 of their next 23 and found themselves tied for the lead with the surging Phillies. The two teams were tied atop the division standings when they faced off in a three-game series in Philadelphia to end the month. St. Louis was built on speed, and that portion of the offense was humming along. But the speedsters at the top of the lineup needed someone to drive them in, and that job fell primarily to George Hendrick, who happened to be in one of the biggest slumps of his Cardinals career.

Hendrick grew up in the Watts section of south Los Angeles and did not play organized sports. His first love was basketball, but he also excelled at baseball, and it was in a semipro game where he caught the eye of the New York Mets director of player development, a man named Whitey Herzog. The Mets had the second overall selection in the 1968 draft and coveted Hendrick, but the Oakland A's made him the top pick in the draft. Hendrick made his major league debut in 1971 and filled in for an injured Reggie Jackson in the 1972 World Series against the Cincinnati Reds. After tearing up the minor leagues and contributing to a World Series-winning team, Hendrick felt he was ready to assume the everyday center field duties heading into 1973. But the A's disagreed and acquired Bill North from the Cubs in a trade and sent Hendrick to Cleveland. It was there that he began to fulfill the potential that baseball insiders felt he had. He slugged 21 homers and drove in 61 runs in 1974 and made the American League All-Star team in 1974 and '75.

But as talented as he was, he was also a bit temperamental, and there was a perception that he took plays off. After Hendrick let a ball drop behind him in center field with Gaylord Perry on the mound, Perry stood in front of Hendrick's locker after the game and announced he never wanted to pitch again if Hendrick was in center field.[65] Hendrick also had problems with Cleveland manager Ken Aspromonte, including an incident in 1974 where Hendrick pulled a hamstring muscle. Aspromonte said he'd put Hendrick back in the lineup when Hendrick told him he was healthy. The only problem was that Hendrick was refusing to speak to Aspromonte, even if it meant not playing. "I am not going to talk to him," Hendrick told the *Sporting News*. "I don't have anything to say to him. It's no secret I don't care for the man, but I don't want to get into the reasons. I don't want to attack anybody. I just want to leave it at that."[66]

New York Daily News columnist Dick Young reported that the fallout between the two men came when Aspromonte lit into his team following a tough series in Boston. The Indians had a scheduled off day following the series, but Aspromonte announced a workout and said no one was exempt, even if there was a death in the family. Unbeknownst to Aspromonte, Hendrick's mother was gravely ill at the time. According to Young, the two stopped speaking at that point.[67]

Hendrick ended up in St. Louis after a brief stint with the Padres, but, no matter where he went, he put up good numbers, averaging 21 home runs and 77 RBI per season from 1973 through 1981, often in lineups with little protection. He entered June of 1982 batting a respectable .279 with nine home runs and 26 RBI and then went into a tailspin. In his next 24 games, Hendrick hit just .198 with two home runs. Perhaps not coincidentally, Hendrick's slump coincided with the Cardinals losing their lead in the National League East, but on June 29 he broke out in a big way when he homered and drove in seven in a 15–3 win over the Phillies. Hendrick didn't talk to the media, but his teammates were quick to chime in on his behalf. "I know I've been pressing," said first baseman Keith Hernandez. "George is human. I'm sure he probably was doing the same thing. George has been getting a lot of breaking balls. He hates them. Sometimes he lays off them and sometimes he goes after them. He's decided he's going to hit the crap out of them now."[68]

The win proved to be the only one St. Louis could muster in a three-game series at Veterans Stadium, and the Cardinals would need Hendrick to continue to mash breaking balls, and everything else, if they wanted to hold onto what seemed like a certain division title at the beginning of the month.

A day after Hendrick's breakout, San Diego's Broderick Perkins stepped into the batter's box against Dodgers reliever Tom Niedenfuer in the top of the ninth with his team holding a 5–4 lead. Perkins sent a Niedenfuer offering into the seats for a 6–4 lead, to which Niedenfuer responded by hitting the next batter he faced, Joe Lefebvre, in the head. Just the latest chapter in what was becoming a heated rivalry between the two clubs. "They've hit 14 home runs off us and they didn't get their hats spun once," said Padres manager Dick Williams. "We hit one homer and our guy gets hit. Is that Dodger Blue? Is that what it's all about?"[69]

Niedenfuer was fined $500 for the pitch, but that wasn't quite enough for one Padre, who thought Dodgers manager Tommy Lasorda should have been fined as well. "They ought to fine the fat little Italian who ordered the pitch," said Kurt Bevacqua. "He's got nothing to worry about. He knows if a fight breaks out, it'll be over by the time he gets there from the dugout."[70]

"I have never ever told a pitcher to throw at anybody. Nor will I ever," said Lasorda when told of Bevacqua's comments. But he wasn't finished. "And if I ever did, I certainly wouldn't make him throw at a fucking .130 hitter like . . . fucking Bevacqua who couldn't hit water if he fell out of a fucking boat. I guaran-fucking-tee you this: When I was going to pitch against a fucking team that had guys on it like Bevacqua, I'd send a fucking limousine to get the cocksucker to make sure he was in the motherfucking lineup because I'd kick that cocksucker's ass any fucking day of the week. He's a mother fucking big mouth, I'll tell you that."[71]

While Lasorda's comments did not make the papers verbatim, the gist of them was conveyed. Bevacqua may not have been hitting, but many of his teammates were, including Perkins, who carried a .301 batting average into July. Ruppert Jones led the National League in batting through most of June, and Tim Flannery hit .304 in his first 27 games filling in for the injured Juan Bonilla.

In spring training, Williams told his team he did not care about individual statistics, but he shared a unique scoring system he used to judge the performance of his players. He handed out pluses for advancing a runner from second base to third base with no one out and for driving in runners from third with less than two outs. In both cases, players who failed in those situations were given a minus. Once the players understood the system and bought in, the results showed. "They kept advancing runners from second to third and scoring them with groundballs," said Dodgers first baseman Steve Garvey after an early season series. "It was an example of good, fundamental baseball."[72]

"When we execute, we win; when we fail to execute, we lose," said Williams, who teamed with pitching coach Norm Sherry to cut down on walks.[73] The duo tracked the number of walks allowed to leadoff batters, opposing pitchers, and walked batters who eventually scored. In a June game against the Pirates, San Diego starter John Curtis took a 5–4 lead into the sixth inning but walked Pittsburgh's leadoff hitter. Williams trudged to the mound, said, "John, we can't defense a base on balls," and pulled him.[74] The Padres held on to win the game.

The emphasis on throwing strikes paid off. Leading the charge was Tim Lollar, who was second in the NL in wins a year after posting an ERA of 6.10. Ground ball specialist Chris Welsh added five wins, as did Curtis and Juan Eichelberger, who narrowly missed throwing a no-hitter against the Cubs at the beginning of the month. The Padres were playing good baseball, and they were gaining confidence. "I think we're the team to beat in the West Division," said shortstop Garry Templeton. "We've proven we can beat the Dodgers and that we can handle Atlanta."[75] "You look at San Diego and their lineup doesn't excite you," said Cubs manager Lee Elia. "But they make contact, they hit the ball to the opposite field, they have movement on the bases. How do you handle a team like that? If they keep playing the way they're playing, they'll be in the race right up until the end."[76]

STANDINGS AS OF JUNE 30

Table 5.1. American League East and West

AL East				AL West			
Team	Wins	Losses	GB	Team	Wins	Losses	GB
Boston	44	29	-	California	43	30	-
Milwaukee	42	31	2.0	Kansas City	41	32	3.0
Detroit	38	33	5.0	Chicago	40	33	4.0
Baltimore	38	33	5.0	Seattle	40	36	5.5
Cleveland	36	36	7.5	Oakland	33	45	13.5
New York	33	37	9.5	Texas	28	40	13.5
Toronto	33	40	11.0	Minnesota	20	56	25.5

Table 5.2. National League East and West

NL East				NL West			
Team	Wins	Losses	GB	Team	Wins	Losses	GB
Philadelphia	42	33	-	Atlanta	45	29	-
St. Louis	43	34	-	San Diego	42	32	3.0
Montreal	40	32	0.5	L. A. Dodgers	41	37	6.0
Pittsburgh	35	36	5.0	San Francisco	35	42	11.5
New York	36	39	6.0	Houston	31	44	14.5
Chicago	29	40	14.0	Cincinnati	31	44	14.5

6. JULY

I'm Really Kinda Busy

> **Great Ballplayers Drink Miller Lite Because It's Less Filling.**
> **I Know. I Asked One.**
> —Bob Uecker, Mr. Baseball (1982 print advertisement)

Robert George Uecker was born in Milwaukee in 1934, the son of Swiss immigrants who came to Wisconsin in 1920. After a stint in the Army, he signed with his hometown Milwaukee Braves in 1956 and spent six years in the major leagues with the Braves, Cardinals, and Phillies before being released in April of 1968. Uecker's playing career was unremarkable. He hit an even .200 in 297 career games, and, while he was a member of the 1964 World Series-winning Cardinals, he didn't play an inning in any of the team's seven-game series wins over the Yankees. He did garner attention prior to Game Two, though. A Dixieland band was entertaining the crowd, and, when they took a break, Uecker walked over and picked up a tuba and tried to shag fly balls with it. He caught a few in the bell, but the tuba did not fare well, emerging from the incident with several dents. Photos of the stunt appeared in newspapers across the country the following day and the fans in attendance loved it. Cardinals management was not amused and fined Uecker for the cost of the repairs.

Once he retired, Uecker took a public relations position with the Braves before returning to Milwaukee in the early 1970s as a scout and then a broadcaster. It was also during this time that he emerged on the national stage. He made appearances on Merv Griffin's, Mike Douglas's, and David Frost's television shows, but it was his relationship with Johnny Carson that made him a star. Uecker's deadpan delivery while discussing his lack of success on the baseball field made him a regular on

The Tonight Show. He would regale Carson and the audience with tales of his ineptitude, like the time Carson showed a photo of Uecker celebrating in the locker room with teammates pouring beer over his head. Uecker claimed the photo was taken before a game and his teammates were celebrating because he wasn't in the lineup. The chemistry between Carson and Uecker made for great television, and it was Carson who gave him the nickname "Mr. Baseball." He may not have been talented on the field, but he was extremely talented behind the microphone, and Brewers fans came to love him both for his personality and his broadcasting ability. That personality and local popularity helped land him his own Miller Lite commercial in 1982. The ad featured people recognizing him outside a bar and then locking him out. The spot ended with him peering through the window and remarking, "Wow, they're having a good time in there."[1]

The Miller Brewing Company had been involved in baseball in Milwaukee since 1953 when Frederick C. Miller, the great-grandson of the brewery's founder, helped bring the Boston Braves to the city. When Bud Selig bought the Seattle Pilots and moved them to Milwaukee in 1970, Miller once again became a major sponsor, and, as the second largest brewing company in the United States (behind Anheuser-Busch) they eventually gained naming rights to the Brewers' new ballpark, which opened in 2001 in the shadow of Milwaukee County Stadium.

The 1982 Brewers were definitely having a good time under new manager Harvey Kuenn. Since taking over for Buck Rodgers the previous month, Kuenn turned the Brewers into a juggernaut. On Saturday, July 3, a Milwaukee County Stadium record crowd of 55,716 watched the Brewers hit four home runs, including two by Cecil Cooper, in a 7–0 win over the Boston Red Sox to move into a first-place tie in the American League East. It was the sixteenth straight game in which they'd hit at least one homer. "It's amazing, it really is," said Kuenn. "You think to yourself, 'Will it ever end?' Now I'm saying, 'No.' I don't think it's going to end."[2]

"Those guys are amazing," said Cooper of his teammates. "They are simply awesome. I've never seen a display like we've had. Some teams don't do that in a season. It ain't no fluke, either. It's a reality."[3]

Another reality was that shortstop Robin Yount was now one of the best players in the American League. The Brewers selected Yount with the third overall pick in the 1973 draft out of Taft High School in Woodland Hills, California. He played just 64 games in the New York/Penn League

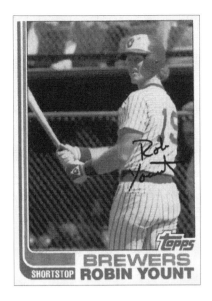

Figure 9: Robin Yount led the American League in hits (210), doubles (46) and total bases (346) and won his first MVP Award. 1982 Topps® trading cards used courtesy of The Topps Company, Inc.

before making his big-league debut the following April at age eighteen. Now twenty-six, Yount was in his ninth season and considered one of the best players in the game. "There is the MVP in the American League," said teammate Gorman Thomas as he watched Yount take batting practice. "If he's not, there's no justice. He can cool off the rest of the season and still walk off with it. There's nothing he can't do. Hit, throw, field, you name it. He's the best shortstop in baseball. Period."[4] Thomas would get no arguments from Kansas City lefty Larry Gura. After Yount homered against Gura in his first two at bats in a July game, Gura instructed his catcher to simply tell Yount what pitch was coming. The strategy worked, as Yount grounded out to third base in his next at bat. "What could he do besides hit another one out?" asked Gura.[5]

Yount's first-half performance, a .327 batting average with 15 homers and 57 RBI, earned him the starting nod for the All-Star Game. Outfielder Ben Oglivie and pitcher Rollie Fingers also received All-Star honors, but notably absent were Thomas and starting pitcher Pete Vuckovich. Thomas's twenty-two homers led the American League, while Vuckovich's ten wins were tied for the most in the AL. After the Brewers beat Kansas City on July 9, Thomas popped open a bottle of champagne to "celebrate" the fact that he and Vuckovich had been snubbed for the All-Star Game. "I bought a bottle for me and a bottle for Vukie, for being overlooked," said Thomas. "That's life in the big city, I guess."[6]

The big city hosting the All-Star Game was Montreal, the first time the game would be played outside of the United States. It was also notable that the manager of the American League squad was Oakland's Billy Martin. Traditionally, the opposing managers in the previous year's World Series have the honor of managing the All-Star Game. Tommy Lasorda of the Dodgers was there, but Yankees manager Bob Lemon had been fired. Since Martin managed the 1981 AL runner-up, he got the nod to manage the All-Star Game and deal with the inevitable criticism about his roster.

Martin opted not to bring Vuckovich and Chicago's LaMarr Hoyt, who also posted ten wins in the first half, because pitchers usually only throw an inning or two and Martin wanted to stock his roster with relief pitchers. Not surprisingly, Lasorda did not like questions about players he left off the roster, saying, "If St. Peter picked this team, he'd be criticized."[7] Lasorda would definitely be criticized if the National League squad didn't emerge victorious, as the National League had lost only one All-Star Game between 1963 and 1981.

"The object of the game is to win," said National Leaguer Pete Rose. "To go out there and not think about winning is letting down the people who voted for you. Of course, the object is to have fun, but that's winning. I spell fun by winning."[8]

"I never really felt that winning or losing was the object of the game," said Red Sox American Leaguer catcher Carlton Fisk. "Just representing your team and being voted as an All Star is a thrill. Being able to rub elbows with all of the guys you've played against all year in the same locker room is a thrill. I don't know if our attitude is different. I don't know if it's because of this type of camaraderie that we don't get our game faces on like Pete Rose with that killer instinct."[9]

Rose drew the starting nod at first base for the NL squad, his fifteenth All-Star appearance in the past sixteen years. Rose's Phillies teammates Manny Trillo (second base) and Mike Schmidt (third base) joined him as starters. Cincinnati's Dave Concepcion was the starting shortstop, while Atlanta's Dale Murphy played right field. The remaining four slots were taken by players from the host Expos: Tim Raines in left; Andre Dawson in center; Gary Carter behind the plate; and Steve Rogers got the start on the mound, the first pitcher since 1960 (Whitey Ford of the Yankees) to start an All-Star Game in his home park.

Billy Martin's American League squad had Milwaukee's Cecil Cooper at first, with Yount at shortstop, Kansas City's George Brett at third, and California's Bobby Grich at second. Grich was joined by teammates

Reggie Jackson in right field and Fred Lynn in center, while Oakland's Rickey Henderson drew the start in left field. Chicago's Carlton Fisk was behind the plate, and Boston's Dennis Eckersley was the starting pitcher.

After Henderson led off the game with a single to left, the cat and mouse game between him, Rogers, and Carter began. Henderson had an amazing 84 stolen bases at the All-Star break, and Rogers did his best to keep him close to first by stepping off the mound and throwing over to Rose several times. Henderson finally took off, and Brett slapped a single to left to advance him to third, where he later scored on a Jackson sacrifice fly to give the AL a 1–0 lead.

The NL got on the board in the second inning when Dale Murphy drew a two-out walk from Eckersley and Dave Concepcion took advantage of a hanging slider. Carlton Fisk called for a pitch on the outer half, but Eckersley missed. The pitch was up and tailing inside, and Concepcion smacked it just inside the foul pole down the left field line for a two-run homer. In a National League lineup full of sluggers, it was Concepcion, a man with exactly one home run in 1982, who hit the first homer and put the NL up 2–1.

"It was a slider, up and in," Concepcion said after the game. "I don't think it broke, and I was able to get it pretty good."[10]

"He yanked it," said Eckersley. "I was hoping it would hook foul. You know it's a bad pitch when you throw it and you say to yourself, 'Break!'"[11]

The NL tacked on another run in the third when Ruppert Jones, pinch hitting for Rogers, hit Eckersley's first pitch in the bottom of the third off the wall in right-center field, narrowly missing a home run of his own. Jones scored on a Rose sacrifice fly, and the NL capped their scoring in the sixth inning when Montreal's Al Oliver led off with a double and came in to score on a Gary Carter single.

The AL threatened in each of the final three innings, but Cincinnati's Mario Soto struck out the side in the seventh, including both Kansas City's Willie Wilson and Buddy Bell of the Rangers with runners on second and third. The Americans put two aboard in the eighth as well after Fernando Valenzuela walked two, forcing Lasorda to replace him with Greg Minton to face Detroit's power-hitting catcher Lance Parrish with two outs. "He's a low-ball hitter," Lasorda told the Giants' Minton. "Keep the ball inside on him and keep it up."[12]

While Minton received a scouting report on Parrish, third base coach Dick Howser was giving Parrish the lowdown on Minton, saying, "He's a sinkerballer. He just stays right downstairs. He'll make you swing at the ball below your knees. You gotta make him get the ball up. He pitches down, down, down."[13]

Minton's first pitch was in on Parrish's hands, but he fought it off, breaking his bat in the process and sending a high chopper over the mound for what looked like an infield single. But Ozzie Smith, who had replaced Concepcion at shortstop, short-hopped the ball on the first base side of the field and nipped Parrish at first to end the inning. "Anybody but Ozzie Smith and anybody but Parrish running and that might be a base hit," said ABC color commentator Don Drysdale.[14] "That, ladies and gentlemen, is a Big . . . League . . . Play," added Keith Jackson.[15]

Minton got Ben Oglivie to fly out to begin the ninth inning but walked Rickey Henderson, prompting Lasorda to bring in the left-handed Steve Howe, a Dodger, to face Twins left-hander Kent Hrbek. It took Howe all of one pitch to retire Hrbek on a fly out, prompting Lasorda to emerge from the National League dugout to replace him with Reds righty Tom Hume, with the right-handed Buddy Bell due up.

"Great job," Lasorda said. "I'm going to bring in [Tom] Hume."

"OK, fine," said Howe, "but you aren't getting the ball."

"What do you mean?" asked Lasorda.

"This is my ball. I got him out, and I might never make it here again. I'm taking it with me."[16]

Home plate umpire Doug Harvey made his way to the mound, and when Lasorda asked if Howe could keep the ball, the man they called God didn't miss the opportunity.

"Hell no," said Harvey with a wink. "What did he do?"

"He got an out on one pitch," replied Lasorda.[17] Hume induced Bell to fly out, and the game was over. The National League won 4–1, their eleventh straight All-Star Game victory, and Steve Rogers became the first pitcher to earn an All-Star win in his home ballpark since the Reds' Johnny Vander Meer in 1938.

The National League's dominance was, again, a main topic of discussion in both locker rooms, but *Montreal Gazette* columnist Michael Farber summed things up well when he wrote:

So, the party—more than a year in the making—is over, and everything turned out as we thought.
The city, which loves a good time, sparkled.
    The organizers really put on a good spread, with plenty of schmaltz for good digestion.

Too bad the American League had to put a lampshade over its head.[18]

Concepcion's home run and stellar defensive play earned him MVP honors for the evening, but there was no doubt who the fan-favorites were. The five Expos players who saw time in front of the home fans drew rave reviews for their play. In addition to Rogers getting the win, Carter driving in a run, and Oliver starting a rally, Tim Raines drew a walk in two plate appearances and added a stolen base while Andre Dawson went 1-for-4. Surprisingly, it wasn't Carter who received the most votes, or Dawson who drew the longest and loudest applause in pregame introductions. That honor went to Al Oliver, who had been a member of the Expos for just a few months. Oliver entered the game with a .321 batting average, but not even the rabid Expos fans could stuff the ballot box enough to unseat Pete Rose as the NL starter. They showed their appreciation with a standing ovation, and the gesture did not go unnoticed.

"It was unreal," said Oliver. "I was holding back tears. I didn't expect that type of ovation. But like [Dodgers outfielder] Dusty Baker told me, 'That's a lifetime ovation', I guess for all the things I've done in thirteen years in the league. It was a long time coming."[19]

"I was really thrilled with the way the Montreal Expos played in front of their home fans," said Carter. "Tim Raines stole a base, Oliver had two hits, Dawson had a hit and Steve Rogers was super. I'm sure this will be a good carry-over for when we start the second half."[20]

Carter and the Expos *needed* something to build on after a horrid start to July. They entered the month just a half game out of first place but lost ten of thirteen heading into the All-Star break to drop four games behind in the NL East. On the same day his teammates were set to play the All-Star Game, Montreal shortstop Chris Speier told the media he expected his manager, Jim Fanning, to be fired if the losing continued. "That's just a personal observation," said Speier. "If we don't do well, changes will be made. It's only common sense. The main problem is consistency. When you lead the league in home runs and ERA and have so many losses, you're not being consistent."[21]

But Speier pointed to one other aspect that could signal the downfall of Fanning's reign, and Montreal's season, when he said, "There's a definite lack of unity on the club. When you have losses on the field, the back-biting becomes more prevalent. Everybody has got to stop pointing fingers and look at themselves. It's the same old stuff, but I thought I'd say it. Maybe it will shake some people up."[22]

Speier's comments brought Montreal's internal issues out in the open. Expos fans had been holding up banners at Olympic Stadium calling for Fanning's firing, but public comments from the team's shortstop gave some of his teammates permission to address the situation. "It's not Jim Fanning's fault," said Oliver. "All he can do is post the lineup each day. It's our fault. I think there have been some occasions this year where players have not hustled, have not busted their rears. And I think they know it."[23]

The Expos began the second half of the season with a ten-game West Coast swing beginning in San Diego. When they arrived, Speier didn't back away from his comments, but he did apologize for their timing. "We should be thinking about only one thing right now and that's pulling together," he told the Montreal media while lounging by the pool at the team hotel. "The timing was not fair since Fanning has enough to think about. Several of the players are going all out every day. They should be the ones (not Fanning) to remind others to keep hustling when that is necessary."[24] This time Speier's words inspired his teammates to a four-game sweep of the Padres to open the road trip. The offense put up 23 runs in the series while the pitching staff stayed in lockdown mode, prompting some optimism from Oliver, who said, "The way we hit in this series is great. If we can make our hits count, we will make a move. We know we have the pitching."[25]

"We have the best pitching in baseball," said pitcher David Palmer. "The way we bunched our hits is what we need to take over."[26]

For the Expos to take over, they would have to pass both the Phillies and the Cardinals, who spent most of July swapping the lead in the NL East. The two teams were tied for the lead when the month began, but St. Louis won five of their first six games of the month to take a two-game lead. One surprising contributor was rookie pitcher John Stuper, who made his debut at the beginning of June. He faced the Dodgers in his second start and gave up two runs in five innings but did not factor into the decision in a game the Cardinals eventually lost 5–3. On the flight home, veteran lefty Jim Kaat pulled Stuper aside and explained all the things he had to work on if he wanted to have success in the big leagues. Stuper was an eighteenth-round draft pick who had spent four and a half years in the minor leagues. Kaat was forty-three years old and in his twenty-fourth season in the major leagues. He faced Ted Williams as a rookie, was a three-time All-Star, finished fifth in the AL MVP voting in 1966, when Stuper was all of nine years old, and had won 16 Gold Gloves. Stuper took his advice to heart.

Stuper's other valuable lesson came from late-night television. Unable to sleep one evening, he watched an episode of the *Whitey Herzog Show,* featuring his manager. When asked on the show about Stuper, Herzog said the rookie wasn't throwing as hard as he could and seemed nervous. Figuring he had nothing to lose, Stuper changed his approach and went 4–1 over his next five starts. His luck ran out when he surrendered five runs to Cincinnati in just two innings on July 15 to earn his second loss of the season. The loss was the third straight for St. Louis and dropped them a game behind Philadelphia in the division.

On Opening Night in Philadelphia, new Phillies owner Bill Giles had turned to general manager Paul Owens and said he thought the team they had assembled was the best they'd ever put on the field. The Phillies then began the season by losing 11 of their first 14 games. "We didn't realize it would take so long for the newly acquired players to blend in with the others," said Giles. "In addition, we had a new manager [Pat Corrales] and a new coaching staff. Throw in injuries to Mike Schmidt and [closer] Tug McGraw and right there you have a pretty legitimate reason for the slow start. It took time for everything to gel."[27]

"In April we were buried, and everyone was beginning to wonder," said Corrales. "But Mike Schmidt was hurt, there were other injuries and then [a] flu epidemic hit us. I knew we had the talent and character to get back in the race, but I thought it would take longer. To me, the skid stopped when Mike Schmidt came back on May 1 in San Diego. Just his presence in the lineup gave everyone more confidence."[28]

Corrales was right. The Phillies were 6–13 when Schmidt returned to the lineup. But from early May through mid-July the team went 45–26 and moved into first place in the division. In addition to Schmidt, the Phillies were also bolstered by Steve Carlton, who continued to pitch well after a slow start. Like the Expos, Philadelphia also began the second half on a West Coast swing, and Carlton shut out the Dodgers 1–0 to run his record to 13–8. In doing so, he passed Cincinnati's Mario Soto for the league lead in strikeouts, took over the league lead in innings pitched, tied Fernando Valenzuela for the league lead in complete games, and tied Steve Rogers for the league lead in shutouts. Carlton was famous for not speaking to the media, but Corrales was happy to sing the praises of his ace. "All I know is when I send him out to the mound,

I have a lot better chance to win the game than the other manager does," he said.[29]

While the Phillies were on the way up, the Oakland A's were on the way down, and there was plenty of blame to go around, most notably the starting rotation. Oakland's starting five, Steve McCatty, Matt Keough, Rick Langford, Mike Norris, and Brian Kingman, graced the cover of *Sports Illustrated* in 1981 under the headline, "The Amazing A's and their Five Aces." A year later, those five pitchers had surrendered 61 home runs in Oakland's first 88 games and sported a combined ERA of 4.66. Injuries to McCatty and Norris played a role, but so did just plain poor performance. Kingman had been dubbed one of Martin's aces by *Sports Illustrated* despite an 8–20 record in 1980. He followed that up with a 3–6 record in 1981 and was sent to the minors to begin 1982. Unhappy with the demotion, Kingman didn't report to Triple-A Tacoma until the end of April. Martin wasn't pleased, but as Oakland's team ERA crept toward 5.00, and McCatty and Norris went down with tendonitis, the Oakland skipper didn't have many options and begrudgingly summoned Kingman.

"The guys in Tacoma said I'd never pitch for him again," said Kingman. "I figured if they needed me, they'd call me. This is a business. I'm going to pitch as good as I can and maybe I can make him as happy as he was mad."[30]

"If he pitches well now, everything is history," said Martin. "He should thank the Lord that he has the opportunity to pitch in the big leagues again."[31]

Once back in Oakland, Kingman went 0–5 in his first six starts and nearly came to blows with Martin outside the team hotel in Kansas City. But what the 0–5 record failed to show was that his teammates only scored six combined runs in his starts. The losing streak finally came to an end when he threw a complete game to beat Cleveland 7–3, his first win at the big-league level in 13 months. "It's a very important day for Brian Kingman," said Martin. "He got his confidence back. There were times today when I could have taken him out. Anybody else, I probably would have. But for Kingman to go nine innings and win . . . nothing can replace that. We never gave up on him, really. We've always liked his arm."[32]

Two days later, Martin picked up a landmark win of his own when Oakland beat the Yankees 6–3. For Martin, it was career win number 1,000 as a manager, and the fact that it came against the Yankees made it that much sweeter. When asked about his tenure in Oakland compared to his tumultuous time in New York under George Steinbrenner, Martin replied, "All I'm going to say about that is that [Yankees manager] Gene Michael has my sympathy. I'm glad I'm over here and not over there. That's the kind of stuff that can wear anyone out, and who knows it better than me?"[33]

But the good times in "The Town" did not last. Oakland headed east for a 13-game road trip and got swept by the Yankees to drop 14 games behind California in the American League West. "You can't do it without the horses," Steinbrenner told Martin. "You've got the best owners I've seen since I came into baseball. They'll get them for you."[34]

"It's pretty bad when the other side feels sorry for you," said Martin. "That was nice of him to come by. I have in my own mind what has to be done, but I won't throw in the sponge. This is the lowest I've been in my whole life, but I'm not out."[35]

Despite their problems as a team, there was one important reason for fans to continue to watch the A's: Rickey Henderson was still running wild. Shortly after the All-Star break, Henderson stole two bases against the Indians to run his season total to 89. At that point, the Indians were the only *team* in the American League that had more stolen bases than Henderson did by himself. "Ricky is probably the most feared offensive force in the game," said Reggie Jackson. "I was leading the league in homers, but I'd fear him more than me. With him, if he gets on base, it's a triple."[36]

After spending much of June in first place in the American League West, Jackson and the Angels endured an eight-game losing streak that dropped them behind Kansas City. Rod Carew was battling soreness in his right hand as a result of an early season fight against the Twins. In the top of the sixth inning on April 16, Angels starter Bruce Kison hit Minnesota's Gary Gaetti with a pitch. Following baseball mores of the time, Minnesota starter Darrell Jackson, whom the Angels pounded for six runs on seven hits in his previous start, was expected to hit an Angels player in retaliation. But instead of plunking a California player in the ribs or the thigh, Jackson threw at Bobby Grich's head. Two pitches later, Grich hit a tapper to the mound and turned left on his way to first base, straight at Jackson. Grich was ejected, but Carew had his hand stepped on in the melee. "My right hand, the steering wheel of my swing, began throbbing. Several bones got chipped," he wrote in his 2020 autobiography, *One Tough Out*. Over his next 25 games, the 1978 AL batting champ hit just .217. The bones healed, but his hand bothered him for the rest of the season, and he wasn't the only star on the Angels whose bat had gone silent. Grich's batting average fell 22 points between early June and mid-July, while former All-Stars Don Baylor and Fred Lynn also suffered through tough times at the plate. Still, there was no panic.

"Our hitting left a little to be desired in the first half of the season," said general manager Buzzie Bavasi. "I look for more production in the second half. There's no way you can hold down guys like Fred Lynn, Reggie Jackson, Rod Carew, Don Baylor, and Bobby Grich."[37]

"Maybe it's because we've gotten such good pitching and defense and been involved in so many close games," added Baylor. "But sometimes we seem to get two or three quick runs, then say, 'OK now we will play defense.' We haven't busted loose for the five or six run inning as often as we can."[38]

The pitching staff got an unexpected boost from a man who wasn't even on the Angels roster when the season began. When the Dodgers released Dave Goltz, the Angels brought him in to be reunited with manager Gene Mauch. The result was a return to form and a return of confidence for the thirty-three-year-old righty. Goltz replaced an injured Kison in the rotation and responded by allowing just three hits and one run over seven innings to pick up his first win in eleven months. "I was relaxed all the time," said Goltz. "I was just doing what I know I can do for a very good team. I was out there with the knowledge that the manager had confidence in me, that means a lot."[39] When asked how long it had been since the manager felt confidence in him, he answered "2½ years."[40] When Goltz got to L.A., the Dodgers told him to throw an overhand curveball and abandon his knuckle curve, arguably his best pitch, and thus the main reason he won 96 games with the Twins over seven full seasons. He returned to the knuckle curve when he got to the Angels, and the results were immediate. After going 9–19 with the Dodgers, he won four of his first five starts with the Angels. "Dave's philosophy had changed or been changed (with the Dodgers)," said Mauch. "I had never, ever regarded Dave as a sinkerball pitcher and all I kept hearing was that he didn't have his sinkerball. We'll see how it works out, but I didn't get Goltz to sit him."[41]

Goltz's resurgence came at roughly the same time the Angels bats woke up. Among those getting hot was Lynn, who noticed a flaw in his mechanics after watching film from his rookie season when he won the Rookie of the Year and MVP awards. Once corrected, the new mechanics resulted in an 11-game stretch in which he hit .463 with 6 homers and 20 RBI. "It was just a matter of time before the team started hitting like this," said Lynn. "Everybody thought that this team was going to mash people every day. That's what we're starting to do."[42]

One potential concern for Mauch and the Angels was the bullpen. Doug Corbet pitched well after initially coming over from Minnesota but struggled in June and July. Don Aase was 3–2 with four saves but was lost for the season with an elbow injury. Mauch was running out of options. During one particularly tough stretch, opposing pinch-hitters went 8-for-12 with seven walks against Angels relievers. California had the talent to win the division, but history had shown it is difficult to go deep in the postseason without a strong bullpen.

Across town, the Dodgers were also dealing with slumps, injuries, and an ineffective bullpen. Utility-man Derrel Thomas went down with a leg injury and Steve Garvey pulled a hamstring, prompting L.A. to call up slugging first baseman Mike Marshall from Triple-A Albuquerque. Thomas went to the disabled list, but Garvey did not, and there was speculation that his consecutive game streak, which stood at more than 1,000, was the only reason. Over a 14-game span, Garvey played just one complete game. In the others, he would start at first base and then leave after a few innings or enter games late as a pinch-hitter. Lasorda claimed that the streak had no bearing on his lineup decisions, but evidence suggested otherwise and opened both Lasorda and Garvey up for criticism.

"I could never put the streak ahead of what the team was trying to do," said Pete Rose after Garvey made a pinch-hitting appearance against the Phillies.[43] Rose was currently working on a steak of more than 500 straight games, but he was not a fan of what seemed to be the Dodgers' efforts to keep Garvey's streak alive. "I've missed nine games (in 20 seasons), but none because of an injury," Rose added. "I broke streaks off because I needed the rest. I never, never went for game streaks. If I had gone for a streak like that, I'd have 1,400, maybe more, in a row by now."[44]

Lasorda bristled when asked why he pinch-hit Garvey, a right-handed hitter, against Phillies pitcher Dick Ruthven, also a righty, when lefty Jorge Orta was available on the Dodgers' bench. "Are you telling me Garvey can't hit right handers?" Lasorda asked. "I wanted Garvey to hit," he said, his voice rising. "I know who I'm supposed to send up in that situation. I'm going to put the right guy up in that situation."[45]

Lasorda may have felt that way, but he was likely in the minority. On the same day Lasorda pinch-hit Garvey against the Phillies, the

Los Angeles Times published several letters from angry fans criticizing the decision to keep the gimpy first baseman on the active roster. The feelings of many were summed up succinctly by one who wrote, "Steve Garvey's streak is a mockery that is getting more preposterous and nauseating each day."[46]

There was off-the-field controversy as well when former Dodger Don Newcombe was quoted in a California newspaper as saying he felt between 70 and 80 percent of professional baseball players were using some sort of mind-altering substance. "I'm talking about all kinds of alcohol," he said. "Beer . . . champagne . . . wine . . . and when you get into the area of drugs, I mean Valium, cocaine, and marijuana."[47]

Newcombe was a four-time All-Star and a former Rookie of the Year whose career was derailed by a drinking problem. By the time he retired after 1960 he was, in his words, "a stupefied, wife-abusing, child-frightening, falling-down drunk"[48] who pawned his World Series ring to buy booze. Newcombe turned his life around and became very vocal in the fight against alcohol abuse. He began his own foundation and held multiple positions with the Dodgers, including creating the Dodger Drug and Alcoholic Awareness Program.

At the time, however, Dodgers players and management were not happy with Newcombe's assessment, which forced him to clarify his remarks, saying he didn't think there was specifically a problem on the Dodgers, just that if there was it should be dealt with and not hidden. L.A.'s team doctor Robert Woods said Newcombe was "laying it on a little heavy" with his comments. "He looks on drinking with a great deal of horror," said Woods. "The kids like their beer. If you took that away, there'd probably be a rebellion. If there were any heavy users, they couldn't perform as well as they do. I don't think there are any kids using marijuana or any drugs at all. I know no one is using cocaine or heroin and none of them were on Quaaludes."[49]

At age seventy, Woods was one of the longest-tenured members of the Dodgers extended staff, and though his position was part-time, he had seen a lot. That knowledge apparently did not extend to recognizing the signs of cocaine abuse, as Steve Howe detailed in his autobiography, *Between the Lines*. "Through nearly the entire 1982 baseball season, I snorted 2 grams or more per day," he wrote. "In little more than a year, my habit had grown from a cozy campfire into a full blown, life threatening, homewrecking California brush fire."[50]

Howe began using cocaine as a rookie in 1980, a season in which he won Rookie of the Year honors. By 1982 he, like Raines, had formed a serious habit. But unlike Raines, Howe didn't seek help. The problem became so bad that he was snorting coke in the back of the team bus. His wife, Cindy, tried to calm him down, but after she became pregnant and stopped going on the road with him, his abuse intensified. "I was already snorting as much as I could without dipping a straw into a baggie in the bullpen, but [with Cindy at home] it was easier to get away with it. The only restrictive influences in my life were baseball and guilt."[51]

Yet, contrary to Wood's assessment, Howe was still effective enough to make the All-Star team and was probably the best relief pitcher in a disappointing Dodgers bullpen. The defending World Series champs were slipping further and further down in the NL West standings. "I can't quite put my finger on why they're not playing better ball," said Mets catcher John Stearns. "It seems they've got as much talent as they've ever had."[52]

"We need to score more runs and we need better relief pitching," said Lasorda. "And the two teams in front of us have been getting a lot of breaks, I don't expect them to play as well in the second half."[53]

Lasorda was right. One of the teams the Dodgers were chasing was the San Diego Padres, who went into the All-Star break with a record of 50–36. But, like the Dodgers, the Padres had troubles with injuries and inconsistency. San Diego opened the second half of the season by dropping their first five games before finally beating the Phillies at home on July 20. Immediately following that game, however, the Padres suffered another loss when police arrested outfielder Alan Wiggins for suspicion of cocaine possession.

San Diego called up Wiggins from Triple-A Hawaii at the beginning of May, and he became an impact player, batting .263 and stealing 29 bases in 35 attempts. Now he was gone, another casualty of baseball's growing cocaine problem. "My kids tell me about this happening with 12–13-year-old kids," said general manager Jack McKeon. "There is a lot of this in society. The consequences are more severe when you're a public figure. The whole country has to sit back and (grasp) the seriousness of this problem."[54]

"You can't say it is an innocent mistake with something like that," said catcher Terry Kennedy. "I was surprised in a way and not surprised in a way. I don't know how athletes can get close to it [drugs] with all that has happened. I'm sure the league has people all over the place. With what I've read, I'm surprised it hasn't scared more guys away."[55]

Wiggins met with team president Ballard Smith briefly following his arrest and then voluntarily checked himself into a rehabilitation center.

Losing Wiggins was a blow to the Padres, but that blow was softened by the debut of an outfielder named Tony Gwynn. The twenty-two-year-old Gwynn was a third-round draft pick in 1981 out of San Diego State University and had done nothing but hit since joining the Padres organization. He won the Northwest League batting title in 1981 with a .331 average, was promoted to Double-A Amarillo and hit .462 in 23 games, then went to the Arizona Fall League and hit .386. "Tony is the one player in a hundred who could jump from Double-A to the big leagues," said McKeon in spring training.[56]

"He is ready right now," added Williams. "The kid I had in Montreal, (Terry) Francona has a real good batting stroke. But in everything else, there's no comparison; Gwynn's so much better."[57]

The Padres were determined not to rush Gwynn and sent him to Hawaii, where he hit .328 in 93 games. He made his Padres debut at home against the Phillies on July 19, doubling off Sid Monge in the eighth inning for his first career hit. He singled in his next at bat, prompting Phillies first baseman Pete Rose, who had collected career hit number 3,800 earlier in the game, to shake his hand and say, "What are you trying to do, kid, catch me in one night?"[58]

The Padres would need Gwynn to keep hitting. They faced the Braves, the team they were chasing, at the end of July in a four-game series in Atlanta, the first of fourteen between the two teams that would probably decide the NL West. Atlanta swept the Padres to knock them nine games off the pace, but the Braves would soon face their own problems.

The Cincinnati Reds had been struggling all year, both on and off the field. At the beginning of July, Cincinnati lost a 3–1 game to the Cardinals in St. Louis only to find that thieves had broken into their locker room and made off with some valuables, including Tom Seaver's wallet. Two days later, the Reds trailed the Pirates 6–2 in the top of the ninth and scored 6 runs to take the lead only to see Pittsburgh score 5 in the bottom of the frame and win the game on Jason Thompson's bases-loaded walk-off double. On July 21, with their record at 34–58, the Reds fired manager John McNamara. The same John McNamara who led Cincinnati to a division title in 1979 and the best record in baseball in 1981. But some of the players on the 1981 Cincinnati Reds had a fatal flaw, at least in the eyes of team management: They were expensive. Thus, they needed to go, and McNamara was asked to shape a young, inexperienced roster into a winner. The young players Cincinnati was counting on were not producing, the veterans weren't faring much better, and McNamara took the fall. The Reds final game under McNamara was a microcosm of their season. Starting pitcher Bruce Berenyi allowed three runs in seven innings, but his teammates managed just one run on five hits and went 0-for-7 with runners in scoring position. The 3–1 defeat was Cincinnati's twentieth in their past twenty-four games.

"Cincinnati appears to be stuck with that most unappetizing of baseball sub-species," wrote Bill Conlin in the *Sporting News*, "a bad young team. The front office went into the season crowing that the Ravaged Reds would be at least competitive and, if the pitching held up, perhaps good enough to win the West. It appears that [the Reds] will have to bite the bullet with what they've got for years to come and pray that the farm system suddenly produces a fresh breed of stars. [General Manager Dick] Wagner's only consolation is that the Reds are finally out of stars ready to declare free agency."[59]

At the time of McNamara's dismissal, the Reds had scored the fewest runs in the NL and lacked a .300 hitter. Combined with the fact that their pitching staff led the league in walks, things were not looking good in Cincinnati. McNamara was out and was replaced by Russ Nixon. "Only in this conservative city can people still say, 'Nixon's the One.' Russ, not Richard," wrote Tim Sullivan in the *Cincinnati Enquirer*.[60] The forty-seven-year-old Nixon grew up in Cincinnati, attended Western Hills High School, the same school that produced Pete Rose, and had been a coach in the Reds organization since 1970. "I just hope the Reds can play aggressive, heads up, sound baseball," he said. "One thing the players must realize is that if they make the same mistakes over and over, they're going to be missing some money."[61]

When Nixon took up residence in his new office, he found a note from McNamara on his desk that read, "Congratulations. Best wishes. Good luck. If I can help in any way, call. Tell the players I said thanks. I've been proud to be part of the team."[62]

Western Hills High School could claim two of their alums as major league managers for exactly one week. Just seven days after Nixon took over in Cincinnati, Don Zimmer, Western Hills class of 1949, was officially fired by the Texas Rangers in one of the most bizarre transactions of the season. When Zimmer returned home from a 12-game road trip on July 25, one in which the Rangers won just twice, his wife, Soot, told him "the Rangers called earlier. You're to be in Mr. Chiles' office at 10:00 o'clock tomorrow morning."[63]

The subject of the meeting was not a surprise to Zimmer, especially considering he'd been convinced he was going to be fired a month earlier. Zimmer recounted the meeting in his book, *Zim*. "Mr. Manager,"

Chiles said, "we're going to make a change. We're going to make a manager change. Here's what I want you to do, I want you to manage the club Tuesday and Wednesday, and we'll announce it on Thursday."[64]

It was perhaps the first time-delay managerial firing in baseball history, and Zimmer balked at the plan for one important reason. He had a tee time scheduled for Thursday, and he was not at all excited about skipping golf to sit at a press conference to announce his own firing. Word of the ridiculous situation leaked to the media, and when Zimmer arrived at the ballpark for Wednesday's game against the Brewers, he figured Chiles would make the move before the game, thus allowing Zimmer to get a good night's sleep and make his tee time. Instead, Chiles called Zimmer into his office and said, "OK, everything is right on schedule. You manage tonight and we'll announce it after the game."[65] Zimmer was dumbfounded. When he went to home plate to exchange the lineup cards before Wednesday night's game, he received a standing ovation from the 11,000 fans in attendance. "Everyone in the ballpark knew I was fired," said Zimmer. "That's how dumb a baseball man this guy [Chiles] was."[66]

Once the game began, Milwaukee scored two runs in the top of the first inning on two separate errors and pushed another run across in the top of the eighth to win 3–2. Zimmer's odd run as Rangers manager was over. He was sitting in his office when a Rangers employee frantically approached to tell him that everyone was waiting for him in the lunchroom. No one thought to tell Zimmer exactly where his firing was to take place, so he wound up being late.[67]

"You know this guy sitting next to me is a good man and a good friend," said Chiles, "and he's been nothing but a good manager."

"So why are you firing him?" asked a member of the media.

"Someday you'll understand," said Chiles. "We did it for personal reasons."

"I never murdered anyone. I never robbed a bank," said Zimmer. "So, whatever your personal reasons you're talking about, I don't know what they are."[68]

The coup de grace came later that evening when Zimmer was out to dinner with some friends. While sitting at his table, former Rangers owner Brad Corbett approached them. Corbett led an investment group that purchased the Rangers in 1974 and was not shy about spending money. He brought in high-priced players like Richie Zisk, Bobby Bonds, and Al Oliver, but when the Rangers failed to win consistently, he sold the team to Chiles in 1980. The former owner approached Zimmer's table and said, "This guy Chiles is even making me look good. There's no way you should have been fired."[69] Corbett looked at Zimmer's wrist and asked to see the former manager's watch. "That's no watch for you. Here, look at this one," he said, pointing to the Rolex he was wearing. "Here let's make a switch. You take mine."[70]

Leaving the Rangers marked the second time in three seasons that Zimmer had been fired, but at least this time he got a nice watch out of the deal. The entire situation was ridiculous, and the press blasted Chiles and his partners, especially when Chiles accused the local media of being afflicted with "Watergate Syndrome" while at the same time admitting that he had lied when asked if Zimmer's job was safe once word of the firing leaked.

"As long as the decisions are being made on the whims of oilmen who know nothing about baseball, the Rangers are going to be in big, big trouble," wrote Peter Gammons in the *Sporting News*. "They laughed at [former Rangers owners] Bob Short and Corbett, but never as much as anyone's laughing at what Chiles, Rankin, et al. have done this season."[71]

"The calliope is playing its old familiar tune at Arlington Stadium," wrote Jim Reeves in the *Sporting News*. "The ringmasters may change, but the circus known as the Texas Rangers continues to come up with new tricks. If they can't find new ones, they simply rework the old gags."[72]

In New York, George Steinbrenner was up to his old tricks as well and broke out one of his favorites: messing with a superstar outfielder. When Dave Winfield signed his contract with the Yankees in December of 1980, the deal included a provision that Steinbrenner would "either contribute, or cause to be contributed, $3 million to the David M. Winfield Foundation, at a minimum of $300,000 per year over ten years,"[73] with payments to be issued quarterly. According to Winfield, it took Steinbrenner less than a year to stop making those payments, and the situation came to a head in July of 1982 when Winfield sued Steinbrenner on behalf of his foundation. Rather than taking care of his obligations, Steinbrenner took to the newspapers to publicly criticize his star outfielder.

"Dave Winfield is an outstanding athlete but he's not a superstar in the sense that Reggie Jackson is," said Steinbrenner in comparing Winfield to the other outfielder he helped run out of New York. "Winfield can't rise to the occasion. He can't carry the club the way Reggie does. David would best be served to concentrate on earning his large salary as a superstar, which he is supposed to be."[74] When asked if the lawsuit could affect Winfield's on-field performance, George answered, "I don't know. But if he says it won't work and he wants to be traded, I don't think any team would be willing to take him at those prices. I'm not saying I want to lose him, but I doubt if anybody would want him."[75]

Winfield knew he could not win a public PR battle with Steinbrenner, but he was also a proud man and wasn't about to slink away, especially when the deal Steinbrenner had reneged on would have benefitted needy kids. On the day George's comments hit the papers, Winfield homered twice against the Indians. Over the next six games, he hit .500 with 6 home runs and 12 RBI. "If he thinks he's going to upset me, he's messing with the wrong guy," he said. "It didn't bother me, what he said about me as a player. I don't need that kind of motivating tactic. If he wants Reggie Jackson, then why did he let him become a free agent? And if he wants him back, he should go get him. . . . All I know is that I play hard and do my job and produce. Everybody knows that Yankee Stadium affects the production of righthanded hitters. If they had moved the fences in a little, then my stats would reflect superstar numbers. But that doesn't mean I want to be traded. I intend to stay . . . and collect."[76]

Making matters worse, Reggie Jackson weighed in on the current state of his former team, saying, "They've got three guys trying to do what I did—Mayberry, Collins and Griffey—and they're paying them close to $3 million when they could have had me for $1 million. But it worked out the best for me. I'm in a more relaxed atmosphere. I miss the city, the fans, and the guys, but George made it so tough. A human being can only take so much."[77]

There was another member of the organization who was upset with Steinbrenner, and, unlike Winfield, he wanted out. Tommy John began the season with a 4–4 record and a 2.48 ERA but struggled in June and July. His problems mirrored those of Ron Guidry and 1981 Rookie of the Year Dave Righetti, who was eventually sent down to Triple-A Columbus.

"Going into spring training, you had to figure that Guidry, Righetti, and myself were good for 60 wins," said John in mid-July. "Nobody expected me and Gator [Guidry] to be losing and Righetti to be in the minors. But we can't lose confidence in ourselves and the club can't lose confidence in us. That's the main thing. If we're going to get back in the race and win, we will win because Gator, Righetti, and myself pitch well."[78]

The Yankees didn't share John's optimism and bumped him from the rotation. An upset John requested a trade, presenting a problem for

Steinbrenner. John was thirty-nine years old, and his contract called for him to make more than $750,000 in 1983. The list of teams willing to take him on was a short one. Vice president of baseball operations Bill Bergesch talked to the New York papers and sent John over the edge when he said, "Tommy John should show more appreciation for what the Yankees did for him last year."[79]

John took the comments as a reference to a near-fatal fall suffered by his son, Travis, in 1981. Shortly after the second half of the season began, John was in Detroit with the Yankees when Travis, then two and a half years old, fell out of a third-floor window of the family home and was badly injured. John missed one start and spent the rest of the season flying back and forth between home and Yankees games.

John saw Bergesch in the visitor's clubhouse in Texas and asked for a word in private. The two retreated to the laundry room, and the conversation that ensued was not cordial. Bergesch claimed he was misquoted, but John said he'd heard it from four different writers, all of whom had the same quote. "If you ever bring Travis John into this again, I'll kick your ass," John reportedly told Bergesch.[80] Then things got out of hand. "Something snapped," said John in his 1991 book, *T. J.: My 26 Years in Baseball.* "I got in his face, screaming at the top of my lungs. I called the guy every name in the book, using language that would wrinkle your clothes. I was hoping he'd make a move to shove me or something, because I was ready to flatten him. The whole club heard the outburst. When I got done, I was shaking. I could not calm down."[81]

Once the outburst was over, Yogi Berra, who witnessed the scene, remarked to John, "Boy. You were mad."[82]

The confrontation made the papers, and Bergesch denied he was referencing Travis John's fall, saying, "I did say I was disappointed that Tommy didn't show more appreciation for the things Mr. Steinbrenner did for him last year. I'm sorry for the interpretation he put on it, but it wasn't intended. Like the rest of the country, I had great sympathy for Tommy John and his family in that thing. I wouldn't want to do anything to embarrass or insult his family. I just meant that he showed no appreciation for the other things Mr. Steinbrenner did for him and I still feel that way."[83]

"If Travis John's name was mentioned, it was mentioned by Tommy, not us," said Steinbrenner. Then he went on the offensive. "He mentioned it because he's weak and he's looking for a crutch. I would never say anything like that, and I would never allow any of my people to say anything like that. If they did, they'd have to answer to me. It's become the popular thing to lay it on the big guy, to blame Steinbrenner, and Tommy just joined the crowd. If anybody exploited his son, he did. I've done more for kids than Tommy John will do in a lifetime. I didn't pull him out of the starting rotation, but I backed my manager up for doing it. He sure as hell hasn't pitched like a $750,000 pitcher."[84]

While the Yankees' season was slowly slipping away, the Baltimore Orioles were quietly getting back in the race in the American League East. In Earl Weaver's final season, the Birds were hoping to give him one last shot at the postseason, and there were signs of hope after a very slow start. Offensively, the team was still led by first baseman Eddie Murray, who continued to put up tremendous numbers.

One of twelve children, Murray grew up in the Watts neighborhood of Los Angeles and was just nine years old when the 1965 riots decimated the area. The memories of bullets hitting a water tower near his family's home were jarring, but he also had pleasant memories of his childhood, of loving parents who did all they could to provide for him and his siblings. Eddie grew up playing the game with his brothers, using tennis balls and the lids of Crisco cans as substitutes for baseballs. "I don't know how it started but I think it helped us a lot hitting curveballs later on," Murray said. "You could make that lid do wicked things if you were pitching, and you only had about ½-inch area to hit it."

Hitting Crisco lids paid off when Murray was drafted in the third round by the Orioles in 1973. Baltimore converted him to a switch hitter in 1975, and just two years later he won the American League Rookie of the Year Award. In December of 1980, he became the highest-paid player in team history when he signed a six-year deal that paid him more than $1 million per season. He celebrated by having a jeweler make him a necklace that read, *Just Regular*. "When someone asks me what it's like to be a millionaire, I point to the necklace," Murray said. "I like to think I'm the same person I was when I was playing ball for fun with my brothers in Los Angeles."[85]

He may have been a regular guy off the field, but on it, he was one of the most feared hitters in the game. His 22 home runs and 78 RBI in 1981 both led the American League in the strike-shortened season, and, despite battling a wrist injury, he was still batting above .300 in 1982 with his signature power. Murray was locked in at first base, but the Baltimore infield did see a change in July.

At the beginning of the month, Weaver moved rookie third baseman Cal Ripken Jr. to shortstop and installed Floyd Rayford at third. Weaver had the lineup he wanted, but it wasn't necessarily the one the Orioles front office wanted. Some questioned the move, thinking Ripken would move back to third base in 1983, but Weaver's plan all along was for Ripken to play shortstop. "It's always been easier to find a third baseman who can hit the ball out of the park than a shortstop," Weaver said. "You never know, Rip might be a helluva shortstop, too. He's played the position before."[86]

Ripken had played shortstop in three different stints in the minor leagues, but the man who was supposed to play shortstop at Memorial Stadium for years to come was named Bobby Bonner. Bonner was billed as the second coming of Mark Belanger, the Orioles' slick fielding shortstop from 1968 through 1981. Baltimore selected Bonner in the third round of the 1978 draft, and he dazzled the front office with his fielding prowess in the minor leagues. But it was one play, followed by one Weaver outburst, that had shattered his confidence and derailed his once promising career.

Bonner made his major league debut in September of 1980 with the Orioles in the heat of a pennant race. On September 14, in just his second game, Bonner misplayed a hard-hit ground ball in the eleventh inning that allowed the Blue Jays to tie the game. Toronto eventually won it in 13, dropping the Orioles five games behind the Yankees in the American League East. "Where the hell did we get this guy?" Weaver yelled. "He's supposed to be our best shortstop prospect? He couldn't catch anything!"[87]

In his book, *The Only Way I Know*, Cal Ripken Jr. said his father, the Orioles third base coach, indicated the ball was an extremely tough play on wet Astroturf, but that didn't matter to Weaver. The only thing that did was that the Orioles lost the game and would eventually finish second that season despite winning 100 games. "Quite a few players said that (Bonner) crumbled on the spot and never recovered," said Ripken. "Mike [Boddicker] said he saw it in Bobby's eyes."[88]

The Topps trading card company issued an "Orioles Future Stars" card in 1982 featuring Ripken, Bonner, and a pitcher named Jeff Schneider, who went to the Angels in the DeCinces trade. Bonner hit .169 in 40 games before being sent to the minor leagues in July while Ripken hit .326 with 6 home runs in his first 22 games at his new position. The

Orioles went 15–7 in those games to pull to within two games of the division lead. After being nearly 10 games off the pace in late May, Baltimore was on the move.

Also on the move were Joe Torre's Atlanta Braves, who, after a brief stumble following the All-Star break, took a nine-game lead over the San Diego Padres in the National League West. The lead was 10.5 games over the third-place Dodgers, who came to Atlanta for a series that could make or break their season.

"This is not a terrific looking club right now," wrote Mark Heisler in the *Los Angeles Times*. "The defending world champions warmed up for what is surely their last stand by continuing to make fundamental errors in bunches, to give away runs and then, to seem to accept it . . . 10½ games out, with his team playing terrible, emotionless baseball, [Dodgers manager Tommy] Lasorda is still into his Joe Cool act."[89]

By contrast, the Atlanta media was singing the praises of Torre and his team. Jesse Outlar wrote in the *Atlanta Constitution*, "You can't fault the manager for playing it cool as he puffs victory cigars and watches his team threaten to turn the race into a runaway. If the Braves take the four-game series with the Los Angeles Dodgers, they should have clear sailing to the pennant."[90]

The Braves were playing good baseball, and ticket sales were brisk, so much so that Braves owner Ted Turner decided to create some extra seating. Since moving to Atlanta in 1966, the Braves had a teepee in the left field stands that became the domain of a mascot named Chief Noc-A-Homa. A college student from nearby Georgia State originally played the part of the Chief, but in 1969 a man named Levi Walker, a member of the Odawa Tribe, approached the team with an idea. "I went to the Braves in full uniform and said, 'you got a white guy doing this job.' I told them if you want to hire a bartender, you bring in someone who can make drinks. I told the Braves you want a real Noc-A-Homa, you need a real Indian and that was me.'"[91]

Chief Noc-A-Homa became a staple at Braves games, emerging from his teepee located on a platform to do a war dance whenever Atlanta hit a home run. But business was business, and Ted Turner wanted to sell more tickets, so he gave the order to remove the Chief's platform to free up more seats just as the Dodgers were headed to town. Once there, L.A. swept a doubleheader on July 30 to cut two games off the Atlanta lead in the division and finished the four-game sweep two days later. Unfortunately for the Braves, the losing would continue, and their once safe lead would be put in danger.

STANDINGS AS OF JULY 31

Table 6.1. American League East and West

AL East				AL West			
Team	Wins	Losses	GB	Team	Wins	Losses	GB
Milwaukee	58	42	-	California	58	44	-
Boston	58	43	0.5	Kansas City	56	44	1.0
Baltimore	54	44	3.0	Chicago	51	49	6.0
New York	50	47	6.5	Seattle	52	50	6.0
Detroit	51	49	7.0	Oakland	44	60	15.0
Cleveland	49	50	8.5	Texas	39	59	17.0
Toronto	48	52	10.0	Minnesota	34	69	25.5

Table 6.2. National League East and West

NL East				NL West			
Team	Wins	Losses	GB	Team	Wins	Losses	GB
Philadelphia	58	42	-	Atlanta	61	40	-
St. Louis	58	44	1.0	San Diego	55	48	7.0
Pittsburgh	53	46	4.5	L.A. Dodgers	55	49	7.5
Montreal	53	47	5.0	San Francisco	49	54	13.0
New York	45	56	13.5	Houston	46	55	15.0
Chicago	40	65	20.5	Cincinnati	38	65	24.0

7. AUGUST

Awesome! Totally Awesome!

Beer and baseball just go together. It's what you need when the Jays are down 7–0.
—Toronto Blue Jays fan Gary Newfield

For the first five-plus years of their team's existence, Toronto Blue Jays fans endured multiple last-place finishes, often played in lousy weather, and without beer, despite the team being partially owned by the Labatt's brewery. "When Toronto came into the American League in 1977, it was known as a far different town than the other Canadian Baseball Franchise," wrote the *Los Angeles Times*. "Montreal was Catholic, Latin, and easy-going, while Toronto was Protestant, Anglo-Saxon, and uptight."[1]

That conservative attitude extended all the way to Exhibition Stadium and other arenas, thanks to an Ontario law that prohibited the sale of alcohol at sporting events. But after years of pressure, the Ontario government finally relented and lifted the ban in three stadiums in the province. The taps were scheduled to open in early August 3 when Toronto hosted (who else?) the Milwaukee Brewers, but the Blue Jays concessionaire, VS Services, worked diligently to take advantage of a weekend and warm temperatures and began serving beer on July 30, albeit with strict rules in place. Patrons had to visit concession stands behind the seating area and were limited to two twelve-ounce paper cups of beer per purchase. Sales began one hour before first pitch and ended promptly after the first pitch of the ninth inning, and there were no roving beer vendors in the stands. The first beer was poured by Metro Toronto chairman Paul Godfrey about one hour before game time.

"I wouldn't say it's a monumental event," he said. "The fact that it's been prohibited in the past is all that makes it important. I'm not a beer drinker myself, but this is a good day for sports fans."[2] But not all sports fans were filled with enthusiasm. "If beer brings more people out to the ballpark, I guess that's a good thing," Father Jerome Rohrer told the *Globe and Mail*. "In Milwaukee, they have youth nights and some people get carried away, make fools of themselves and don't even bother to watch the games."[3]

According to estimates, the crowd of 18,262 consumed nearly 15,000 cups of beer and saw their home team beat the Detroit Tigers 6–5, prompting one Canadian newspaper to run the headline, "Baseball and beer—and the Blue Jays even won."[4]

The beer-fueled winning streak was snapped at two when Detroit's Jack Morris beat the Jays 8–5 on August 1, but the days of "dry baseball" in Toronto were finally over. Toronto's loss dropped their record to 48–53 and saw them in the cellar of the division once again. But perhaps an even bigger surprise than beer at Blue Jays games was the fact that the Yankees, who were once also owned by a brewery, the Jacob Ruppert Brewing Company, were a mere 2½ games ahead of the Toronto in the division standings. That's when George Steinbrenner took action, again. On August 3, after a doubleheader sweep at the hands of the Chicago White Sox in which they were outscored 15–2, Steinbrenner fired manager Gene Michael and replaced him with pitching coach Clyde King on an interim basis. "George Steinbrenner, the impatient owner who discards managers the way Elizabeth Taylor goes through husbands, struck again following Tuesday night's . . . doubleheader loss to the Chicago White Sox," wrote the *Ithaca Journal*. "Gene Michael's second term as manager came to a sudden end, the ninth managerial change—involving six people, three of them two-time losers—since Steinbrenner purchased the club in 1973."[5]

Making matters worse, fans began chanting they wanted a refund during the second game of the twin bill, and, amazingly, Steinbrenner agreed. Shortly thereafter, an announcement came across the public address system stating that fans could exchange their tickets for any of six select games later in the season. "During the game," Steinbrenner said, "the fans underneath me were chanting 'Refund! Refund!' and it occurred to me it might be a good idea from a public relations standpoint."[6]

From an external PR standpoint, the move was a stroke of genius. From an internal PR standpoint, it was exactly the opposite. "You're asking me what goes on in that man's head?" asked reliever Goose Gossage. "I can't tell you that."[7] But he didn't stop there, adding, "This cock-sucking place is a fucking joke. The way they boo fucking everybody . . . and all you mothers with a fucking pen and a fucking tape recorder, you can fucking turn it on and take it upstairs . . . to the Fat Man [Steinbrenner]. OK? Because I'm fucking sick of the negative, fucking bullshit. You got that?"[8]

It was the second time in less than twelve months that Steinbrenner had fired Michael as Yankees manager, and he offered typical Steinbrenner logic for the move, saying, "I don't really blame [him]. It's just that I have to do what I have to do." He went on: "And if it doesn't work, I'm perfectly willing to bite the damn bullet on some of these big contracts. There are too many players on this team who are not playing up to their potential. If we don't win this thing, at the end of the season I'm prepared to go with my kids who want to play. If a guy doesn't want to put out for the Yankees than he can damn well sit home on his ass like a big fat toad."[9]

Ten months after being on the brink of their third World Series title in five seasons, the Yankees were imploding. They wouldn't qualify for the playoffs again until 1995, and their problems could be summed up by a Cheech and Chong film released the day after King took the helm: *Things are Tough All Over*.

While Cheech and Chong were driving a cab from Chicago to Las Vegas in their latest box office offering, Joel Youngblood woke up on August 4 in Chicago as a member of the New York Mets. By the time he went to bed that night, he had earned an obscure spot in baseball history. Youngblood was part of a crowded and unhappy Mets outfield rotation consisting of himself, Mookie Wilson, George Foster, Dave Kingman, and Ellis Valentine. On August 4 at Wrigley Field, Youngblood was 0-for-1 on the day with a strikeout when he stepped into the right-handed batter's box and delivered a single off Chicago starter Fergie Jenkins in the top of the third. The single scored two runs and gave the Mets a 3–1 lead in the game, eventually earning Youngblood the game-winning RBI. Later in the inning he was on the bench when the phone rang. The voice on the other end told him to report to the Mets clubhouse, where he was informed that he had just been traded to the Montreal Expos, who were scheduled to play the Phillies later that night in Philadelphia. Youngblood quickly packed and caught a flight to Philadelphia, arriving at Veterans Stadium and entering the game as a defensive replacement.

In the top of the seventh he again stepped into the right-handed batters' box, except this one was 770 miles away from the previous one. "When I got up to the plate against [Steve] Carlton, I felt better than I have felt all year," he said. "I felt comfortable and confident that I can play up to my ability because I'm finally with a club that wants me." He proved his worth right away, delivering an infield single, making him the first player in history to get base hits for two different teams in two different cities in the same day—the pièce de resistance being that both hits had come off future Hall of Fame pitchers. "I had no idea that I'm the first to do what I've done," he said. "I never gave it a thought. I'm just happy to be with a first-class organization and I hope I can get the club into first place. They didn't order me here for tonight, but I felt if I could make it, I wanted them to have the opportunity to use me."[10]

Youngblood helped Montreal to a 5–4 win, but the Expos found themselves seven games out of first place in the National League East. He and his new teammates would really need to step up if Montreal was going to get back in the hunt.

In the American League East, the Boston Red Sox were 2½ games out, their largest deficit of the year, as they entertained the Chicago White Sox a few days later at Fenway Park. The Red Sox had spent much of the season in the chase, extending their lead to five games in June, only to see it shrink and eventually vanish thanks to the Milwaukee Brewers' hot streak. Among those keeping the Red Sox in the race was left fielder Jim Rice.

Rice was Boston's first-round selection in the 1971 draft and had a standout rookie season in 1975, finishing second in the Rookie of the Year balloting and third in the MVP race, with his teammate Fred Lynn taking home both honors. In parts of seven seasons, he carried a .302 lifetime batting average while averaging 27 home runs and 91 RBI per year. But it was his actions on August 7, 1982, that went above and beyond perhaps any seen on a baseball field.

In the bottom of the fourth inning, Rice was in the home dugout at Fenway as his teammate Dave Stapleton faced Chicago pitcher Richard Dotson. Sitting in Field Box 29, row two, seat two, down the first-base line, was a four-year-old boy named Jonathan Keane. Keane was attending the game with his father, Tom, and his younger brother, Matthew. Dotson delivered a pitch, and Stapleton hit a line drive foul ball. Tom Keane heard a crack and assumed the ball had hit the Boston dugout to his right. Instead, the crack he heard was the ball hitting Jonathan's skull. Keane looked and saw his son slumped and bleeding profusely.

Jim Rice had been standing at the top of the steps of the Boston dugout, and even before Keane could truly process what had happened, Rice had leapt into the stands, scooped Jonathan up in his arms, and made a beeline to the Red Sox clubhouse. Boston team doctor Arthur Pappas was seated on the opposite side of the dugout and also headed straight for the clubhouse. "It was the most sickening thing I've ever seen in the stands," said Boston outfielder Rick Miller. "[Keane] didn't have a chance. Jerry [Remy] was in the runway when Jim went by with the kid and Jerry said he almost threw up."[11]

Pappas met Rice in the trainer's room and found the boy nonresponsive and immediately called Children's Hospital to request an ambulance. Fortunately, the hospital was only a mile away, and Pappas estimated that Keane was in the ambulance less than 5 minutes after having been struck. The *Boston Globe* ran a dramatic photograph the following day on the front page of the sports section of Rice carrying a slumped Keane in his arms. His quick actions likely saved the boy's life, but Rice brushed off the idea that he was a hero. "If it was your kid, what would you do?" he asked. "The baby was crying and there was a lot of blood. I think he was more in shock than anything."[12] It was more than shock. Keane suffered a fractured skull but eventually made a full recovery thanks to Rice's quick actions.

After Rice's heroic act, his teammate Mike Torrez narrowly escaped injury when a Ken Singleton line drive glanced off his head above his right ear and bounded into left field. Torrez came out of the game for precautionary X-rays, which proved negative. "It's something you sometimes dream happens to you, but you wake up relieved it's only a dream," said Torrez. "This wasn't a dream, and I was very fortunate."[13]

Unfortunately for the Red Sox, the starting rotation was struggling even before Torrez's scare. Chuck Rainey went 1–1 with a 5.72 ERA in August, Torrez went 0–2 with an ugly 6.28 ERA, and lefty Bob Ojeda surrendered six runs in less than four innings against the Angels and was then lost for the season after falling in the hotel bathtub and injuring his shoulder. By mid-August, Boston saw a one-game lead in the AL East over Milwaukee turn into a 5½-game deficit. In addition to slipping in the tub, the Red Sox were slipping out of the race.

If the Red Sox were slipping, the Houston Astros were in free fall. On August 10, with their record at 49–62, Astros owner John McMullen fired manager Bill Virdon and replaced him with coach Bob Lillis. Virdon spent twelve years in the major leagues as a player, earning NL Rookie of the Year honors in 1955 and winning a World Series with the Pirates in

1960. He took over as Houston's manager in August of 1975 and molded the Astros from perennial losers into perennial contenders. The team finished in second place in the National League West in 1979 and finally won the division in 1980 before eventually losing to the Phillies in the National League Championship Series. The following year, they made it to the NLCS before falling to the Dodgers. Then came the 1982 season, which was an unqualified disaster. Despite a strong starting rotation led by Nolan Ryan, Joe Niekro, Ken Forsch, and Don Sutton, the team went 9–14 in April, and things never improved. At the time of Virdon's dismissal, the Astros were dead last in the National League in team batting average and next to last in home runs and runs scored.

"We made the decision that the Houston Astros were going to need a new manager next year and, in the best interest of both the ballclub and Bill Virdon, this seemed to be the appropriate time to make the change," said McMullen. "This will now give us the next two months to go through a list of possible candidates and begin making our plans for next season."[14]

"We've been expecting something like this because there has been speculation all year that Bill would be fired," said Niekro. "It goes down to the old adage that you can't fire the players, so you fire the manager."[15]

"I have no bitterness toward anybody in the organization," said Virdon. "They paid me for my services. You can't question a man's right to make a change if he's running an organization. My only regret is that we didn't get into the World Series. Some of these players will never have that opportunity again, and that's the one thing every player wants to do."

In the fall of 1979, back when Virdon was guiding the Astros through the heat of the first pennant race in team history, twenty-two-year-old Cameron Crowe was going undercover as a high school student in California to research his first book. He enrolled at San Diego's Clairemont High School under the pseudonym Dave Cameron and began chronicling the lives of students. The resulting book was *Fast Times at Ridgemont High*, which was turned into a film of the same name released on August 13, 1982.

"'Fast Times' is well made and abounds in fresh new talent on both sides of the camera,"[16] wrote Kevin Thomas in the *Los Angeles Times*. Behind the camera, that talent included Crowe and first-time director Amy Heckerling. The film also helped launch the careers of Judge Reinhold, Phoebe Cates, Jennifer Jason Leigh, Forest Whitaker, and Eric Stoltz. But the actor who really established himself was twenty-one-year-old Sean Penn, who was cast as the perpetually stoned surfer Jeff Spicoli.

"Penn is one of the most hilarious presences to hit the screen since the late John Belushi was let loose in 'Animal House,'" wrote Thomas, "especially when he comes against astringent history professor [played by] Ray Walston for whom he defines the constitution of the United States as a set of 'cool rules.'"[17]

Penn came to the set of "Fast Times" after finishing a very different role, one he described as "the conscience of the film," in the military school drama *Taps*. Spicoli became his breakout role, in part because he not only played the role but lived it, both on and off the set. "All through the shooting, you could not address him by his name; you had to call him Spicoli," said casting director Don Phillips. "It was written on his trailer. He made all the kids do that, even though 'Taps' had not yet come out, so nobody knew who the fuck Sean Penn was."[18]

Among those not impressed by Penn's performance, at least initially, was Walston, a veteran actor who had worked in both television and film since 1954. In rehearsing one scene, the script dictated that Spicoli call Walston's character, teacher Mr. Hand, a "dick," but on the fly Penn changed the line and instead called Walston an "old, red-faced motherfucker."[19]

"Walston turned beet red and got crazy pissed off, like 'How dare this kid?'" said Art Linson, one of the film's producers. "But Sean, even then, was trying . . . to get a rise out of him that would be great for the moment. That's a pretty audacious move for a kid no one had heard of yet."[20]

"The morning after we wrapped [shooting], Sean showed up very nicely dressed in slacks and a shirt and jacket, and went around introducing himself to everyone as 'Sean,'" said Heckerling. "But for a long time after the movie, people would ask me, 'What's Sean like?' and I would say, 'Well I only know Spicoli. . . .'"[21]

Despite a limited promotional budget, and a limited initial release, *Fast Times* grossed more than $2.5 million in its first weekend and eventually topped more than $25 million in gross revenues. Penn would go on to win two Academy Awards for his roles in other films.[22]

* * * * *

"You should be able to outmanage them since they don't have a man -ager."[23]

These words of "encouragement" offered to Dodgers manager Tommy Lasorda as he sat in the visitor's clubhouse at Wrigley Field on August 17 were correct thanks to home plate umpire Eric Gregg, who ejected Cubs manager Lee Elia in the eighth inning of that afternoon's contest.

Unfortunately for all involved, the two teams were still tied nine innings later when the game was suspended due to darkness. Elia's ejection came courtesy of a play at the plate in which Cubs shortstop Larry Bowa, all 160 pounds of him, bounced off Dodgers catcher Mike Scioscia, who, in just his third season in the big leagues, was already establishing himself as one of the game's best in terms of blocking the plate. "I thought I got the plate," said Bowa. "It was bang-bang." Elia agreed and came out to argue his case, at which point "there was much feverish head-waggling on both sides, and soon thereafter Gregg ejected Elia." For his part, Scioscia was unfazed by his run-in with Bowa, both thirteen years his senior and forty pounds lighter, telling reporters, "It's OK. I finally got a $100 deductible from State Farm on collisions at home."[24]

The game resumed the following day, and Dodgers relief pitcher Ricky Wright, who got the last out of the bottom of the seventeenth inning, was available to pitch in the eighteenth inning, but Lasorda instead tapped Jerry Reuss, who was slated to start the regularly scheduled game that day.

Reuss retired the Cubs in the eighteenth and his teammate, Steve Sax, led off the top of the nineteenth inning for Los Angeles by drawing a walk. Chicago's acting manager, John Vukovich, was then ejected by Gregg for arguing balls and strikes. Ron Cey led off the top of the twentieth inning with a single to right field but was promptly picked off first base. Cey argued the call, and he too was ejected, as was Lasorda, the third managerial ejection of the contest. With Cey gone, the Dodgers were down to just two players on the bench, both pitchers, so right fielder Pedro Guerrero moved to third base to replace Cey and Fernando Valenzuela headed to the outfield.

"I have been dreaming all my life to play a position other than pitcher," said Valenzuela. "The thrill came when the fans began cheering when I moved out to right field. I felt like a little kid again."[25]

Reuss led off the top of the twenty-first inning with a groundout, but Steve Sax doubled to right field and advanced to third base on a wild pitch. Dusty Baker then lifted a fly ball to right field. Keith Moreland made the catch and threw home to get the tagging Sax at the plate. The throw was high, which allowed Sax to slide between the legs of Cubs catcher Jody Davis in a cloud of dust. Eric Gregg cocked his right arm to signal Sax was out, then changed his mind and signaled safe. "I was over-aggressive," Gregg said. "I started my call and I thought, 'Wait a minute.' My baseball instinct told me to get the call correct. I feel good about the call. I looked at the replay and saw it wasn't close."[26]

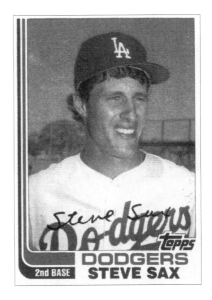

Figure 10: Steve Sax had big shoes to fill in 1982 but took home Rookie of the Year honors after batting .282 and stealing 49 bases. 1982 Topps® trading cards used courtesy of The Topps Company, Inc.

Reuss retired the Cubs in order in the bottom of the twenty-first for a 2–1 victory, the longest game the Dodgers played since they moved to Los Angeles prior to the 1958 season. As Reuss entered the dugout, Lasorda asked him how he felt. "I'm fine," said Reuss. "Then you'll start the regular game and go as long as you can," replied Lasorda.[27] The regularly scheduled game was set to begin in thirty minutes, so Reuss turned to pitching coach Ron Perranoski for advice on how to handle getting ready. "I've never pitched in two games thirty minutes apart. Any idea on how I should warm up?"[28]

"How should I know?" said Perranoski, who pitched in the big leagues for thirteen seasons. "I've never done it either."[29]

Reuss changed uniforms and minutes later was back on the field, where he threw five innings, allowed just two runs, and got the win, his second of the day. The doubleheader sweep, coupled with a Montreal doubleheader sweep of Atlanta the previous day, produced something almost unthinkable just a few weeks prior: a four-game Dodgers lead in the National League West.

On July 29, right about the time the Braves removed Chief Noc-A-Homa's teepee, Atlanta held a nine-game lead in the division. Then they went into a tailspin, losing 19 of their next 21 games. Making matters worse, all but three of the games were against divisional opponents. The skid began on July 30 when the Dodgers came to town. Prior to the series, L.A. shortstop Bill Russell was asked about the upcoming four-game set and replied, "We are what, 10 games out in the loss column? So, we've got to go into Atlanta and just about take 'em all."[30]

They did just that, outscoring Atlanta in the series 30–15. Then came the San Francisco Giants, who took two of three before the Braves headed west for another four-game set with the Dodgers, this one in Los Angeles. "I think this is a great time to play the Dodgers," said third-baseman Bob Horner. "It's time for a little payback. They beat us last weekend, and let's see what we can do to them there."[31]

The answer was . . . nothing. The Dodgers swept the Braves again, including three straight extra-inning walk-off wins. Atlanta had come to town with a 5½-game lead in the division and left with their lead cut to just a game and a half. Two nights later, Al Hrabosky surrendered a seventh-inning home run to Milt May in San Francisco to give the Giants a 3–2 win, and Atlanta's divisional lead was gone. After beginning the season 13–0, the Braves had 49 wins and 49 losses in their next 98 games and found themselves in second place.

"Only in Vegas should one be able to lose so much so fast," wrote Tim Tucker in the *Atlanta Constitution*. "Just 12 days after leading the National League West by 9 games, just 12 days after leading the Los Angeles Dodgers by 10½ games, just 12 days after flashing 'We're World Serious' on the Atlanta Fulton County stadium scoreboard, the Atlanta Braves Wednesday morning find themselves out of 1st place. It's like inheriting a fortune and, 12 days later, filing for bankruptcy."[32]

The Braves lost their next three games before finally beating the Padres 6–5 on August 14, then proceeded to lose again the next afternoon on an extra-inning walk-off single to complete an eleven-game road trip in which they went 1–10. "Can't say that I've ever been through a trip like this," said a bewildered Horner. "Sure can't say that I have."[33]

"We can't really be looking for philosophies now," said manager Joe Torre. "We've got to be looking for more consistency in the way we play. We sure as hell didn't play well again today. We had plenty of opportunities to win."[34]

The final game of the series was a perfect summation of the disastrous trip. Atlanta built a 4–1 lead but coughed it up after Braves defenders lost two balls in the sun and botched two easy double-play balls. Atlanta limped back home and promptly lost the first three games of their ten-game homestand, including a 12–2 pasting at the hands of the Montreal Expos on August 18. "We can still turn it around," said Horner. "But we've been saying that for three weeks."[35]

If the Braves were to turn things around, they'd need Horner to produce. During the 21-game swoon, Horner hit just .188 with 4 homers and 11 RBI. Dale Murphy was even worse, batting .181 with 1 home run and 8 RBI. But as bad as the Atlanta bats were, the bullpen was worse. Hard-throwing rookie Steve Bedrosian went 4–1 in the season's first half, with a 1.64 ERA. During Atlanta's slide, he went 0–5 with a 4.08 ERA. Fellow reliever Rick Camp went 0–3, Hrabosky posted an ERA of 9.00 and was eventually released, and Gene Garber went 0–2 with a .391 batting average against. "What it boils down to is that I haven't been doing my job," said Garber. "It's that simple."[36]

The losing streak finally came to an end on August 19 when Atlanta beat Montreal 5–4. But the bigger story on that evening was the fate of scheduled starting pitcher Pascual Pérez, who arrived at the ballpark just in time to hear the national anthem and watch Phil Niekro pitch in his place. Pérez had received his driver's license earlier in the day and got lost on the way to Atlanta Fulton County Stadium.

Atlanta had acquired Pérez from the Pittsburgh Pirates at the end of June, and he went 5–0 with a 1.26 ERA for the Braves' Triple-A farm club in Richmond, Virginia, before being recalled at the end of July. He was penciled in to start the August 19 game against the Expos and left his apartment that afternoon for the twenty-minute drive to the stadium. His roommates told him to take I-85 and get off at I-20, which would take him straight to the ballpark. But the inexperienced Pérez instead got on I-285 and circled the city . . . for more than three hours. He stopped multiple times for directions but couldn't find his way and eventually turned up at a service station in a panic and nearly out of gas. He had also forgotten his wallet. Fortunately for Pérez, the clerk was a Braves fan and had been listening to the pregame radio show.

"You Pascual Pérez?" asked the clerk. "People been waiting for you at the stadium."[37]

Perez was able to get gas, and directions, and eventually arrived at the ballpark, but not before Niekro got the start in his place. What could have been a disaster gave the Braves a much-needed reason to laugh. Pérez was OK, the Georgia State Patrol and DeKalb County Police, who had been enlisted to find the wayward pitcher, were told to stand down, and the Braves won the game.

Pérez arrived at the ballpark, on time, the following day, paid a $100 fine for being late the previous day, and got ready for his start, but not before enduring lots of ribbing from his teammates. He found a map posted above his locker with the intersections of I-285 and I-20 circled, and, after batting practice, shortstop Rafael Ramírez tied a rope to Pérez's wrist and led him around the clubhouse. "Easy getting here today," said Pérez. "Easy, easy. I followed the map. I know the way now."[38]

He then allowed just one run to the New York Mets over nine and two-thirds innings before being relieved by Bedrosian, who induced an inning-ending groundout. Dale Murphy drew a walk-off walk in the bottom of the tenth inning to give the Braves their first two-game winning streak since July 29. They would eventually stretch the winning streak to six and get back in the race in the National League West. "I just feel the ballclub is back to normal," said a relieved Torre.[39]

"Normal" for the St. Louis Cardinals was hitting the ball in the gaps and stealing bases. By the third week in August, St. Louis had amassed 157 stolen bases, second only to Oakland in all of baseball, but there was one stolen base that stood above the rest.

The Cardinals began the month of August in second place in what was becoming a two-team race with the Phillies for the National League East title, but they regained the lead on August 12 thanks to the pitching, and hitting, of Joaquin Andújar, who gave up just two runs in seven innings of work and delivered a key base hit in a 3–2 win over Pittsburgh. Andújar swung a forty-ounce bat, eleven ounces heaver that his teammate Ozzie Smith wielded, and tended to try to hit every pitch he saw out of the ballpark. But a conversation with St. Louis coach Hub Kittle caused Andujar to change his approach at the plate, and the result was a single to keep a rally going. With Ozzie Smith on third base and no one out, Andújar was supposed to bunt but noticed the corner infielders charging and instead poked a hit to the right side of the infield. A sacrifice and two hits gave the Cardinals the lead and, eventually, the win while Andújar gave Kittle the credit.

"He's my guy," said Andújar. "He taught George Foster how to hit."[40]

"I was tired of seeing him (strike out)," said Kittle. "He's got to make contact."[41]

The Cardinals built their lead to two games by August 22 but found themselves in trouble at home against the Giants. Andújar started the game, and the Cards trailed 4–3 with two outs in the bottom of the ninth and a man on second. With pitcher Doug Bair scheduled up, Whitey Herzog scanned his bench for a pinch-hitter to face the right-handed Greg Minton. The man Herzog normally called on in such situations was reserve outfielder Dane Iorg, but he was unavailable because his wife had delivered their fifth child earlier in the day, so Herzog went with Ken Oberkfell, who had a total of zero pinch-hits in his three years as a member of the Cardinals. "I figured he was due," said Herzog.[42]

Minton delivered a sinker but left it up, and Oberkfell hit it into the gap in right-center field for an RBI double to tie the game at four apiece. The game remained tied until the bottom of the twelfth inning when the Cardinals loaded the bases with two outs. On third base was back-up catcher Glenn Brummer, making just his third appearance of the month. Brummer signed with the Cardinals in 1974 as an undrafted free agent out of Effingham, Illinois, about ninety minutes east of St. Louis. On August 22, 1982, he was making the fiftieth appearance in a career that would span parts of five seasons. It was also perhaps his most memorable.

David Green, back from his hamstring injury, was at the plate for the Cardinals and was down 1–2 in the count with Gary Lavelle on the mound for the Giants when Brummer, on his own, broke for the plate. Lavelle's delivery featured a high leg-kick, and Brummer, who at that point had a grand total of one career stolen base, thought he could take advantage.

"Two down, sacks jammed," said Mike Shannon on the Cardinals radio broadcast. "Lavelle at the belt, checks . . . Brummer's stealing home! He is . . . safe and the Cardinals win! Brummer stole home! The dugout comes out and they congratulate him. You wouldn't believe it! Glenn Brummer . . . steals home and now the Giants are out arguing about the call."[43]

Giants manager Frank Robinson came out to argue not whether Brummer was safe, which he clearly was, but the call on the pitch. Home plate umpire Dave Pallone came out from behind the plate to get a better view of the attempted steal. Brummer slid home safely, but the question was whether the pitch was a strike or a ball. If it was a strike, Green was out, and the inning was over.

"[Giants catcher Milt] May asked me if the guy had gotten under the tag," said Pallone. But Robinson and the rest of the team "were arguing that I hadn't called the pitch. I called it a ball."[44]

"The umpire never made a call on the pitch," said Robinson. "That pitch Lavelle threw was a strike, and Pallone said he called it a ball from the start. That pitch was right down the middle of the plate."[45]

"As far as I could see," said Pallone, "the pitch was out of the strike zone. If I felt like the pitch was a strike, then the inning would have been over."[46]

The actual location of the pitch depended on who you asked. Lavelle and May both said it was a fastball down the middle. Green claimed it was a slider low and away, while Keith Hernandez muddied the waters further when he said he spoke to his father who was watching the Giants broadcast at home and agreed with May and Lavelle. Television replays showed that the pitch was definitely not a slider and definitely not low and away. It was at the belt, but it *may* have been outside. Regardless, Brummer was called safe, and the Cardinals won the game.

"I never would have thought that I'd steal home in my career," said Brummer. "It's like a dream come true that a catcher would try to steal home for the St. Louis Cardinals or anybody else to win a ball game."[47]

"I'll probably never see that again in my career," said Keith Hernandez. "Stealing home plate with two strikes and two outs . . . I'll never see that again. I thought I had seen it all. I have not seen it all."[48]

* * * * *

The following day featured another event someone had never seen before when Gaylord Perry was ejected from a game for the first time in his career for doctoring a baseball. "After 20 years of getting away with the perfect crime, Gaylord Perry finally got caught with his hand in the Vaseline jar," wrote United Press International.[49] Perry ran afoul of home plate umpire Dave Phillips in the seventh inning of the Mariners' game with the Boston Red Sox when he threw Boston outfielder Rick Miller "the best spitter I've ever seen."[50]

"He used to only use it when he needed it," said Red Sox manager Ralph Houk. "But now, maybe because he's lost a lot, he's trying to throw it eight out of every 10 pitches."[51]

Despite his reputation as a spitball pitcher, Perry denied any wrongdoing and went on the offensive, saying, "No other umpire is as bad as Dave Phillips. It was a forkball. Bruce Sutter's forkball does that, too. Are you going to throw him out of a game? Phillips made bad calls all game. He's a crusader."[52]

Phillips issued Perry a warning in the fifth inning for having a foreign substance on the ball, so he felt he was justified in ejecting him in the seventh, saying, "The rule states that if I can tell by the flight of the ball, I can call an illegal pitch. The question was the flight of the ball. By my judgment, it was an illegal pitch, and it wasn't only my judgment, but the judgment of anybody out there who knows baseball. It was an obvious illegal pitch. Gaylord Perry has a history of this stuff. He was in a tough situation with men on 1st and 3rd and he threw an illegal pitch."[53]

The 4–3 loss to the Red Sox dropped Perry's Mariners thirteen games off the pace in the American League West, but still left them four games on top of the Oakland A's, who were in the process of putting up their fourth straight month of sub-.500 baseball. It was a lost season for everyone in Oakland save one man. Rickey Henderson was having a season like no one had seen in the history of the game. He stole his 100th base of the year at the beginning of the month, and as August drew to a close Lou Brock's single-season record of 118 was in danger.

"The only question was whether I'd steal 119 at home or on the road," said Henderson in his 1992 book, *Off Base: Confessions of a Thief.* "That was an important question because the Oakland fans were turning out in record numbers. Billy Ball was attracting a new breed of A's fans to the Coliseum. The year before, despite the strike, we drew 1.3 million people, and that had never been done in Oakland, even in the World Series years of the '70s. In '82 we continued to draw even though we weren't winning."[54]

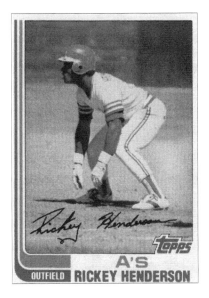

Figure 11: Rickey Henderson set the single-season stolen bases record with 130. It was one of twelve seasons in which he led the league in stolen bases. 1982 Topps® trading cards used courtesy of The Topps Company, Inc.

Henderson stole his 115th base of the season on August 23 at home against the Detroit Tigers, which put the record within striking distance. But Oakland had only one home game left before heading out on a ten-game road trip. The situation called for some creativity, so Billy Martin came up with a plan. Henderson walked in his first plate appearance on August 24, then stole second and third. He was just two away from the record, but he flew out in his next two at bats. The game moved to the eighth inning, in which Fred Stanley drew a leadoff walk to bring Henderson to the plate. Stanley was in the final season of a major league career that began in 1969, but speed was not part of his game. In thirteen seasons heading into 1982, Stanley amassed half as many stolen bases (11) as Henderson did in April of 1982 alone (22). For Henderson to break the record at home, he'd need to get on, and then steal second and third again, but Stanley was in his way. The stakes grew higher when Henderson singled to left field, moving Stanley to second. This was where Martin's plan came in.

Oakland's third-base coach, Clete Boyer, walked over to Stanley and told him to steal third. At the same time, Oakland's first-base coach told Henderson to stay put. If Stanley was cut down on the front end of a double steal, then Henderson wouldn't get credit for a stolen base even if he slid safely into second. With Stanley *off* the bases, the path would be clear for Henderson to steal second and third to set the record. But Detroit manager Sparky Anderson caught on and yelled at his team to let Stanley go.

As Tigers pitcher Jerry Ujdur got set to pitch, Stanley took a large lead off second. Ujdur spun and made a pickoff throw to shortstop Alan Trammell. Stanley didn't move. Anderson then yelled at Trammell not to tag Stanley, so Trammell threw to third baseman Enos Cabell. Again, Stanley didn't move. Cabell threw to second baseman Lou Whitaker, who tagged Stanley out, much to the chagrin of Anderson. Henderson now had a clear path to set the record. Ujdur threw to first three times to keep Henderson close, then finally came home.

"A pitchout," wrote Henderson. "I took off. [Tigers catcher Bill] Fahey threw to 2nd, and I got under the tag. Yes! I've tied Brock. Hallelujah."[55]

Only he hadn't, because umpire Durwood Merrill called Henderson out on the play. Henderson howled in protest, as did the fans and Henderson's teammates. Dwayne Murphy flew out to end the inning and earned an ejection on his way out to his position in center field after expressing his opinion to Merrill. "You're motherbleeping horsebleep. Those were my exact words," Murphy told the *San Francisco Examiner*.[56] Martin came to the defense of Murphy and also got tossed. Oakland won the game 3–0, but Henderson would not break the record in front of the home crowd. The stunt so upset Anderson that he was shaking in his postgame press conference.

"All honor has left this game," he said. "If Fred Stanley isn't fined the biggest figure ever fined, then we have no commissioner of baseball. Fred Stanley has discredited this game; What he did is totally unforgivable. He did something that takes all honor away from the game. I'll never forgive him for it, and I'll think of it every time I see him for the rest of my life."[57] Anderson then turned his ire to Henderson, saying, "He has control of it. He can say no. Somewhere along the line you've got to be a man. If you can steal that many bases, you can steal [them] straight."[58]

Stanley turned the blame on Merrill, saying, "If I get nailed then Durwood should really get fined. He told Billy, 'You had Stanley picked off intentionally.' He was making a judgement right there. He got emotionally involved."[59]

"He thought we had Stanley deliberately picked off," said Martin of Merrill. "We had a double-steal on . . . It's an outrage. Rickey was safe at second without a doubt."[60]

Despite the outrage, the record still belonged to Brock, but not for long. Oakland faced the Brewers to begin their road trip, and Henderson stole one base in the series opener to tie the record. On August 27, the speedster faced a battery of Doc Medich, who was slow to the plate, and Ted Simmons, who wasn't known for his arm. It was a dream matchup. Henderson walked with two outs in the third inning and took his lead. The crowd of more than 41,000 began chanting, "Go! Go! Go!"[61]

"I had butterflies rolling in my stomach," said Henderson. Oakland first-base coach Jackie Moore could see the nerves and did what he could to calm Henderson down. "Jackie called me aside and said, 'Give me a smile.' When I smiled, he said, 'I know now you'll be all right.'"[62]

Medich threw to first four times, drawing boos from the crowd. He then came set and delivered home. Henderson took off. Simmons came up firing but to no avail as Henderson slid into second ahead of the tag. The record was his. He stood up, brushed the dirt from his uniform, and pulled second base from its moorings. Brock emerged from the stands to shake Henderson's hand and pose for photos. Murphy, the man who hit behind Henderson for most of the season, got a hug and a kiss from Henderson. "Believe it or not, I felt just as excited as he did," said Murphy. "The last two, three weeks, every time he ran, I got the chills."[63]

The sacrifices made by Murphy were lost on no one, least of all Henderson, who said, "If I could have split that base in half, I would have given the other half to Dwayne Murphy. He's why I stole so many bases. Dwayne has had to use a lot of patience hitting behind me. He won't hit for a high average behind me because he has to take pitches that he would normally hit. When he does hit it's usually with two strikes on him."[64]

Not content, Henderson walked and stole second again in the sixth inning. He led off the top of the eighth with another walk. With the record behind him, Henderson could finally relax. "Your legs look lighter," said the first-base umpire.[65] Henderson agreed, then stole second and third, giving him four for the game and running his season total to 122. The first-base umpire was Durwood Merrill.

"I'm relieved and exhausted," said Henderson after the game. "Now I can go out and relax a little more and hope the team can pull together and win more games. I want to take some days off, but we need to win, so the days off will come sometime down the road."[66]

With the record firmly, and legitimately, in hand, a few days of rest would not be out of the question. But Martin was having none of it. He wanted Henderson to keep playing and to keep running. "I want him to steal 145 bases," said Martin. "I think that would put the record out of reach. The records that I don't think will be broken are DiMaggio's hitting streak and Gehrig playing in every game for all those years. If Rickey steals 145, he could have one of those kinds of records too."[67]

There was one other stolen base record set in August of 1982, albeit a much less prestigious one. When John Wathan of the Kansas City Royals stole his thirty-first base of the season on August 24, he passed Ray Schalk's 1916 record for the most stolen bases in a season by a catcher. Like Henderson, Wathan received the base as a souvenir and immediately announced what he planned to do with it. "I think I'll make it into a bar stool," he said. "I heard that's what Lou Brock did with the one he got for setting the record. I think I'll put some legs on it, write a little inscription on it, and sit on it when I retire."[68]

The accomplishment was even more impressive considering Wathan missed five weeks after fouling a ball off his foot, breaking a bone near his ankle, on July 5. Once he returned to the lineup, he hit .347 over his next 27 games to help keep the Royals in the hunt in the American League West race. He was not the only member of the team with a hot bat. After a trip to Toronto earlier in the season, the Royals returned home at 2 A.M. to face a line at the US Customs desk. A weary agent asked a weary Frank White if he was bringing anything back into the

United States from Canada. "He's bringing back an 0-for-16," said Hal McRae.[69] White, an outstanding fielder, carried a lifetime .252 batting average into 1982, but success at the plate had eluded him in the early going. Then he caught fire, batting .354 over his next 71 games to raise his batting average to a robust .325. The hot streak included a 4-for-5 day against the Tigers where he hit for the cycle and drove in four. When he uncharacteristically committed two errors in the same game, his teammates jokingly described the six-time Gold Glove winner as "all hit, no field."[70]

White told the *Sporting News* that after ten seasons in the big leagues he was a smarter hitter. With that came a more relaxed approach at the plate, which allowed him to be more selective, take pitches he may have swung at in the past, and take more aggressive cuts at the pitches he liked. "I'm using all fields more and not free-swinging except in certain situations," he said. "I've been on the bottom end [at the plate] too many times and I know how fast things can change. I just like to enjoy it and see if I can keep it going."[71]

Like Wathan, White was also dealing with a bad foot, the result of an arthritic toe that caused him to miss a few games in late July, and doctors told him surgery would be required to relieve the pain. Third baseman George Brett was also facing surgery but hoping to put it off until after the season. In Brett's case, the injury was a bone chip in his wrist that led to tendonitis. The problem became so bad that he had to exit a game on August 13 after a swing sent waves of pain through his hand and up his arm. "All I can do is rest, take cortisone, sit in the whirlpool, tape up, and watch Greg Pryor [his replacement] and hope I can learn something from him," said Brett. The cortisone injections were enough to avoid surgery and get Brett back in the lineup after twelve days, and, a testament to his greatness as a hitter, he actually raised his batting average by ten points over the next seven days. But his power was gone. At the time he left the lineup, Brett was batting .300 with 17 home runs. He would hit just four more over the course of the season's final six weeks.

Injuries would nag Brett, White, and Wathan for the rest of the season, but the one suffered by Willie Wilson was downright scary. In early August, Wilson was leading the American League with a .340 batting average when he was hit in the cheek by a pitch from Detroit's Dan Petry. Wilson left the field on a stretcher and was taken to Kansas City's St. Luke's Hospital for observation. The injury upset the Royals, specifically manager Dick Howser, who felt the pitch had been intentional, but Petry pleaded his innocence. "I'm sorry it happened," he said after the game. "Very, very sorry. It's the first time I've ever hit anyone in the head and I'm never going to *try* to hit someone in the head. The ball just sailed back in on him. It's a common law around the league to pitch Willie Wilson inside."[72]

"Petry was very uptight the rest of the night on the bench," said his manager, Sparky Anderson. "Anybody who would intentionally try to hit a man in the head is the lousiest human I know. I think the world of Petry, so you know what I think happened."[73]

Fortunately for Wilson and the Royals, the injury wasn't as serious as it could have been, and he was released from the hospital the following morning with a bruised and swollen cheek. A team spokesman indicated that the decision on when Wilson would be able to return to the lineup was up to Wilson and Howser. It took the two of them all of one day to decide that Wilson was ready, and he responded by batting .362 over his next 13 games. It appeared that nothing could knock the Royals out of contention.

Kansas City's surge could have vaulted them further up in the standings were it not for the batting heroics of Angels third baseman Doug DeCinces. Prior to 1982, Ted Williams was the only player in American League history to hit three home runs in a single game twice in the same season. In August of 1982, DeCinces did so twice in one week, part of a 14-game span in which he hit an even .500 with 12 homers and 22 RBI. The streak boosted his home run total to 24 and drew a call from the Hall of Fame, which requested his bat as a display piece. DeCinces declined. That bat still had some hits left in it. "It's a great honor," he said, "But they're not going to get it right away."[74]

"I've never seen anything like this," said Angels skipper Gene Mauch. "The way DeCinces is swinging the bat, it doesn't matter who is pitching."[75]

He was still swinging a hot bat when the Angels faced Oakland in a four-game set during which Billy Martin and his pitchers decided to see if they could intimidate him. In the top of the first inning, Oakland starter Mike Norris threw a fastball right at DeCinces's head, sending him ducking for cover. "Oh crap," said A's catcher Mike Heath. "That's not coming from me, Doug." But the disclaimer was not necessary. DeCinces knew exactly where the order had come from. "I knew Billy did those kinds of things," said DeCinces. "I got up and looked in the dugout and Billy's looking at me. The next pitch was a screwball and I hit it as hard as I could. It hit Norris in the left hip and ricocheted almost into our dugout and he went down. I was at first base and I was so intense I yelled, 'I missed! I was aiming for your head.'"

Norris stayed in the game but allowed a single to Reggie Jackson, followed by walks to Fred Lynn and Don Baylor. Bobby Grich reached on an error, and Norris's night was over. He was rewarded for his efforts with a loss and a sore hip, while DeCinces went 2-for-5 in a 9–0 Angels win. He went 0-for-3 the following night and faced Brian Kingman in the third game of the series. Kingman brushed him back in his first at bat and threw a pitch at his head in his second plate appearance. DeCinces had had enough and headed to the mound, bat in hand. The benches emptied, but neither DeCinces nor Kingman was ejected. "I expected that kind of thing from Norris," DeCinces said after the game. "But I never had a problem with Kingman before. I don't condone [fighting], but when I get a pitch behind my head, something has to be done about it."[76]

"I knew DeCinces was angry," said Kingman. "I never expected him to come out to the mound. I turned my back to the plate and when I turned around again, DeCinces was being restrained. Then everything broke loose."[77]

DeCinces responded to Oakland's challenge, but the Angels lost the game and slipped out of first place, half a game behind Kansas City. The Angels regained the lead the following day, but it was obvious that they needed pitching help, and general manager Buzzie Bavasi looked to an unexpected source.

Luis Clemente Tiant y Vega (known as Luis Tiant) made his MLB debut in 1964 and won 64 games for the Cleveland Indians over the next five seasons, including a 21–9 mark in 1968. But his record slipped to 9–20 in 1969, and he was dealt to Minnesota, along with a young third baseman named Graig Nettles, prior to the 1970 season. Tiant's stay in Minnesota was cut short by injury in 1971, and the Twins released him. The only team willing to take a chance on the sore-armed Tiant was the Boston Red Sox. It turned out to be a wise decision. Tiant won 161 games over the next seven seasons and helped the Red Sox come within one game of a World Series title in 1975, where his unusual delivery gained national attention. From the windup, Tiant raised his hands above his head and turned his entire body so his back was facing the catcher before turning back, a jumble of arms and legs, to deliver the ball to the plate.

The delivery was imitated by kids across the country, including Carmen Ronzoni, the character played by Jimmy Baio in the 1977 film, *The Bad News Bears in Breaking Training*. But by August of 1982, Tiant hadn't pitched in the major leagues in nearly a year and was toiling for the Tabasco Plataneros in the Mexican League. That's where he was spotted by Angels scout Cookie Rojas. "When I saw him pitch, his control was good and his velocity was good," said Rojas. "He worked his butt off, according to everybody who saw him pitch there. His arm was back, as good as it's been. He was clocked at 88, 89 miles per hour consistently."[78]

The addition of Tiant to the starting rotation helped, but the Angels were still in desperate need of better pitching, primarily in the bullpen. Don Aase was out with an elbow injury, and Doug Corbett's early success was just a memory. Corbett endured an eight-game stretch in which he walked 12 and gave up 13 runs in 15 1/3 innings and was sent back to the minor leagues. By late August, nearly half of the Angels losses had come in the seventh inning or later, and their bullpen was comprised of five players (Dave Goltz, Bruce Kison, Andy Hassler, Luis Sánchez, and Rick Steirer) with a combined career relief record of 9–6 with just nine saves.[79]

"The Angels continue to play their own version of Russian Roulette," wrote Pete Donovan in the *Los Angeles Times*, "gambling that their big-gun offense can stake them to a sufficient enough lead for the bullpen to hold. They have yet to inflict the fatal wound on themselves, one that would take them out of the race for the American League's West pennant, but they have hurt themselves several times."[80]

The self-inflicted wounds required the Angels to make another pitching move if they wanted to stay in the race, and, with relief help tough to find as August ended, they went in another direction.

Back in the Bronx, Tommy John's situation had gone from bad to worse after his screaming match with Bill Bergesch in Texas, so he decided to test a statement George Steinbrenner made in a team meeting earlier in the season. Steinbrenner had declared that anyone who did not want to be a Yankee would be accommodated. John's opportunity arose when he was approached by Howard Cosell prior to a *Monday Night Baseball* telecast.

"T. J., what's the solution?" asked Cosell.[81]

"The solution is that I don't want to be a Yankee anymore," said John. "I've got to go elsewhere because my stay here has ended."[82]

John followed his proclamation by calling Bergesch repeatedly to ask if he'd been traded yet. A reprieve came not from Bergesch but from Reggie Jackson. Jackson had been extremely supportive in the aftermath of Travis John's accident, often visiting the young boy in the hospital.

Now he was looking for "reimbursement" in the form of innings pitched and wins. He phoned the Johns and asked Tommy's wife, Sally, if Tommy thought he could still pitch. When Sally said yes, Reggie said he'd see what he could do. "Reggie," Sally John implored, "use your influence with Mauch, [Angels owner Gene] Autry, and Buzzie [Bavasi] and see if you can help get Tommy on your team. Because the Yankees will trade him for just about anything."[83]

A few days later, Sally and Reggie got their wish when the Yankees sent Tommy John to the Angels for a player to be named later. The Angels were in Detroit to play the Tigers at 7:30 when the deal was announced. Bob Boone asked when John would arrive and was told sometime around midnight. "Let's stall," he joked.[84]

The Angels were treading water in the American League West, but in the East, the Brewers were rolling, thanks to their strong offense and key contributions from the pitching staff. With his Pac-Man injury behind him, Milwaukee starter Pete Vuckovich was emerging as one of the top pitchers in the league. Vuckovich won six games in July and August; his only loss was a game in which the Brewers were shut out by Minnesota. The run also included a July outing in which he tried to barehand a comebacker and severely cut his hand between his ring and pinky fingers. The wound required four stitches to close, but he bounced back nine days later to throw a complete game against the Royals and pick up another win. By the end of August, he was 29–8 since coming to Milwaukee in the trade with St. Louis prior to the 1981 season. "It's nice, but I can't take full credit," said Vuckovich. "I've done a pretty good job as a pitcher, but I've won a lot of games I could have lost. . . . This is a great team to pitch for. I've gotten some good defense behind me. They've gotten some big hits for me. I can take partial credit, but not all of it."[85]

"To me, he's the ace," said first baseman Cecil Cooper. "You know if you score some runs, you've got a good chance of winning when he's out there. I know my intensity level is up when he's out there. You know he's going to be in there battling."[86]

When Vuckovich, or any other Brewers starter, needed help, he could count on a bullpen anchored by 1981 MVP and Cy Young winner Rollie Fingers, who picked up the 300th save of his career on August 21. Fingers entered the game in the eighth inning with a 3–0 lead and allowed two runs before getting Seattle's Dave Henderson to foul out to end the game and escape with a 3–2 win. Fingers could be excused for being a bit rusty, as the outing against Seattle was his first in nine days. He'd been sidelined recently by a sore elbow and received two cortisone injections to ease the discomfort. The elbow pain didn't concern Fingers, who told reporters he'd dealt with it in previous seasons and expressed confidence that the second injection would clear up the problem. While Fingers was out, rookie Pete Ladd picked up his first career save and quickly gained the trust of manager Harvey Kuenn by posting a 1–0 record with one save and an ERA of 0.96 in his first eight outings. At six foot four and 240 pounds, Ladd was known as "Bigfoot" thanks to his size 15 shoes, but his contributions on the mound were just as big. He struck out two to quash a White Sox rally and earn the win in his Milwaukee debut and had been effective ever since. With Fingers back saving games, Ladd was relegated to spectating and learning as much as he could. "I'm used to pitching every day, but when you have someone like Rollie in front of you, I definitely can wait," he said. "I can learn just by watching him. We've had a lot of close games. I know I can pitch in close games, but I realize they want to use pitchers with experience in there."[87]

The experienced pitchers and big bats allowed the Brewers to go 19–11 in August and build their lead from one game at the beginning of the month to four and a half by the end of the month. Still, the Brewers were far from complacent. "You can't worry about the lead," said Gorman Thomas. "Those things can go awfully fast. A prime example lately would be Atlanta. You just have to take it one day at a time."[88]

Like the Angels, Milwaukee felt they needed additional pitching help. They picked up Doc Medich from the Texas Rangers on August 11 and at the end of the month made an even bigger splash by acquiring veteran righty Don Sutton from Houston. Sutton had gone 13–8 for the Astros and was a welcome addition to the Brewers rotation. Teaming with Vuckovich, Sutton gave Milwaukee a strong 1-2 punch for the stretch-drive. "Milwaukee is an outstanding ballclub and they are in the thick of a pennant race," said Sutton. "If you can't get excited about that you don't have a pulse. It's probably the best thing that could happen to me at this stage of my career. Of all the places that I could have gone to, this is a 9.99 on a scale of 10."[89]

The 1982 season was about to enter its final month, one that would bring lead changes in all four divisions and a thrilling final weekend with some unlikely heroes.

STANDINGS AS OF AUGUST 31

Table 7.1. American League East and West

AL East				AL West			
Team	Wins	Losses	GB	Team	Wins	Losses	GB
Milwaukee	77	53	-	Kansas City	77	55	-
Boston	73	58	4.5	California	75	56	1.5
Baltimore	72	58	5.0	Chicago	68	62	8.0
New York	67	63	10.0	Seattle	62	69	14.5
Detroit	66	64	11.0	Oakland	58	75	19.5
Cleveland	61	67	15.0	Texas	51	79	25.0
Toronto	61	72	17.5	Minnesota	47	84	29.5

Table 7.2. National League East and West

NL East				NL West			
Team	Wins	Losses	GB	Team	Wins	Losses	GB
St. Louis	75	56	-	Atlanta	74	58	-
Philadelphia	73	59	2.5	L.A. Dodgers	74	59	0.5
Montreal	70	62	5.5	San Diego	68	65	6.5
Pittsburgh	70	62	5.5	San Francisco	66	66	8.0
Chicago	58	75	18.0	Houston	63	69	11.0
New York	50	80	24.5	Cincinnati	51	81	23.0

8. SEPTEMBER

A Lot's Happened, and I Really Need You This Year

> The heavy metal trio's main constituency has long been the kids. The kids don't care if the band is considered by many older rock enthusiasts to be second generation derivative. The kids don't care if Neil Peart's lyrics have been dismissed by many as the epitome of hollow minded pretension. And the kids don't care if the band has generally been dubbed overblown and overrated. The kids have just liked Rush— often for just those reasons—and when it comes to rock, the kids are alright.
>
> Bill Provick[1]

Bill Provick's review of *Signals*, the ninth studio release from the Canadian trio, Rush, was typical. Mainstream music critics did not like Rush, an attitude summed up by the *Buffalo News,* who wrote, "To most critics, the music is not authentic, because it is too brainy, too well-played. Not raw enough, not simple enough, to be considered 'cool.'"[2]

Apparently, the fans and the critics did not agree, as *Signals* rocketed to number 1 on the album charts in Canada and took just two months to go platinum in the United States. One single from the album, "New World Man," reached number 1 in the US market, but perhaps the defining cut of the album was "Subdivisions," a song about the feeling of isolation many teens experience while growing up. Neil Peart's lyrics explored the idea that many adolescents must choose between keeping a low profile and blending in or expressing themselves and potentially being ostracized. The idea resonated with many fans of the band, who likely experienced similar choices.

In addition to their musical prowess, the band was known for incorporating visual puns in the artwork that graced their album covers. The back of the LP featured the blueprint of a fictional subdivision with a street called "Line Drive," a tribute to the band's affinity for baseball. The upper left corner featured the school the kids in this fictional subdivision would have attended. Its name was Warren Cromartie Secondary School, named in honor of the Montreal Expos outfielder.

"We had the great pleasure of meeting Warren when we were doing the album," said lead singer Geddy Lee. "He's a rock drummer himself, a big rock fan, primarily a fan of Neil's. He came to visit us and loved being able to see the studio where we work. After the year he's had, if anyone deserves to have a school named after him, it's Warren."[3]

Cromartie and the Expos showed signs of life in early September and clawed their way back into the National League East race. Montreal stood just two and a half games behind division leading St. Louis after play on Sunday, September 12, and just two games behind Philadelphia. The Phillies began a crucial three-game series against the Cardinals the following day at Veterans Stadium as part of a six-game homestand. Those games would be followed by a pair of games against the Cardinals in St. Louis. It was an eight-game stretch that could potentially decide the NL East. "So, what you've got are three dramatic weeks left, teams that are all in pretty good shape and a race that is no longer a very simple one to handicap," wrote Jayson Stark in the *Philadelphia Inquirer*.[4]

The team sitting in first place, St. Louis, came to Philadelphia with their own problems. The Cardinals began the month by losing six of their first ten games without the services of shortstop Ozzie Smith, who suffered a badly bruised thigh earlier in the month. Smith's injury was serious enough for him to stay back in St. Louis while his teammates headed to Philadelphia. In addition to Ozzie, outfielder Lonnie Smith was nursing a sore ankle, leaving the Cardinals extremely shorthanded. "The only thing I can say about those guys is that they are not a better team with their bench people," said Pat Corrales. "I don't care who they put in there. They might fill in and do a good job, but they're not going to do the job both the Smith boys can do."[5]

The Phillies also had an advantage in that they had their ace, Steve Carlton, going in the first game of the series. Carlton was gunning for his twentieth win despite beginning the season 0-4. Since then, he'd gone 19-5 with a 3.01 ERA. Philadelphia got all the offense they needed in the bottom of the first inning of the series opener when Mike Schmidt doubled off Cardinals starter Bob Forsch to score Gary Matthews. Carlton took it from there, allowing just three hits and striking out twelve in a complete game shutout while also hitting a solo home run in the bottom of the fifth inning. The Phillies won the game 2-0 and took over first place in the division.

"Poets have churned out every word in the language trying to define greatness," wrote Stark. "But what Steve Carlton did to the Cardinals defined it better than any words could ever say it. He was simply a great athlete rising to an occasion to which great athletes rise."[6]

"He's the best I've seen," said Corrales, a former major league catcher. "I've seen some great ones, caught some great ones. Here's a man 38 years old, and he's throwing like he's 28. We just came back from Pittsburgh after losing two games to the Pirates and he just goes out there and puts us right back in first place. And that's the difference. You've got that hammer. You've got that stopper."[7]

"We got three hits tonight and we won the ball game and it looked like we won it easily," said Mike Schmidt. "How often do you get three hits and win a game easily?"[8]

The answer is not often, and the Phillies proved that by mustering just eight hits over the final two games of the series. John Stuper shut them out on five hits in Game Two, and Joaquin Andújar shut them out on just three hits in the series finale and the Cardinals regained the lead in the division. In all, the Phillies mustered just eleven hits in the three-game series, three of which came from their pitchers, and scored two runs, hardly a recipe for success. "We've got to turn it around," said outfielder George Vukovich. "We've got to regroup and play better against the Pirates. And we've got to start hitting and scoring runs. We're still only a game and a half back. Tonight was one of those games when nothing goes right. But maybe we got it all out of our system and can come back Friday."[9]

Unfortunately for Vukovich and the Phillies, that was not the case. Pittsburgh came to town and took two of three. Meanwhile, the Cardinals went to New York to play five games in three days and won all five. They followed that up by returning home and taking the first of a two-game series against the Phillies. In the span of seven days, the Cardinals turned a ½-game deficit in the division into a 5½-game lead. Corrales summed up the Phils' chances of winning the division in one word. "Slim," he said. "They [the Cardinals] have to collapse and we have to play like hell."[10]

St. Louis became the first team to clinch their division in 1982 when they beat the Expos a week later. It was the first time they'd qualified for postseason play since losing to the Tigers in the 1968 World Series and was the culmination of a remarkable turnaround engineered by Herzog. In June of 1980, Herzog took over a team that was 18-33, completely overhauled it, and turned it into a winner. From the time he took over until the day they clinched the 1982 NL East title, the Cardinals went 206-163. The additions of Ozzie Smith, Lonnie Smith, Darrell Porter, and Willie McGee turned an underachieving team into a division champion. Herzog's mastery in building a team tailored to their home ballpark was exceeded only by his ability to keep everyone involved and maximize the contributions of the entire roster.

"He knows how to use players and how to use all of them," said catcher Gene Tenace, a three-time World Series champ with the Oakland A's. "He's the best manager I've ever seen," added Keith Hernandez. "Why we won is attitude. It started last year. Whitey knew what he had to do. He's a winner. He knows how to get the most out of his athletes. The things he's done the last few years a blind man could see."[11]

There was one other man whose contribution could not be overlooked and that was bullpen ace Bruce Sutter. Since joining the Cardinals prior to the 1981 season, Sutter had racked up an MLB-high 61 saves and given his teammates, and the opposition, the expectation that the game was over once he took the mound. The 1982 Cardinals put together winning streaks of twelve and eight games, but they never lost more than three straight prior to clinching the division title. "The reason for that," said pitcher Jim Kaat, "is the big guy in the bullpen. When you have a great defense, which we have, and a strong man in the bullpen, you know you're going to win consistently."

Some 250 miles west of St. Louis, Herzog's former team, the Kansas City Royals, were hoping to qualify for the postseason for the fifth time in the past six years. The Royals opened September with a 1½-game lead in the American League West, and that's when the roller-coaster ride began. Four straight losses were followed by six wins in seven games, which were then followed by four straight losses to the lowly Minnesota Twins.

"They seem tight," said Minnesota pitcher Jack O'Conner, who held the Royals hitless through six innings in the series finale. "I think the pressure is getting to them. They're probably cussing and throwing things. I'm sure not going over to their clubhouse." For his part, Minnesota's manager Billy Gardner added, "I don't understand. . . . It seemed like they didn't want to play us. They weren't alert, weren't ready. I didn't think they'd get frustrated."[12]

"Nobody's moping around," countered Royals Manager Dick Howser. "No feeling sorry for ourselves. I see guys diving for balls, sliding into first base, playing hard in every way." Regardless of how hard they played, the Royals needed better pitching. The Twins scored 25 runs in the three-game sweep and grabbed early leads in all three games, forcing Kansas City to play catchup. "We never had a chance all three games," said second baseman Frank White. "It's hard to win when you have to have five or six runs every night."[13]

In contrast, the California Angels were getting outstanding pitching, especially from their starters. Over a ten-game stretch in mid-September, Angels pitchers allowed just 32 runs while the team went 7-3 and tied the Royals for the division lead. That set up a three-game showdown in Anaheim, and whoever won the series would have a lead in the division with ten games remaining. "All we wanted all season was to have this series mean something to us," said Angels shortstop Tim Foli. "To have the chance to determine our own fate."[14]

"It's like Michigan playing Ohio State," said Angels pitcher and Michigan alum Geoff Zahn. "This series is (critical). This is what it's all about. This is what you play for."[15]

As it turned out, both Foli and Zahn played a key role for the Angels in the first game of the series. Foli was a surprise starter after spending the previous two days on the bench with a pinched nerve in his neck and muscle strains in both legs. The thirty-one-year-old wore a neck brace before the game but shed it in time to take the field and rob the Royals of a run with a sparkling play on defense. "I've got all winter to recover," he said. "You don't come this way that often."[16]

The game was tied 1-1 in the bottom of the fifth inning when Foli stepped to the plate to face Royals starter Larry Gura with two out and no one on. The New York Mets made Foli the overall number 1 pick in the 1968 draft out of Notre Dame High School in Sherman Oaks, California, just forty miles from Anaheim Stadium. In his thirteenth season in the big leagues, Foli had a World Series ring from the 1979 Pirates and a mean streak, if not a lot of power. Still, he jumped on a Gura offering and hit it down the left field line for a solo home run and a 2-1 Angels lead. The home run was not without controversy, however. Kansas City left fielder Willie Wilson believed a fan knocked the ball out of his glove and protested vehemently when umpire Jim Evans ran down the line to signal the home run. "All we could see [from the Royals bullpen] was a menagerie of hands and faces," said Royals closer Dan Quisenberry. "We were just shocked to see Foli hit one that far."[17]

A Ron Jackson home run gave the Angels a two-run cushion heading into the ninth inning, but the Royals led off the top of the inning with back-to-back singles off Zahn, who had cruised through the first eight, allowing just one run on six hits. The Royals had their chance, and they knew it. "The whole idea is to get to their bullpen," said Kansas City outfielder Amos Otis before the series began, "because they have no bullpen."[18]

De facto closer Luis Sánchez entered the game and induced three straight groundouts, and the Angels won the series opener 3-2 to take the lead in the division. The win was a sweet one for Zahn, who admitted after the game that he wasn't a big fan of the Royals. "It's probably because they've always been good," he said, "but it may also be because they've always had an attitude of extreme cockiness. I don't like to see it on my club and I don't like to see it on others. I simply get more excited when I beat the Royals and more disappointed when I lose."[19]

Prior to the second game, Quisenberry told reporters the Royals were in a must-win situation. The two teams had another three-game series approaching in Kansas City, but the Royals couldn't afford to let this one slip away. "It would be tremendously depressing if we lost tonight," he said. "No matter how well we play at home I'd hate to be in a situation where we go into that series two or more games behind. I'd hate to be in a situation where we'd have to sweep."[20]

A few hours later, Quisenberry surrendered a ninth-inning RBI single to California's Daryl Sconiers, and the Angels suddenly had a two-game lead in the division. Sconiers had been hitless in ten previous plate appearances but seemed unfazed by pinch-hitting in the bottom of the ninth with two men on in the middle of a pennant race. "I didn't feel a bit nervous," he said. "Reggie [Jackson] and [Rod] Carew told me to stay low, so I squatted more than usual and looked to make contact with Quisenberry's sinker. I'd never faced him before, but I was confident I would make contact as Daryl Sconiers always does."[21]

"That was a rotten way to lose," said a reporter to Quisenberry in the visiting clubhouse.

"Does it bother you a lot?" Quisenberry asked.

"No," she said. "Does it bother you a lot?"

"You're the one complaining about it," replied Quisenberry. "When a team is going good, those ground balls are hits. We've lived that way a lot of times. I don't like to say luck, because I don't believe in it, so I'll say I think it's a case of providence . . . Rhode Island." Turning serious, he added, "I did my best to accomplish what I tried to do, which is get groundballs," he said. "They hit four. One was an out, the other three weren't. Those hits were nothing I should be ashamed of. Sconiers didn't get his hit on a pitch that made me say, 'Oops,' when I threw it."[22]

The Royals were in trouble, and their problems got worse when the Angels completed the sweep the following day to take a three-game lead in the division. "That series was huge as far as us establishing ourselves and the Royals knowing that we were better than them," said Doug DeCinces. "You can't let the Royals stick around. They were a great team. Any team George Brett is leading is a great team."

The Royals lingered, but California wrapped up the division title on the final weekend. The big question was who they would face in the American League Championship Series, and that, as well as who would face the Cardinals in the NLCS, came down to a dramatic final day.

It took the Atlanta Braves less than two weeks in late July and early August to squander a nine-game cushion in the National League West, but Joe Torre's club turned things around at the end of August to win seven of eight and build a 2½-game lead on September 3. Then disaster struck . . . again. The Braves won just four of their next thirteen games, including a spell in which they dropped five of seven to Houston and Cincinnati, the two worst teams in the National League. Atlanta was playing lackluster baseball, and everyone knew it, though no one seemed to know how to fix it.

"I feel like, the last four games, even the last five, we've been flat." said starting pitcher Rick Camp after a 5-2 loss to the Reds on September 17. "I know we shouldn't be going through something like this right now, but we are. I can't begin to explain it."[23]

"The flatness was there again tonight, and it's crazy in September of a pennant race," said Torre. "As Yogi Berra said, 'It's not over till it's over,' and we're far from finished. Our biggest problem right now is that we aren't hitting."[24]

An observer in the other dugout thought it might be more than that. "They may be exhausted," said Reds catcher Johnny Bench. "The Braves have had a lot of pressure on them all year. They've let Houston beat them, and they let us beat them. They're America's Team and that's a lot of pressure for them day in and day out. Now they just can't let anything get too far away."[25]

The loss to Cincinnati dropped the Braves to 3½ games behind Los Angeles in the division, and then the teams abruptly swapped roles, with Atlanta winning six of their next ten and the Dodgers dropping eight of nine. The pressure that Johnny Bench speculated the Braves were feeling had now shifted squarely onto the shoulders of the Dodgers. When asked how he felt after the 4-3 loss that knocked his team out of first place, L.A. manager Tommy Lasorda wasn't in the mood for introspection. "What are you, a damn psychiatrist?" he snapped. "That's a stupid question."[26]

The good news for Lasorda was that the Braves were coming to town for a two-game series. A sweep would give L.A. the lead heading into the final few days of the season. Getting swept could spell disaster. "It's great for the West Division, great for the National League and great for the fans," said Lasorda, "But it's not too easy on the managers."[27]

Further complicating matters was that the National League West was still a three-team race, but it was the San Francisco Giants, not the San Diego Padres, who were now in the hunt despite a tumultuous season. The 1981 Giants posted the fourth-best team ERA in all of baseball, then traded all five of their starting pitchers before Opening Day in 1982 in what general manager Tom Haller called a youth movement. The youth movement encompassed only the starting rotation, apparently, since the Giants' Opening Day infield had an average age of thirty-four. Their new projected starting rotation had amassed a total of 19 major-league wins the previous season.[28] After a rough start the Giants suddenly got hot. From August 1 through September 28 they went 35-19 and climbed back in the race. While the Dodgers and Braves split their two-game set in L.A., the Giants swept Houston, meaning just one game separated the top three teams in the National League West heading into the final weekend of the season.

Things were similarly tight in the American League East. Harvey's Wallbangers rolled into September after having spent all of August either in the lead or tied for it. They brought a 4½-game cushion into a September 2 doubleheader against Cleveland when disaster struck. Milwaukee held a 2-1 lead in the ninth inning of Game One when closer Rollie Fingers went down with an elbow injury—and this time it was neither Pac-Man nor a mud fight that was to blame.

"It was a burning sensation," said Fingers. "I didn't feel anything snap. It was just over the course of three or four pitches. It kept getting worse and worse. It wasn't any one particular pitch. It was just a little sting at the beginning, then I got to about the 4th or 5th pitch and said, 'that's it.' I knew it was something bad."[29]

Starter Doc Medich was in the trainer's room in the Brewers clubhouse when Fingers came in. Medich earned his nickname by studying medicine at the University of Pittsburgh and had already decided that 1982 would be his final season in baseball before retiring to pursue medicine. On two separate occasions, Medich went into the stands to aid fans who were suffering heart attacks,[30] which made him more qualified than most baseball players to diagnose what he saw when Fingers entered the room.

"I could see this wad of muscle had separated from the bone," recalled Medich, "I knew right away he had ruptured the flexor muscle and torn the tendon off. I knew exactly what would happen next, what it would take to fix it. I knew he wouldn't be back."[31] Hoping for a miracle, Fingers rested his arm for about a week before trying to throw in the bullpen and feeling the same stinging sensation. Despite losing Fingers, the Brewers still held a 4½-game lead over Boston in the division. The Baltimore Orioles were in third place, five games back, but they were beginning to turn things around in the home stretch of Earl Weaver's final season as manager. On July 26, the Orioles were just two games out but then lost sixteen of their next twenty-three games to drop 7½ games off the pace in mid-August. That streak was followed by an incredible string of seventeen wins in eighteen games. Suddenly, the Orioles were back, and things got interesting when they faced the Brewers in a three-game series at the end of September. Milwaukee pounded Baltimore starter Mike Flanagan to take the series opener 15-6, but the Orioles evened the series the following day. The pivotal third game took place on September 26, and the key play was made by a rookie who had just joined the team at the beginning of the month.

The Orioles selected John Shelby in the first round of the 1977 January draft out of Columbia State Community College in Columbia, Tennessee. Nicknamed "T-Bone" due to his svelte six-foot-one, 175-pound frame, Shelby hit .279 for Baltimore's Triple-A Rochester Red Wings in 1982 despite battling bone spurs in his right (throwing) elbow that would require off-season surgery. When he reported to the Orioles on September 1, Weaver asked him if he could make a good throw if he had to. Shelby answered that he could likely make one and only one. He got his fourth start of the season in the series finale with the Brewers on Sunday, September 26. Baltimore was three games out and, with just eight games remaining, needed a win badly. The Orioles took a 3-1 lead into the eighth inning when starter Dennis Martinez faltered. Robin Yount's single to left field scored Charlie Moore to make it a 3-2 game with a runner on third. Weaver lifted Dennis Martinez, a righty, and brought in the left-handed Tippy Martinez to face Milwaukee's Cecil Cooper with the game, and potentially Baltimore's season, on the line. Cooper hit a fly ball to center field, and Shelby took a few steps back, paused, then charged forward. He caught the ball on the run and unleashed a throw, the only one he had left, to Orioles catcher Rick Dempsey. At third base, Milwaukee's Bob Skube tagged up and headed home. "I wanted to keep the throw low enough to hit the cutoff man," said Shelby, "so, if we didn't get him at the plate, the go ahead run [on first base] wouldn't get down to second."[32]

"When the throw was on the way, I was saying to myself, 'Hit. Hit. Hit.,' so I'd be ready for the contact, give a blow instead of take it," said Dempsey.[33] Shelby's throw bounced once and arrived at the plate just before Skube, who had to decide whether to take the Orioles catcher out or try to slide under the tag. "He gave me the plate," said Skube. "I slid through his legs and he tagged me in the chest. It was close. My legs were close to the plate, if not on it, when he made the tag."[34]

Home plate umpire Jim McKeon signaled out, and, in case there was any doubt, he had help. "It's the first time I ever saw 25 players call out one runner," said Orioles pitching coach Ray Miller.[35] Baltimore tacked on two more runs in the top of the ninth and won the game 5-2 to cut Milwaukee's division lead to two with seven games remaining.

The two teams were set to face off one more time, on the final weekend of the season, in Baltimore, in a four-game series. The division title in the American League East, as well as the National League West, would come down to the final weekend of the regular season. Over the course of three days, six teams would play ten games in three cities to determine two winners.

* * * * *

Don Sutton arrived at Baltimore's Memorial Stadium on Friday, October 1, feeling a bit run down. At thirty-seven years of age, and with more than 4,100 regular season innings under his belt, he was used to the feeling at the end of the season. His team had just taken two of three games from the Boston Red Sox and held a three-game lead over Baltimore in the

American League East with four games remaining. His main goal was to nip whatever was ailing him, rest up, and be ready for the American League Championship Series.

Sutton found Brewers trainer John Adam and asked him to contact the Orioles team doctor for a shot of penicillin. The doctor balked initially but relented when Sutton reassured him that he often took a shot at this time of the year as a preventative measure. His Brewers would be facing the Orioles in a doubleheader later in the afternoon, and a split would ensure the division title. With their ace, Pete Vuckovich, starting the first game of the twin bill, followed by 17-game winner Mike Caldwell in the nightcap, Sutton was looking forward to a relaxing evening on the bench.

Baltimore took a 3-1 lead in the second inning of Game One thanks to back-to-back singles from Joe Nolan and Rich Dauer. The Birds added single runs in each of the next two innings and won 8-3, then beat the Brewers again in the second game 7-1. After trailing Milwaukee by four games just a week earlier, Baltimore had won five of seven to cut Milwaukee's lead to a single game with two left to play.

"If we win Saturday, then I wouldn't sleep too well if I were them," said outfielder Jim Dwyer, who went 3-for-3 in the first game.[36] There was no panic in the visitors' clubhouse as manager Harvey Kuenn remained stoic. "I'll tell my club the same thing I've said . . . play, relax, and have a good time," he said. "Why not? We're still one game up. It will not carry over into tomorrow. I'm sure we'll bounce back. If they [the Orioles] don't win, it's all over for them."[37]

On the West Coast, the Atlanta Braves held the lead in the National League West, but it was a slim one-game margin over the Dodgers and Giants, who were tied for second. Atlanta opened a three-game series against the Padres in San Diego, while the Dodgers and Giants faced off in San Francisco. The NL West was very much in play.

Like Don Sutton, Phil Niekro had logged more than 4,100 innings in his major league career. But Sutton had ten postseason starts while Niekro had but one, and it had not gone well. Niekro started Game One of the 1969 National League Championship Series and allowed nine runs in eight innings of work in a loss to the eventual World Champion New York Mets. He desperately wanted to get back to the postseason, and a strong performance against the Padres on October 1, 1982, would go a long way toward accomplishing that goal.

Niekro cruised through the first five innings, but, unfortunately for Atlanta, so did Padres starter Eric Show. The game was tied 0-0 in the top of the sixth when Atlanta pushed a run across to take a 1-0 lead. Two innings later, Niekro sent a Show fastball 350 feet into the night for a two-run home run, his first since 1976, to give the Braves a 3-0 lead.

"Nothing Phil does really surprises me," said Dale Murphy, who led the National League in home runs. "But a home run in that situation maybe surprised me a little bit. Maybe I should borrow his bat tomorrow; that's farther than I hit them."[38]

Niekro then returned to the mound and retired the Padres in order in the eighth and ninth innings to secure the 4-0 win. Niekro hadn't allowed an earned run since September 18, and the Braves were on the cusp of going to the playoffs for the first time since 1969.

"He knows how much this championship means to the city of Atlanta," said catcher Bruce Benedict. "And after the last two games he's pitched, I think everybody realizes how much a championship and a World Series in Atlanta would mean to Phil Niekro. He's really taken charge of this thing."[39]

"It means a lot to everybody else in this clubhouse, too," said Niekro. "We've all been working toward this for 160 games, not to mention six weeks of spring training. We've been through everything a team could possibly go through. Everybody kept talking about the Dodgers, about how they had all the experience. We heard people say we were choking in August. Then we got hot again. Then, according to some people, we started choking again. But still, with two games left, we're one game ahead."[40]

Up the California coast, the Dodgers were also involved in a pitchers' duel. L.A.'s Jerry Reuss and San Francisco's Fred Breining were locked in a 0-0 game through seven innings when Steve Sax led off the top of the eighth with a walk. Dusty Baker singled, and Steve Garvey also walked to load the bases. With the left-handed swinging Rick Monday due up, Giants manager Frank Robinson emerged from the dugout to talk to his starter.

"I told him, 'you dug a hole for yourself, now get yourself out of it,'" said Robinson.[41] Lefty Al Holland was loose in the bullpen, but Robinson decided to stick with the right-handed Breining, knowing Dodgers manager Tommy Lasorda likely would have brought in a pinch-hitter to face Holland.

"I appreciate him leaving me in," said Breining. "I wanted to keep going. I just threw a forkball that got away. I didn't keep it down."[42]

Monday hit that hanging forkball into the right field stands for a grand slam and an eventual 4-0 win.

"Where was the pitch?" a reporter asked Monday after the game.[43]

"Out of the park," he replied.[44]

"He's been doing that a lot for us for a few years, coming up and getting the big home run," said Lasorda. "We needed it tonight, desperately. And he hit it a ton."[45]

The win kept the Dodgers within one game of Atlanta and put the Giants in a precarious position, summed up by John Hillyer in the *San Francisco Examiner*, who wrote, "The third-place Giants need a miracle—two victories plus two Atlanta losses, in which case they would visit the Braves for a one-game playoff [on] Monday."[46]

* * * * *

Don Sutton awoke in his Baltimore hotel room on Saturday, October 2, in a sweat. He was running a fever, and when he lifted his shirt, he saw a severe rash on his abdomen. Perhaps the penicillin shot was not such a good idea after all. He made his way to the ballpark and quickly found the Brewers trainer. When Sutton lifted his shirt, Adam's heart sank.

"He was covered with welts—red, angry looking welts," recalled Adam. "I'm thinking, 'we're all in trouble now.'"[47]

Adam called the Orioles doctor, who gave Sutton a cortisone injection to counteract the reaction to the penicillin. Still, there was no need to panic. Despite being swept in the doubleheader the previous day, Milwaukee just needed to win on Saturday. That would give Sutton plenty of time to rest before starting Game One of the ALCS. Milwaukee starter Doc Medich surrendered hits to four of the first five men he faced and then committed a balk, and Baltimore took a 3-0 lead. The Brewers tied the game in the fourth, but the Orioles scored four in the bottom of the frame and tacked on another four in the eighth inning for an 11-3 win. The Brewers had lost four straight, and the reason was obvious. In the four losses, Milwaukee pitchers allowed 35 runs and 62 hits. The division was tied with a winner-take-all game set for the following afternoon, and the pitching matchup was a fans' dream. Jim Palmer would take the hill for the Orioles, while Sutton, rash and all, would pitch for the Brewers. The two had been in opposing dugouts in a big situation before when the Orioles faced the Dodgers in the 1966 World Series. Both had been rookies back then, and Sutton did not pitch in the series, which the Orioles swept four games to none. Now, sixteen years later, the two had amassed 520 combined wins and would go head-to-head for the first time.

"I won't be trying any harder to win this game than if we were playing the Orioles for fifth place," said Sutton. "That's just the way I am. I want to win the first game of the season as much as the last. But if you don't get excited and have your pulse quicken in a situation like this, then you're in the wrong business."[48]

"I think the whole thing is a dream," said Kuenn, "coming down to one game, a shootout with Palmer against Sutton."[49]

Kuenn was still unaware that his starting pitcher was under the weather. Sutton and Adam had kept the information to themselves, but that didn't mean it wasn't top of mind, at least for Adam, who spent a restless night at the team hotel. Sutton went out to dinner with Brewers general manager Harry Dalton and some teammates but never said a word about his condition. Later that evening, Gorman Thomas peered out the window of his hotel room and saw Brewers owner Bud Selig walking back and forth and smoking Tiparillo cigars. "He was out there pacing, in front of the shops, in front of the restaurant. Just watching him do that, I said to myself, 'Bud you better get some sleep. We've got a big game tomorrow.'"[50]

The Braves had a big game as well, thanks to their 4-2 win over the Padres. Atlanta was just a game away from wrapping up the National League West, and they were anxious to get it over with and focus on the playoffs.

"I just can't wait to come to the park Sunday and lock this thing up," said shortstop Jerry Royster. "I think we'll break out and get a bunch of runs and finish this thing right. It's down to one game, and all the other things that have happened this year mean nothing now. It's down to this, and here we are."[51]

"All season, I've told the team, 'Don't get excited until you see the finish line,'" said Joe Torre. "Now we see the finish line. It's right here, right in front of us, one win away. I'm just glad tomorrow's game is in the afternoon, so I don't have to wait all day for it. I know I'll be trying to snore about 6:00 AM, and my eyes will be wide open."[52]

The Dodgers would wake up on Sunday morning with a chance to force a playoff game on Monday, thanks to their 15-2 win over the Giants on Saturday. L.A. scored six runs in the top of the second inning and built a 10-0 lead before Frank Robinson pulled his starters, despite technically having a chance to win the game. When asked after the game why he did it, his answer was concise. "Technically, you go out and play, then," he said. "What game were you watching? Did Lasorda numb your guys' brains that much?"[53]

For the second day in a row, an in-game decision from Robinson came under heavy scrutiny. While many felt the game, and the season, was lost, some did not, and they weren't shy about expressing their feelings.

"I was hoping to play the whole game," said second baseman Joe Morgan, "even down 10-0. I didn't like to see it end that way. I'd rather have seen the last out."[54]

Third baseman Darrell Evans agreed, saying, "I wasn't very happy about it. I'm not the manager, of course, and it would have been the biggest comeback of the year. But you're not out of it until the game is over. I was disappointed."[55]

Robinson explained he pulled his starters so they could get plenty of rest before Sunday's game. The Dodgers/Giants rivalry still mattered, and the fact that the Giants were eliminated did nothing to ease tensions. "If we can't do it, we're not going to let them do it," he said.[56] The San Francisco Giants hadn't won a division title since 1971, and it wouldn't happen in 1982, either. That left them just one thing to play for on the final day of the season: the role of spoiler.

Don Sutton awoke on the morning of Sunday, October 3, feeling better. The cortisone injection had done its job. He made his way downstairs at the team hotel and was eating breakfast when Howard Cosell, who would be calling the game along with Keith Jackson for ABC, slipped into his booth and asked how it felt to be going against Jim Palmer in the big game. "Why don't you ask Jim how it feels to go against me in the big game?" Sutton asked.[57] Cosell boomed with laughter and began to ask another question, but Sutton shooed him away. He arrived at the ballpark a bit later and found Adam with an anticipatory look in his eyes. When Sutton game him a thumbs-up, Adam breathed a sigh of relief. He felt even better when Sutton whispered, "I'm going to pitch my ass off and win this game."[58]

Sutton was in the trainers' room getting taped when Robin Yount poked his head in the door. The normally reserved Yount offered some advice *and* some encouragement, saying, "Don't make us have to score five runs and we'll kick Palmer's ass."[59] A grin crossed Sutton's face, but

Yount's proclamation also showed how much the game meant to him and the rest of the team. The Brewers did not want to get swept and watch the playoffs on TV.

In the home clubhouse, Palmer was preparing for his most important start since the 1979 World Series. The righty began the season with a 2-3 record, then reeled off 15 wins in his next 19 decisions. Big games were nothing new to Jim Palmer. Over his career, he'd pitched in six All-Star Games and five World Series, but this game had an additional element.

"I really wanted it," he said in his book, *Together We Were Eleven Foot Nine*. "For the come from behind of it all and for the team and for . . . OK I had a lump in my throat for the maniac I'd been playing under for all those years. We all did. We wanted to win it for Earl, for all he's done for us, with us, at us, by us, and to us."[60]

In fifteen seasons on the Baltimore bench, Earl Weaver had won four American League pennants and a World Series title. If the Orioles lost on Sunday, his managerial career would be over. If they won, he'd have a shot to go out as a World Champion. The weight of the moment was not lost on the Orioles players, and they were tight. The locker room was silent. None of the usual joking around, none of the usual insults that can be heard in baseball clubhouses from the major leagues to high school. Just . . . silence. Then Weaver entered the room and gathered his team.

"I want to tell all of you guys how proud I am of you,'" said Weaver. "This is going to be my last game as an Oriole manager. And you've all made my job easy."[61]

Weaver then grew quiet, weighing the gravity of the moment. He took a deep breath and said, "I don't care what happens today, I'm telling you guys you had a great year."[62]

Second baseman Rich Dauer let out an exaggerated sigh of relief. "Whew!" he said. "I thought for a minute you were going to tell us you changed your mind, and you weren't going to retire."[63]

The entire room burst into laughter. The tension was broken. The Brewers were ready, and now so were the Orioles.

More than 51,000 fans, many carrying brooms in hope of a sweep, jammed Baltimore's Memorial Stadium on Sunday afternoon for the season finale while millions more watched on ABC. The NFL Players' Association had gone on strike on September 20, so the Orioles and Brewers took center stage. It also meant that the stadium turf was in perfect shape, unmarred by divots and unscarred by the lines normally on the field for the Baltimore Colts.

"The trophy will rest in the Orioles Nest," read a homemade sign hanging from the facade of the third-base stands as Palmer and the Orioles took the field for the showdown between the teams with the two best records in baseball in 1982. Paul Molitor led off the game with a flyout to right field, bringing to the plate Robin Yount, who was looking to make good on his pregame promise to Sutton after going hitless in his previous nine at bats in the series.

Despite his mini-slump, Yount was enjoying the finest season of his nine-year career. Through 161 games, the Brewers shortstop was batting .328 with 27 home runs and 112 RBI, all of which were career highs. He was greeted with chants of "MVP" from the Milwaukee fans during the final week of the season each time he came to bat. But he still had work to do. The Orioles had been able to shut Yount down with a steady diet of pitches on the outer half, and Palmer and catcher Rick Dempsey saw no reason to deviate from that plan. Yount was behind in the count 1-2 when Palmer tried to finish him off with a curveball low and away, but the pitch missed its mark. He tried the same pitch again with the same results to run the count full. His next pitch was a belt-high fastball on the outer half, and Yount pounced on it, sending it about five rows deep into the right-field bleachers to give Milwaukee a 1-0 lead.

The Orioles bounced back in the bottom of the first. With one out, rookie Glenn Gulliver dropped a perfect bunt down the third-base line. Molitor charged and scooped the ball, but his throw sailed past first baseman Cecil Cooper and down the right field line, allowing Gulliver to advance to second. Sutton retired the next batter before walking Eddie Murray to bring up left fielder John Lowenstein.

Lowenstein's father, Balzer, was stationed at Pearl Harbor on December 7, 1941, and moved his family to Wolf Point, Montana, where his son, John, was born. The family relocated to Southern California, where John established himself as a baseball star. He graduated from the University of California, Riverside, with a bachelor's degree in an-thropology and was drafted in the eighteenth round by the Cleveland Indians. Once he reached the major leagues in 1970, Lowenstein estab-lished himself as one of the game's great characters, giving rise to the L.A.C., or Lowenstein Apathy Club.

"Cheering is bad for a player because it gives him a false sense of im-portance," Lowenstein told the *Sporting News* in 1975. "Booing indicates a fan really cares enough about him to get mad, which is negative, too. But a fan who really doesn't care one way or another about him, won't boo or cheer. That is an ideal kind of club member."[64]

The Indians began receiving hundreds of letters from people pledging disinterest in Lowenstein's career and promised to hold a day for him while the team was on the road. Four years later, Lowenstein made his way to Baltimore, where he became a vital cog in Earl Weaver's platoon system. Splitting time with the right-handed hitting Gary Roenicke in 1982, Lowenstein hit .324 against right-handed pitching and had his best season. He was perfectly suited to face Sutton, and, with two outs, he hit a sinking line drive to right field. Brewers right fielder Charlie Moore fielded the ball on a hop and came up firing to catcher Ted Simmons.

"Gulliver, coming around third," said Jackson, on the television broadcast. "Here's the throw . . . and he stopped for a moment and he's a dead duck."[65]

Baltimore third base coach Cal Ripken Sr. was halfway down the line imploring Gulliver to hold, but the rookie either missed the sign or ignored it. Once he realized his mistake, it was too late. Simmons ran him down and applied a hard tag to end the inning. Moore spent four seasons as the Brewers' primary catcher but moved to right field when the team acquired Simmons from the Cardinals prior to the 1981 season. The twenty-nine-year-old may not have covered as much ground as other right fielders, but he had a catcher's arm, and this throw was right on target. Milwaukee tacked on another run in the top of the second inning when Gorman Thomas walked and moved to third on an errant pickoff throw from Palmer before scoring on a ground out to take a 2-0 lead.

At about the same time, nearly 3,000 miles to the west, Dodgers third baseman Ron Cey stepped to the plate against Giants starter Bill Laskey at San Francisco's Candlestick Park. Cey entered the game batting .252 with 23 home runs and 77 RBI. He'd been L.A.'s regular third baseman for the past ten seasons, but Pedro Guerrero, who spent a majority of his time in the outfield in 1982, was L.A.'s third baseman of the future. He was seven years Cey's junior and slugged 32 homers with 100 RBI in 1982. Sunday, October 3, would be Cey's final game in Dodger Blue. Over the previous nine games, he had hit a paltry .103, but he'd had success against the Giants this season as five of his 23 home runs had come against San Francisco. Laskey's 1-1 pitch was a letter-high fastball, and Cey sent it over the fence in left field for a 2-0 Dodgers lead in the top of the second inning. Five hundred miles south of Candlestick

Park, San Diego starter Tim Lollar got Braves second baseman Glenn Hubbard to pop out to end the top of the second in their game to keep things scoreless.

Back in Baltimore, Paul Molitor led off the top of the third with a deep fly out to center field to bring Yount back to the plate. Prior to the series, Palmer sat down with rookie Storm Davis, who won the night before, and explained how to pitch to Yount. Davis had executed the plan to perfection. "The thing about Storm was you could practically program him," said Palmer. "Tell him what to throw and he'd just throw it. I talked him through the whole Brewers lineup, including Robin Yount, who was almost unstoppable, and Storm just went out and did it like a pitching machine."[66]

Palmer looked to his own advice to handle Yount the second time around. Behind in the count, 2-1, Palmer threw Yount a thigh-high fastball, and Yount turned on it, sending it over the wall in left-center field for a 3-0 Brewers lead. "Everything that worked on Yount the game before didn't work on Sunday. I threw him a low and away fastball and he put it high and away into the right field stands. He did it the next time up, too. Some days you just know that guys who are hitting can even hit the pitches they aren't supposed to be able to hit and Yount did, over the left field wall."[67]

In San Francisco, Dodgers starter Fernando Valenzuela was in trouble. Darrell Evans led off the bottom of the second with a single; then Jeffrey Leonard doubled, sending Evans to third and forcing Tommy Lasorda to begin warming up Joe Beckwith in the bullpen. A walk to Bob Brenly loaded the bases with no one out to bring up shortstop Johnnie LeMaster. LeMaster was in his seventh season in the big leagues and was not known for his offensive prowess. Fans in San Francisco expressed so much displeasure that he once wore "Boo" rather than "LeMaster" on the back of his jersey during a game in 1979. But Valenzuela walked the light-hitting shortstop on five pitches to force in a run. Laskey then bounced into a double play to push another across. The Dodgers and Giants were tied at two.

Back in Baltimore, home plate umpire Don Denkinger made his way to the pitching mound prior to the bottom of the third inning to speak to Sutton. In the world of doctoring baseballs, Sutton was no Gaylord Perry, but many felt he and Perry were kindred spirits. Like Perry, Sutton had only been caught doctoring a baseball once. That incident came in 1978. But, again like Perry, Sutton used the possibility of doctoring a ball as a mental edge over his opponents. In a *Washington Post* arti-cle, Thomas Boswell said Sutton "has been accused of cutting, scuffing, sandpapering, and generally disfiguring balls in so many ways that he says, 'I ought to get a Black & Decker commercial out of it. The only fun I get now is hiding dirty notes in my uniform pockets for the umpires to find when they search me.'"[68]

Sutton didn't have any dirty notes in his pockets, but he did have a conversation with Denkinger, which he recounted after the game, telling reporters, "Denkinger told me that somehow a scuffed ball had gotten in the game. He told me he'd appreciate it if he didn't happen to find another one. I told him, 'I'd be pleased, too. It's hard throwing strikes with a scuffed ball.'"[69]

Sutton retired Al Bumbry leading off the inning, which brought Glenn Gulliver to the plate. Gulliver was the shortstop on an Eastern Michigan team that advanced to the championship game of the College World Series in 1976. They were defeated by an Arizona State team that featured thirteen players who would later appear in the major leagues, Atlanta's Bob Horner and L.A.'s Ken Landreaux among them. Gulliver knew what it was like to bat in pressure situations, but this was some-thing different. Not only was his team trailing in a winner-take-all game, but his mistake earlier in the contest had potentially cost the Orioles a run.

With the count even at 2-2, Sutton left a fastball up in the zone, and Gulliver hit it down the right field line for a home run to make it 3-1 Milwaukee. It was his first RBI in more than a month and also his first, and only, career home run. Veteran Ken Singleton came to the plate next and sent a long drive to deep center field, but Gorman Thomas made a leaping catch at the wall, likely saving another home run. Sutton escaped further harm in the inning, but the Orioles had another run, and perhaps some confidence.

The Braves and Padres were scoreless through four innings when Atlanta's Tommy Harper homered off San Diego starter Tim Lollar to give the Braves a 1-0 lead. But just as quickly as Harper put Atlanta on top, he gave the lead right back. Tony Gwynn led off the bottom of the fifth inning and lifted a fly ball down the left field line. Harper had a chance to catch the ball but dropped it in foul territory, and Gwynn later singled. Two more singles and a walk to Lollar tied the game at one and brought Alan Wiggins, back from his drug issues, to the plate with the bases loaded. Wiggins hit a sinking line drive to left field that got under Harper's glove and scooted to the wall for a bases-clearing triple. Atlanta's 1-0 lead became a 5-1 deficit a few batters later after Wiggins scored on a sacrifice fly.

The Braves loaded the bases in the top of the seventh, but relief pitcher Dave Dravecky got Rufino Linares to ground into a fielder's choice for the first out. Joe Torre summoned Bob Horner, who hadn't played since hyperextending his elbow on September 18, as a pinch-hitter. Horner lifted a fly ball to center, but it wasn't deep enough to score the runner from third. Dravecky then struck out Claudell Washington; the Braves had blown a bases-loaded, no-out opportunity. And time was running out.

At the same time the Braves were squandering their opportunity, the Dodgers were mounting a threat in San Francisco. Three straight seventh-inning singles loaded the bases with one out to bring L.A. shortstop Bill Russell to the plate. Frank Robinson brought in his All-Star reliever Greg Minton to face Russell, who had ten hits in his last eighteen at-bats. With the count at 2-1, Dodgers broadcaster Vin Scully warned the viewers to be on the lookout for the squeeze. "If there's an ideal count for a squeeze play, this is the count," he said. The camera pulled wide to show Russell at the plate and Rick Monday at third base. "Keep your eye on Monday. . . ."[70]

Also aware of the situation, Robinson pulled all of his infielders in. Minton went into his motion, and Monday broke for the plate. Russell squared to bunt, but the pitch was on the outer half, and he had to go into defensive mode. If he didn't make contact, Monday was out, and the rally would be squelched. He stabbed at the ball and fouled it off.

With the count now two and two, Russell fouled off another pitch, then swung through a nasty sinker on the outside corner to strike out. The bases were still loaded, but now there were two outs, and Tommy Lasorda made the only move he had left. He pinch-hit Jorge Orta for Valenzuela, who hadn't allowed a base runner since the third inning. As Orta strode to the plate, KTTV cameras cut away to a shot of Dodgers owner Peter O'Malley sitting behind the L.A. dugout with a transistor radio held to his left ear. Scully explained the radio was tuned to the Padres/Braves game. He'd just listened to the Braves blow their shot and was hoping his team wouldn't do the same. The Giants faithful were chanting, "Beat L.A.!" and Scully reset the scene. "2-2 . . . seventh inning . . . an excruciating afternoon," he said.[71] Now Minton induced Orta to hit a high hopper to second baseman Joe Morgan, who under-handed the ball to Reggie Smith at first to end the threat. Still tied. The Dodgers season wasn't over, but they had just missed their best opportunity to extend it.

Tom Niedenfuer replaced Valenzuela in the bottom of the eighth inning and allowed a leadoff single to Bob Brenly. Frank Robinson brought in Champ Summers to pinch hit, and Niedenfuer threw a fastball that caught too much of the plate. Summers turned on it. "A drive to right field," said Scully. "Hooking into the corner it is . . . off the fence. It bounces by Monday . . . Here comes Brenly and they're gonna stop him at third!"[72]

Steve Garvey caught Monday's relay throw and began walking toward the mound as the Candlestick Park crowd went wild. As Brenly stood at third waving his arms back and forth, Lasorda emerged from the visitors' dugout to talk to Niedenfuer. Minton was due up, and Robinson faced the same dilemma his counterpart had the previous half-inning, a rally with the pitcher scheduled to hit. Unlike Lasorda, Robinson let Minton hit, and Niedenfuer struck him out with a curveball that buckled the knees of the Giants reliever for the first out of the inning to bring up lefty Max Venable. The managerial chess game was in full swing now as Lasorda brought Terry Forster in from the bullpen, prompting Robinson to counter with righty Jim Wohlford.

"Oh, what a day," exclaimed Scully. "Ninth inning in San Diego, 5-1, Padres. Bottom of the seventh here, 2-2. Four to one, Milwaukee leading Baltimore."[73]

Forster got Wohlford to swing through a biting slider for strike three, and the Giants were down to their final out of the inning. "He's not out of the woods, yet," said Scully. "Two down in the seventh inning and the dangerous Joe Morgan coming up."[74] In his second season in San Francisco, the thirty-nine-year-old Morgan had enjoyed his best year since 1977. Playing in a ballpark just across the bay from where he went to high school, Morgan was batting .289 at the beginning of the day with 13 home runs. He wasn't the same player who won back-to-back National League MVP awards in 1975 and 1976, but he could still hit, and Lasorda knew it.

The PA system played the theme from *Jaws*, as Morgan dug in and took a fastball up and in for ball one. Forster had a base open, but slugger Jack Clark was looming in the on-deck circle. Forster had to go after Morgan, who took a pitch low and away for a strike, then fouled off the next offering. Morgan stepped out of the box and stretched a bit, then got back in to take his practice swings and do his trademark chicken flap with his left elbow. Dodgers catcher Steve Yeager called for a pitch low and away, but Forster left it out over the plate.

"Drive to right field!" said Scully, "back goes Monday, it's . . . gone."[75]

"I used my A-No. 1 swing, and I knew it was a homer as soon as I hit the ball," Morgan said.[76] The three-run shot gave the Giants a 5-2 lead, and the Candlestick Park crowd of close to 50,000 went berserk, cheering, jumping up and down, stranger hugging stranger. In typical Scully fashion, he let the moment speak for itself on the Dodgers broadcast, letting more than a minute pass before saying another word.

In San Diego, the Braves were trailing 5-1 and down to their final few outs. But before panic could set in, word arrived of what had just happened in San Francisco. "When I was batting, [Padres catcher] Terry Kennedy told me, 'The Giants have runners on second and third,'" said Jerry Royster. "Then, after I flew out and was running back across the field, he told me, 'Morgan hit a three-run homer.' All of a sudden, I didn't worry about flying out."[77] Royster returned to the Braves dugout and told Joe Torre, "Morgan hit a three-run homer. We're going to win the pennant."[78]

At Memorial Stadium, the Baltimore Orioles were putting together their own rally. Sutton issued back-to-back one-out walks to Lowenstein and Jim Dwyer. Clad in a straw cowboy hat, an orange Orioles t-shirt, cut off denim shorts, and tube socks, Orioles superfan "Wild Bill" Hagy stood atop the Baltimore dugout and led the crowd in his signature cheer. A cab driver by day, Hagy had first endeared himself to Orioles fans, and Orioles management, with his cheers in the summer of 1979. He would contort his body to spell the name of the home team and the crowd would yell out each letter. "O-R-I-O-L-E-S, Orioles!" "He'd say he was just going to get a beer or go to the bathroom," said a friend, "but then, all of a sudden, you'd see him up on the dugout leading cheers."[79]

While Hagy was leading cheers on top of the dugout, Baltimore outfielder Dan Ford was leading them inside it, waving a towel and trying to get his teammates excited. Sutton's second straight walk brought Kuenn out of the Milwaukee dugout to talk to his pitcher and also to give relievers Jim Slaton and Bob McClure more time in the bullpen.

"So, fatigue has beset Don Sutton," said Cosell on the ABC broadcast, "who did everything that he was asked to do. By his manager, by his team. He hung in there. . . . And he's gonna leave him!"[80]

"Absolutely," said Keith Jackson, "because Sutton says he's alright."[81]

As Kuenn headed back to the dugout, Sutton focused on getting the next Orioles hitter, Cal Ripken, Jr., who was five years old when Sutton made his major league debut. Sutton's first pitch was a fastball that Ripken hit hard down the left field line then hooked foul. Had it stayed fair it likely would have been a bases-clearing double. Instead, it was just strike one, and pitch number 110 of the game for Sutton. His next offering was another fastball, which Ripken swung under for strike two before going on to bounce into a fielders' choice for the second out of the inning. With catcher Rick Dempsey due up, Weaver called on Terry Crowley to pinch-hit. Crowley was in his fourteenth season in the major leagues, nearly all of which had been spent coming off the bench in situations like this. "When the heat's on, he admits his concentration is better," said Jackson. "And the heat's on."[82]

The count went to 2-2, and the stadium PA blared the "charge" bugle theme for seemingly the thousandth time. Sutton delivered, and so did Crowley, sending a base hit to center field to score John Lowenstein and send Ripken to third. It was 5-2, Milwaukee. Kuenn stuck with Sutton, and Weaver brought in reserve catcher Joe Nolan to pinch-hit for Rich Dauer. Again, the count went to 2-2. Simmons set up on the outer half of the plate, and Sutton hit his spot, but Nolan lifted a slicing line drive down the left field line.

"Oglivie . . . a hard run to the corner," said Jackson.[83] Then nothing more, as Oglivie attempted a desperate sliding catch out of view of the ABC cameras. For an instant Jackson, Cosell, and everyone watching at home had no idea what happened. Then Oglivie appeared and showed his glove to the umpire, who was running down the line.

"He made the catch," said Jackson. "Crashing into the wall, feet first. Sliding across the gravel . . . Ben Oglivie makes the catch to retire the side."[84]

"If he doesn't make that catch, the whole dynamics of the game at that point might change," said Mike Caldwell. "That was a catch that a lot of average fans or non-baseball people might not even recognize. As far as that game went, that was a hell of a moment to make a hell of a catch. That took the wind right out of their sails."[85]

"Three things involved here," added Cosell, when ABC showed a replay of the catch. "Instancy of judgement, superb reflexes, absence of physical fear."[86]

The ABC broadcast then cut to San Francisco for the top of the ninth inning. The Dodgers trailed the Giants 5-3 after a Dusty Baker double scored Ken Landreaux in the eighth inning, but they needed another rally to extend their season. Ron Cey led off the top of the ninth and hit a bullet down the third base line, but Evans snared it on his backhand side and threw Cey out by a step at first.

"Evans taking away a sure double for Cey," said Scully, "and the Dodgers expending one of their three precious outs."[87]

With Minton still in the game, Lasorda went to his bench once again and brought in the left-handed swinging Ron Roenicke. Minton's career high in innings pitched prior to 1982 was 91⅓ in 1980. He was now working his 123rd inning of the season, but he didn't mind, telling the media after the game, "The last thing on my mind was my arm."[88] Minton threw a 1-2 tailing fastball that was clearly outside, but home plate umpire Frank Pulli rang Roenicke up for the second out. Roenicke voiced his displeasure on the way back to the dugout to no avail. The Dodgers were down to their final out.

In San Diego, the Braves gathered around televisions in the visitors' clubhouse at Jack Murphy Stadium. They'd lost their game 5-1, but if Minton could retire Bill Russell it wouldn't matter. They'd be division champs.

Back in San Francisco, Giants fans were on their feet. If they couldn't win, keeping the Dodgers from winning was a close second. "It would have been a lot less painful," said Scully, "had Atlanta just won in San Diego. Now, of course, this crowd is on its feet, enjoying the writhing last moments of a Dodger ballclub one step from the end of the year."[89]

Russel took a fastball for strike one, and Giants catcher Bob Brenly threw the ball back to Minton nearly as hard as it had come in. Minton threw another fastball, and Russell swung.

"Ground ball to Evans," said Scully as Evans threw to Reggie Smith at first base. "Good bye '82."[90]

The Giants celebrated at the mound as if they had won the division rather than having been eliminated a day before. As one final twist of the knife, the PA system at Candlestick Park played the Tony Bennett hit "I Left My Heart in San Francisco" as the Dodgers' dugout emptied. The Atlanta Braves were the champions of the National League West.

"This is worth all the years I've waited," said Phil Niekro as his teammates poured champagne over his head. "This is what I talked about, what I wanted, all these years. It's all been worthwhile. But a western division championship isn't all we want. We want a National League Pennant, and a World Series championship, too. That's what the next two weeks are for."[91]

While the Braves were celebrating, the Brewers were blowing the game open in Baltimore, scoring five runs in the top of the ninth to take a 10-2 lead. Bob McClure replaced Sutton to mop up in the bottom of the ninth and got Gary Roenicke, Ron's older brother, to fly out to Oglivie to end the game. The Brewers celebrated on the pitchers' mound, then Cooper, who made multiple sparkling defensive plays at first base and hit a solo homer, made his way to the first base seats to congratulate Bud Selig. The Brewers owner, Tiparillo in hand, hugged his starting first baseman.

The Orioles had just been eliminated, but the fans had some unfinished business and began chanting, "We want Earl!" Weaver emerged from home dugout, tears in his eyes, to accept the love of the fans of Baltimore while Hagy led cheers from the pitchers' mound.

O-R-I-O-L-E-S . . . Orioles!

"Goodbye, Earl, and you deserve it," said Cosell. "You've been one of the greatest managers in the history of the game."[92]

The playoffs were set. Milwaukee would face the California Angels in the American League Championship Series while Atlanta would battle the St. Louis Cardinals in the NLCS.

FINAL STANDINGS

Table 8.1. American League East and West

AL East				AL West			
Team	Wins	Losses	GB	Team	Wins	Losses	GB
Milwaukee	95	67	-	California	93	69	-
Baltimore	94	68	1.0	Kansas City	90	72	3.0
Boston	89	73	6	Chicago	87	75	6.0
Detroit	83	79	12.0	Seattle	76	86	17.0
New York	79	83	16.0	Oakland	68	94	25.0
Cleveland	78	84	17.0	Texas	64	98	29.0
Toronto	78	84	17.0	Minnesota	60	102	33.0

Table 8.2. National League East and West

NL East				NL West			
Team	Wins	Losses	GB	Team	Wins	Losses	GB
St. Louis	92	70	-	Atlanta	89	73	-
Philadelphia	89	73	3.0	L.A. Dodgers	88	74	1.0
Montreal	86	76	6.0	San Francisco	87	75	2.0
Pittsburgh	84	78	8.0	San Diego	81	81	8.0
Chicago	73	89	19.0	Houston	77	85	12.0
New York	65	97	27.0	Cincinnati	61	101	28.0

9. THE PLAYOFFS

How Much for Something in the First Ten Rows?

"The Superstation has brought [Braves] games to the country all year, and now we're being denied bringing any more during this part of the year," complained WTBS vice president for administration Jim Kitchell. "This is a major loss. I can't recall any other decision of this magnitude that Ted [Turner] has lost."[1]

Atlanta Braves owner Ted Turner's loss meant that WTBS, which he also owned, would not be permitted to televise the National League Championship Series between the Braves and the Cardinals, a decision that would likely cost him millions of dollars in advertising revenue. Under ABC television's broadcast contract, local flagship stations could broadcast to their home markets, but a US District Court in New York ruled that WTBS's national reach on cable systems would cause "irreparable harm"[2] to ABC and issued an injunction preventing WTBS from showing the playoff series on their network. Rather than finding Braves baseball on Channel 17, viewers would have to settle for *The Flintstones*, *Leave it to Beaver*, and *The Brady Bunch*.

There were no such issues in the American League Championship Series, as the California Angels hosted the Milwaukee Brewers on October 5 on ABC. Keith Jackson provided the play-by-play while Earl Weaver and Jim Palmer added color commentary. The Lettermen, a 1960s pop trio, sang the national anthem at Anaheim Stadium in front of an AL playoff record crowd of 64,406 fans eager to see the league's top two offensive teams go head-to-head.

Tommy John got the start for the Angels and set the visiting Brewers down in order. In the bottom of the first, Milwaukee starter Mike Caldwell didn't fare as well. Brian Downing led off the inning for the Angels with a check-swing blooper over second base to bring up Doug

DeCinces. Up in the ABC booth, Palmer relayed a conversation he'd had about Caldwell prior to the game with Milwaukee's bullpen coach Larry Haney.

"[Caldwell's] biggest problem is that he tries to throw hard," Palmer recalled Haney telling him. "If he throws more than 84 miles-per-hour, he's throwing too hard."[3]

Two pitches later, Caldwell threw a slow breaking ball to Doug DeCinces, who hit a slow tapper back to the mound. Caldwell fielded it cleanly but then made a bad throw to second baseman Jim Gantner, allowing DeCinces to reach safely. Instead of a double-play, Caldwell now had runners on first and second with no one out. Don Baylor drove Downing home later in the inning with a sacrifice fly to give the Angels a 1–0 lead.

With the big crowd still buzzing, Ted Simmons led off the top of the second inning against John. Anaheim Stadium had been the Angels' home for seventeen seasons, but they'd shared the facility with the L.A. Rams of the NFL since 1980. More than 20,000 seats were added that year, which meant more revenue for the Rams, but the additional seating also blocked what once had been the beautiful views of local mountains. Long a proponent of home runs, Weaver said he liked the new configuration because the ball traveled better than in the past. Simmons singled to center to bring Gorman Thomas to the plate. On the broadcast, ABC played a brief interview with Thomas, who assessed Tommy John as a pitcher.

"All he throws is a sinker. He'll throw an occasional slider, he'll throw an occasional spitball, if you want to call it that," Thomas said with a grin. "He keeps the ball away all the time. I'd say 98% of his pitches go where he wants them to go."[4]

John's second pitch must have been one of the 2 percent because it missed its intended location, and Thomas hit it high and deep down the left field line for a two-run homer. The Brewers added another run in the top of the third inning to make it 3–1. After the inning, John sat on the bench with his head in his hands. He'd been acquired for exactly this moment, and now he felt that he'd let his new team down. It was then that Don Baylor made his way over to him. "Hey, T. J., get your head up," Baylor said. "If you hold them at three runs, I'm personally good for four runs against Caldwell. So, if you hold them there, you win 4–3. I guarantee it."[5]

Downing reached base again to lead off the bottom of the third, this time with a walk. While most major league players were stars in high school, Brian Downing was anything but. He didn't even make his high school team until he was a senior, then walked on to the baseball team at Cypress Junior College, where his main job was to keep the scorebook. In one season at Cypress, he amassed a total of three at bats with his lone hit coming off future major leaguer Al Hrabosky. But his aggressiveness and attitude caught the eye of a Chicago White Sox "bird dog scout" named Bill Lentini. Rather than tell the White Sox Downing only had three at-bats, he told them Downing hit .333 and Chicago could sign him on the cheap, which they did. Downing made his debut with the White Sox in 1973, then went to the Angels after the 1977 season as part of a six-player deal and blossomed, making the All-Star team in 1979. "If you put Brian Downing's heart in a lion," said Reggie Jackson, "the lion would be tougher for it."[6]

With Downing on first base, DeCinces stepped in against Caldwell and singled to center field. Bobby Grich then singled past Robin Yount into left field to score Downing and make it a 3–2 game. All Caldwell had to do now was face four former American League MVPs in a row, beginning with Don Baylor, who won the award in 1979.

"Boy, is he a big guy," said Keith Jackson.

"If you wanted a perfect physique for baseball, you'd take a body like Don Baylor's," added Palmer.

"Or football," quipped Weaver.[7]

Caldwell's next pitch was up in the strike zone, and Baylor hit it off the wall in right-center field, just above the 386-foot marker, for a triple that brought home DeCinces and Grich. Baylor scored on Reggie Jackson's ground out, and the Angels had a 4–3 lead. Baylor capped his day by driving home two more runs the following inning, for a total of five in the game, and California took Game One 8–3.

"In batting practice, I wondered if I'd get a ball out of the infield," Baylor said after the game. "Obviously I got my swing down once the game started."[8]

"In this series, you have to keep each team away from the big inning," said Kuenn. "Once they got the lead and added two runs, we couldn't play the kind of ball we wanted to play. We hit the ball hard, but we didn't score enough runs early off Tommy John."[9]

After a shaky start, John surrendered just three hits over the final six innings to pick up the win. It wasn't a good start for the Brewers, but there was one bright spot. In the bottom of the seventh inning, Harvey Kuenn sent rookie Pete Ladd to the mound to, as one Brewer put it, "protect our 3–8 lead."[10] At this point in his career, Ladd had all of 30 major league innings under his belt, and in his first postseason game he had to face Reggie Jackson, Fred Lynn, and Rod Carew. Undaunted, Ladd struck out all three of them. "I've been hearing all those theories for a long time about our pitching staff being a weak spot," said Brewers pitching coach Cal McLish. "But since we put together a strong bullpen, I don't believe any of that. We'll be back tomorrow night."[11]

The following afternoon, the Cardinals hosted the Braves in Game One of the National League Championship Series on ABC with two of the hottest pitchers in the league going head-to-head. Phil Niekro ended the regular season with back-to-back shutouts and Joaquin Andújar got the start for St. Louis after winning his last seven decisions of the season.

Claudell Washington led off the game for Atlanta with a double off Andújar and later scored on a Chris Chambliss single to give the Braves a 1–0 lead. From there, Andújar allowed just one hit through the next four innings. Unfortunately for the Cardinals, Andujar was bested by Niekro, who took a shutout into the bottom of the fifth inning when rain began to fall. Home plate umpire Billy Williams called the teams off the field with one out in the inning, and then the rain got heavy. Nearly two and a half hours later, the game was called, just two outs shy of it being official. It was as if the four-plus innings never happened.

"I think any pitcher would have been disappointed, figuring that maybe another two or three pitches he could get two outs," said Niekro. "To be honest, I pitched in more rain than was falling when Billy called time. But if they thought it was raining too hard, it's their decision. The game is done, and there's nothing you can do about it."[12]

"I haven't heard one (bad) thing about their decision by our players," said Braves catcher Bruce Benedict. "We're behind it 100%. We'd like to beat the Cardinals on an even scale, and I'm sure they would like to beat us on an even scale. If we'd played five innings today, led 1–0 and gotten a win, that would have been—not unfair—but unfortunate. It's probably best that we start over tomorrow and play a nine-inning game and see who wins."[13]

The weather was much nicer the following afternoon in Anaheim as the Brewers and Angels got set for Game Two of their series. The pitching matchup featured two right-handers who, despite their physical differences, were much alike. Bruce Kison got the start for California, but, by all rights, he shouldn't have been in the big leagues. Kison stood six foot four and was generously listed at 180 pounds. After signing a five-year deal with the Angels prior to 1980, he won only four games before being diagnosed in June of 1980 with damage to the ulnar nerve in his right elbow and metacarpal tendon in his wrist that required career-threatening surgery. He emerged from surgery with paralysis in his pitching hand and offered to return some of his salary to the Angels. General manager Buzzie Bavasi declined, and Kison vowed to return, saying, "I wanted to prove to people that I'm not the kind of person that lets others down."[14] He went 1–1 with a 3.48 ERA in 1981 and followed that up with a 10–5 mark in 1982. Like Kison, Brewers starter Pete Vuckovich stood six foot four but was listed at 220 pounds, which may have been giving him the benefit of the doubt. Vuckovich was not only lucky to be in the big leagues, he was lucky to be alive. Vuckovich was born with the umbilical cord wrapped around his neck, had a tumor removed from his head at age three, had an appendicitis attack in high school that nearly killed him, drove a car off an eighty-foot embankment and walked away, and was nearly electrocuted by a 15,000-volt reactor while working for an electrical contractor, all before he turned twenty-one. "When your time comes, it comes," he told the *Chicago Tribune's* Bob Verdi in spring training. "If it's not your time, you're not going anywhere. Now do you know why I say that someone can rip a line drive off my head and I don't get too excited?"[15]

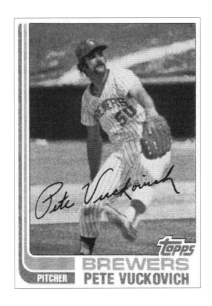

Figure 12: Pete Vuckovich won eighteen games and a Cy Young for the Brewers in 1982, but pitching through a shoulder injury likely caused a premature end to his career. 1982 Topps® trading cards used courtesy of The Topps Company, Inc.

Kison allowed a first-inning single to Robin Yount but escaped unharmed, and, as Vuckovich was taking his warmup pitches before the bottom of the first inning, Palmer mentioned that the big Brewers righty had taken two cortisone injections in September to help alleviate some shoulder pain. What Palmer, and nearly everyone else, didn't know was that Vuckovich's shoulder pain was due to a torn rotator cuff. That hadn't stopped him from taking the ball every fourth day in September, including an 11-inning outing against the Red Sox on September 20. Vuckovich retired the Angels in order in the bottom of the first but got in trouble the following inning. Fred Lynn singled to center field to bring up DeCinces, who had one hit in 25 career at bats against Vuckovich. But when Vuke threw him a belt-high fastball, DeCinces drove it to left-center field for a double to send Lynn to third. Vuckovich then hit Bobby Grich in the thigh to load the bases. Tim Foli singled to left to give the Angels a 1–0 lead, and Bob Boone's squeeze bunt plated DeCinces to make it 2–0.

One inning later, Reggie Jackson sent a Vuckovich offering to deep center field for a home run and his record-setting eighteenth ALCS RBI. "I feel blessed," Jackson said after the game. "If I never get another hit, I'll be . . . well, I'll be pissed off, but I'll also be appreciative of what I've already accomplished."[16]

California led 4–0 when Paul Molitor stepped in against Kison in the top of the fifth inning and a runner on first. Molitor sent a sinking line drive to center field that Lynn dove for, but the ball got past him and went to the wall. It was an easy inside-the-park home run for Molitor and cut the Angels' lead in half. But Kison gave Milwaukee nothing for the remainder of the game, retiring all twelve men he faced en route to a complete-game win, 4–2. Milwaukee found themselves down two games to none in the best of five series. It was a deficit from which no team had ever recovered.

"I'm no mathematical genius," said Mauch, "but I know winning one of three is a hell of a lot easier than three of five. It's no walk in the park to beat this team three in a row, but the players want to do it, and I'm with them."[17]

"When you look at the super pitching we've been getting and the way we've been playing for the last month, I think it's a pretty tall order for any team to win three in a row from us," said Lynn. "The way we've been playing, we're just not going to give anything away. They are going to have to take it."[18]

With a two-games-to-none advantage, Angels team owner Gene Autry requisitioned a DC-10 to take the team and their families to Milwaukee, thinking that from there they would head straight to either

Atlanta or St. Louis. Many of the players packed for a week, and Baylor's wife didn't even make the trip to Milwaukee for Game Three. She told her husband she'd meet him in the National League city prior to Game One of the World Series.

Back in St. Louis, skies were clear, and temperatures were in the high sixties for Game One Part II. Cardinals starter Bob Forsch watched his older brother Ken's Angels take a 2–0 lead in the ALCS, and the prospect of facing him in the World Series was likely in the back of his mind as he shut down the Braves lineup through the first two innings. Unfortunately for Forsch, Atlanta starter Pascual Pérez matched his efforts.

The Redbirds' Willie McGee led off the bottom of the third inning after finishing his rookie season with a .296 batting average, 56 RBI, and 24 stolen bases. He'd been a key weapon for Herzog all season, but a casual fan may have thought he was playing hurt. McGee's gait was awkward as he strode to the plate, as if he was limping on both legs. But once he got going he was as fast as any player in baseball. McGee smoked a ball past Atlanta first baseman Chris Chambliss and down the right field line, prompting cries of, "watch him run, watch McGee run!" from Tommy Lasorda in the ABC booth.[19] By the time the ball caromed in the corner and kicked past Washington toward center field, McGee was halfway to third base.

"He's gonna get a home run!" yelled Lasorda.[20] Washington picked up the ball and prepared to fire home in a fruitless attempt to throw McGee out at the plate. But just as Washington retrieved the ball, McGee stopped at third base. The rookie hadn't seen coach Chuck Hiller waving him home, and by the time he realized his mistake it was too late.

"He could have had five bases if he wanted!" yelled play-by-play man Al Michaels as cameras showed a distraught McGee, hands on his knees staring at the ground at third base.[21] Ozzie Smith came to the plate with one thing on his mind: bring McGee home.

Torre knew Smith often hit the ball on the ground, so he pulled his infield in, hoping to cut McGee down at the plate on an infield chopper. But Smith surprised Torre by lifting a fly ball to center field, allowing McGee to tag and score. The Cardinals had their first run of the series, and an ABC graphic showed just how important a fact that was. In the 80 games in which St. Louis scored first, they went 63–17.

Forsch cruised until the top of the sixth inning, when it looked like the Braves might tie the game. Washington led off with a single to bring Rafael Ramírez to the plate. Forsch's first pitch was a ball, and on the broadcast, Lasorda said now was the perfect time for a hit-and-run play. Behind in the count, Forsch would likely throw a fastball, and Ramírez was known to struggle with breaking pitches. As Forsch went into his delivery, Washington took off but had gotten a bad jump. The pitch was outside, and Ramírez swung through it for strike two. Cardinals catcher Darrell Porter came up firing, but his throw bounced before it reached second base. Washington went into his slide but popped up short of the bag. Though Porter's throw skipped, it was accurate, and Washington was out. Back in charge, Forsch induced a weak grounder for the second out of the inning to bring up Dale Murphy.

Murphy entered 1982 wanting to prove himself, and he'd done just that, turning in his finest season in the big leagues. Two years after leading the league in strikeouts, Murphy instead led in games played (162) and RBI (109), while batting .281 with 36 home runs. He'd be named MVP in a few weeks. Now, trailing 1–0 in the sixth inning, it was time to deliver. Murphy swung at Forsch's first pitch and hit a weak pop fly to short center field that Ozzie Smith flagged down for the final out of the inning. Through six innings, Forsch had allowed just three hits and no runs.

Lonnie Smith led off the bottom of the inning with a check-swing infield single, and now it was the Cardinals turn to play hit and run. With Keith Hernandez at the plate, Smith took off, and Hernandez executed perfectly, sending the ball through the hole at shortstop and advancing Smith to third. George Hendrick poked a short line drive to center field to score Smith and give St. Louis a 2–0 lead. From there, the Cardinals blew the game open. In a half-inning that took thirty minutes to play, the Cardinals scored five times and took Game One 7–0.

"I've seen this team play too many games to read anything into the way we played tonight," said Torre. "We are capable of very good things on the field, and we're capable of being sloppy. Will probably come out tomorrow and kick someone."[22]

"If we'd been able to get some runs early tonight it probably would have been altogether different," said Murphy. "A loss . . . but it's just one game, as long as we come back tomorrow and play hard."[23]

Murphy and the Braves didn't get the chance the next day as rain wiped out the game for the second time in three days, but it also allowed Torre to juggle his rotation and bring Phil Niekro back for Game Two.

"When the pitcher-shy Braves won the National League Pennant in 1948, the theme was (Warren) Spahn, (Johnny) Sain, and rain," wrote Jesse Outlar in the *Atlanta Constitution*. "Before the monsoon N.L. Championship Series ends, the slogan may be Niekro, rain, and Niekro."[24]

After posting a win/loss record of 71–76 from 1977 through 1980, Niekro, at age forty-three, won 17 games against just four losses, while leading the team in starts and innings pitched. His record included a remarkable 14–1 mark on the road, his lone loss coming against the Phillies in May when his team was shut out 1–0. "We have been rained out twice here in three days," said Niekro, "and it has been raining in Atlanta the past two days, so before the series is over, maybe I'll get to start three or four games."[25]

By contrast, it was a beautiful day in Milwaukee as the Brewers hosted the Angels for Game Three of ALCS. Gene Mauch gave the ball to Geoff Zahn, who won a career-high eighteen games in 1982, while Don Sutton got the starting nod for Milwaukee. Don Denkinger was the second base umpire for Game Three, but he had been behind the plate in Baltimore and questioned Sutton about the scuffed baseball that had appeared in the final game of the regular season. Denkinger "clarified" the situation on the ABC broadcast.

"Mr. Sutton, coming from the National League, maybe was not aware of how we deal with that in the American League, that it's illegal to throw a scuffed baseball," Denkinger told Keith Jackson. "I informed him that it was illegal to throw a scuffed baseball in the American League and, from now on, if I find a scuffed baseball that he's thrown that he would have to be ejected."

"[Don] said, 'That's fine with me. I didn't realize it was my responsibility. But now that you've told me we'll go from there.'"[26]

The 2:05 P.M. local start meant that shadows would play a big role in the game, and neither team got much offense in the early going. As the game progressed to the third inning, the pitcher's mound was in bright sunlight while the batter's box was in the shade. Making matters worse, the ball would move from sun to shade as it danced through the shadows of the light stanchions on the first-base side of the field. Sutton shut out the Angels through the first four, and his teammates finally got to Zahn in the bottom of the frame.

Robin Yount led off with a walk and scored on Cecil Cooper's double down the right field line. Ted Simmons singled up the middle to put runners on the corners for Gorman Thomas, who lifted a sacrifice fly to center field to give Milwaukee a 2–0 lead. Simmons later scored on

Don Money's sac fly to give the Brewers a 3–0 lead after four innings and chase Zahn, who was replaced by Mike Witt.

It stayed that way until the seventh inning when Don Baylor led off for the Angels with a walk to bring DeCinces to the plate. In DeCinces's previous at bat, home plate umpire Rich Garcia had gone out to the pitcher's mound to check the baseball Sutton was using for any irregularities but found none. DeCinces was 3-for-9 in the series when he stepped in, his right foot in the back corner of the box and his left one about twelve inches closer to the plate. Television viewers could read nearly all of the name on the back of his jersey. His closed stance invited the pitcher to throw the ball on the inner half of the plate, but Sutton went up and away for ball one. His next pitch was thigh-high on the outer half of the plate, a perfect pitch for DeCinces to drive to right field. But the ball dropped at the last moment, and DeCinces topped it, the ball going straight down, hitting the front of the plate, then bouncing up to hit him in the nose. The pain DeCinces experienced was intense, if familiar. It was the fifth time DeCinces had broken his nose as a major leaguer, and he slumped near the on-deck circle, head in hands, as assistant trainer Ned Bergert came out to tend to him. As Bergert assessed the situation, DeCinces sat up and slammed his batting helmet to the ground in frustration.

"He threw that ball and the bottom dropped out of it," DeCinces said. "I felt like I was on my game and I was playing strong and I knew I was a real cog on the team. I couldn't let myself come out of the game. [I struck out] because my eyes were watering. I was just struggling to see the ball. I was angry, too because I knew Sutton was cheating. I remember looking at him and him looking at me and thinking, 'You cheating sack of crap, now I've got a broken nose.'"[27]

DeCinces's mood didn't improve when Sutton escaped the inning unharmed and Don Money walked to lead off the home half of the inning. Kuenn summoned Marshall Edwards to pinch-run for Money, and Charlie Moore sacrificed Edwards to second. Jim Gantner flew out to center field to move Edwards to third base and bring up Molitor.

With the count at 2–2, Mike Witt threw Molitor a hanging breaking ball that he sent into the left field bleachers for a two-run homer and a 5–0 Milwaukee lead. California finally got to Sutton in the top of the eighth, but Pete Ladd shut the Angels down in the ninth, and the Brewers won the game 5–3 to stay alive. It was the second time in less than a week that Sutton had saved the Brewers' season.

"Sutton has now won five games for us, two under the toughest possible conditions," said Simmons. "We've twice faced elimination, and he's kept us alive. That tells you a lot about the kind of competitor he is."

"We were shut down for seven innings by one of the cleverest pitchers of the last 15 years," said Mauch, who didn't accuse Sutton of any wrongdoing. "He's capable of taking the straight out of the ball without defacing it."

There was rain in the forecast for the following afternoon when the Brewers and Angels would play Game Four, and Mauch surprised many when he named Tommy John, on just three days' rest, as his starter. Thirteen-game winner Ken Forsch hadn't started a game since September 29, but he'd also struggled against the Brewers in his lone outing against them, so Mauch decided to go with John.

"Gene didn't tell me why, he just said he was going with T. J.," said Forsch. "He doesn't owe me an explanation. It's his decision and it's a hard one. I'm not mad or angry, just disappointed."[28]

"Gene asked me before the game how I felt and if I could go tomorrow," John told the media after Game Three. "I told him I was fine and could pitch."[29]

The players said the right things in public, but some had their doubts. "Forsch was there," said DeCinces later. "We felt comfortable with Kenny going but I guess (Mauch) didn't, so he starts Tommy John and we're going, what? Why are we doing that? If we have to go to a 5th game, let Tommy pitch then."

"I must have been in front of my locker for two hours answering questions about the move," John wrote in his autobiography, *T. J.: My 26 Years in Baseball*. "Even at night at the hotel, writers kept calling. Gene was a good guy and a good manager, and I thought he took a lot of unfair heat because of that decision. The move itself wasn't that bad, but his timing was horrible."[30]

The rain predicted for Saturday afternoon arrived on schedule, but it wasn't heavy enough to postpone the game, just push back its start, both teams waiting out a delay of nearly two hours. In addition to the rain delay, many Angels players had something else on their minds. Two wildfires were raging through southern California, and the neighborhood where Lynn, DeCinces, Zahn, Downing, and other players lived lay directly in its path. Before it was contained, the blaze consumed nearly a hundred homes. Lynn's house suffered minor damage, but fortunately no other players' homes were affected.

When the rain in Milwaukee finally subsided, John took the mound against the Brewers' Moose Haas, who posted an 11–8 record in 1982, including an early season win over the Angels. Haas had been Milwaukee's second-round selection in the 1974 draft and made his major league debut in 1976 at the age of twenty. Two years later, he was 2–0 and coming off a 14-strikeout performance against the Yankees when he injured his elbow and threw just 12 2/3 innings the rest of the season. But Haas bounced back, posting double-digit wins in 1979, 1980, and the strike-shortened 1981 season. But 1981 ended on a sour note when he was roughed up by the Yankees in Game Five of the American League Division Series, a contest that ended Milwaukee's season. Now he was looking to atone for that performance in another elimination game.

Haas shut the Angels down in the first two innings; then, once again, the rain began to fall, this time accompanied by winds gusting to nearly twenty miles per hour. Ted Simmons led off the bottom of the second inning with a walk. John struck out Gorman Thomas, but Simmons moved to second on a wild pitch to Don Money, prompting Angels catcher Bob Boone to head to the mound for a discussion with his visibly frustrated pitcher. John had walked just one hitter in his Game One start, but now he'd already walked two of the first four batters he'd faced *and* thrown a wild pitch. His frustration grew when Money took ball four to put runners on first and second with reserve outfielder Mark Brouhard, a former Angels draft pick, on deck.

Brouhard was taking the place of left fielder Ben Oglivie, who injured his ribs when he slammed into the outfield wall late in Game Three. During the regular season, Oglivie's 32 home runs were second on the team only to Gorman Thomas's 34 while Brouhard had only four and hadn't started a game in more than a month. It wasn't an ideal spot for the Brewers. John got behind in the count 2–1, and, on the broadcast, Keith Jackson noted that he'd thrown 33 pitches, with 17 of them outside the strike zone, prompting Earl Weaver to remark, "That's not Tommy John."[31]

John's next pitch was a knee-high breaking ball on the outer half of the plate that the right-handed hitting Brouhard turned into a slow rolling single into center field to score Simmons. Fred Lynn came up firing to third, but his throw hit Money and caromed down the left field line. DeCinces retrieved the ball and threw home to get Money, but his throw was high and sailed into the stands, allowing both Money and Brouhard to score and giving the Brewers a 3–0 lead. They added three more in the bottom of the fourth to chase John. "(Tommy) had absolutely nothing," recalled DeCinces. "It wasn't his fault. He took the ball. He thought he could do it. Gene was playing a hunch. His hunch backfired."

Milwaukee took a 7–1 lead into the top of the eighth when Baylor hit Haas's 136th pitch of the day into the left field bleachers for a grand slam to cut the lead to two, but the Brewers tacked on two more in the bottom of the inning to win the game 9–5 and force a decisive Game Five.

"In the aftermath of his Phillies' 1964 September collapse, Gene Mauch compiled a list of the mistakes he'd made that year and vowed never to repeat them," wrote Ross Newhan in the *Los Angeles Times*. "So much for good intentions."[32]

"I could never find the groove," said John. "I was missing, missing, missing, I could have had three days' rest or a months' rest and it wouldn't have made a difference. It's just unfortunate that I couldn't do the job."[33]

When pressed on whether he second-guessed his decision, a defiant Mauch stood his ground, telling the media, "I do what I have to do. I do now and I did then. There's not enough room for me to second guess myself. It's all taken up."[34]

Temperatures were in the 70s with clear skies that evening in St. Louis as the Cardinals hosted the Braves in Game Two of the NLCS. John Stuper got the start for Whitey Herzog, with Phil Niekro taking the mound once again for Atlanta. St. Louis took a 1–0 lead in the bottom of the first inning on a Niekro wild pitch, but Atlanta scored two in the top of the third when Rafael Ramírez's line drive skipped under the glove of Willie McGee in center field and went to the wall. Ramírez came all the way around to score on the three-base error. McGee had a chance to get back in the good graces of his teammates when he faced Atlanta reliever Gene Garber in the bottom of the eighth with runners on first and third. It had not been a good day for the St. Louis rookie. In addition to making a costly error, McGee was also 0-for-3 with three strikeouts. Now he was faced with the challenge of facing the sidewinding delivery of Gene Garber, who had allowed just three runs in his last 30 innings.

Garber got ahead of McGee in the count 1–2, then threw a pitch at McGee's knees about four inches off the plate. McGee was initially fooled but managed to get his bat on the ball and tap a slow roller to second. Atlanta second baseman Glenn Hubbard forced George Hendrick out at second on the play, but Darrell Porter came home to tie the game at three.

Bruce Sutter shut down Atlanta in the top of the ninth inning, and David Green led off the bottom of the ninth with a single to left field. Then Tommy Herr sacrificed Green to second to bring Ken Oberkfell to the plate, and the managerial battle heated up. Torre had a base open and Bruce Sutter on deck, so walking Oberkfell could set up an inning-ending double play and force Herzog to either let Sutter hit or remove him from the game for a pinch hitter. In addition, Oberkfell had six hits in nine career at bats against Garber.

Torre went to the mound to talk to his pitcher, and the consensus was to pitch to Oberkfell, knowing that Herzog would likely bring in Dane Iorg to hit for Sutter. Keith Hernandez was due up after Iorg, so Torre and Garber picked their poison in the form of the Cardinals third baseman.

In the ABC broadcast booth, Tommy Lasorda was surprised Torre chose to face Oberkfell but said he'd not likely get a good pitch to hit, suggesting Atlanta may try to get him to chase a bad ball and get himself out. Garber's first pitch was on the inner half of the plate, and Oberkfell ripped it foul down the right field line. Oberkfell turned to Atlanta catcher Bruce Benedict and asked if they were still going to pitch to him. Benedict said they were. The next pitch started in but broke over the middle of the plate. Oberkfell swung and lifted it over center fielder Brett Butler's head to easily score Green and give the Cardinals a 4–3 win and two games to none series advantage. Like Mauch, Torre had gambled and lost, and his team was now facing an elimination game. And like Mauch, Torre stuck to his guns. "I had no thought of walking Oberkfell," he said after the game, "because then we'd have to pitch to Iorg and Keith Hernandez. If you know Iorg would have hit into a double play, fine. But you don't know that. (Garber) knows how to pitch with a base open better than anyone else on the team . . . he just gave him too good a pitch."[35]

The series would move to Atlanta the following day for Game Three and Herzog had good reason to not be overconfident. "We've still got to win one ball game," he said. "We're two up, but you saw what happened to Milwaukee. Nothing is sure in this game . . . and the Braves have proven time and time again this season that they can come back."[36]

Back on the West Coast the next afternoon, the mood was tense in the Angels clubhouse. Their homes might have been safe, but their season was in danger of going up in flames, and Don Baylor sensed impending doom.

"We'd given a great team in a great baseball town momentum," he wrote in his autobiography. "Sure, there was another way to look at it. Reggie (Jackson) and Roddie (Carew) weren't hitting. Our pitching was a mess, and we could still win it all. That was the attitude I wanted us to have before Game Five. Instead, I felt tension. In Gene, in 25 players, in (team owner Gene) Autry."[37]

The pitching matchup was a repeat of Game Two, with the lanky Bruce Kison going for the Angels against the bulky Pete Vuckovich for Milwaukee, each on three days' rest. Downing doubled off Vuckovich to lead off the game and bring Carew to the plate. The former batting champion was struggling in the ALCS, with three hits in fourteen at bats, but he was still one of the best hitters in the game, along with one of the best bunters. Paul Molitor creeped in at third base in anticipation of a possible bunt, but Carew lifted a fly ball to left for the first out of the inning. That brought in another struggling member of the Angels in Reggie Jackson. Mr. October homered in Game Two but had just one hit since. Vuckovich induced Jackson to line out to third base for the second out, but when Molitor tried to double Downing off second base, his throw hit the runner, allowing Downing to advance to third. Fred Lynn sliced a single to left, his ninth hit in fifteen at bats, to score Downing, and the Angels grabbed a 1–0 lead.

The Brewers evened things in the bottom of the first when Molitor scored on an error. But Lynn came through again in his next at bat with another single to left to score Bob Boone. Vuckovich was already up to fifty pitches in the game when DeCinces stepped into batter's box in the top of the fourth inning and doubled down the left field line. Bobby Grich was called on to lay down a sacrifice bunt and sent it down the first base line. Cecil Cooper fielded it cleanly, looked DeCinces back to second, then tagged Grich. But Grich wasn't out. When Cooper looked the runner back, he transferred the ball to his throwing hand in case he needed to make a play on DeCinces, then tagged Grich with an empty glove. It was a huge mistake, and the Angels tacked on another run to make it 3–1 when Bob Boone's sacrifice bunt scored DeCinces two batters later.

Ben Oglivie, back after missing Game Four, homered to make it 3–2 in the bottom of the fourth inning, but the Angels threatened again in the fifth. Jackson drew a one-out walk and tried to advance to third when Lynn smacked his third hit of the day to Charlie Moore in right field. Moore charged the ball and fired a laser beam to Molitor at third, who tagged out the stunned Jackson. "I just charged in and the ball came up perfect for me," recalled Moore. "I grabbed it and let go of it as quick as I could. I guess it was one of the best throws I made in my career. The next hitter (Don Baylor) got a base hit, also. If I hadn't made that play, it would have been a big inning."[38]

Moore's throw may have thwarted an Angels rally, but the Brewers still trailed 3–2 heading into the bottom of the seventh. Don Money popped out to begin the inning, but Milwaukee loaded the bases with two out against Luis Sánchez, who had relieved Kison in the sixth inning. Mauch strode to the mound to talk to his pitcher with lefty Andy Hassler and righty Steve Renko up in the California bullpen and Cooper at bat.

"If you want to see the real Cecil Cooper perform, you'd better lower the lights and clear the hall," wrote Mike Littwin in the *Los Angeles Times* the following day. "He reacts to the spotlight like a guy making a prison break. Maybe that's because whenever Cooper gets the chance to really show what he can do, he doesn't."[39]

Littwin's criticism was harsh, but it wasn't far removed from the truth. During the regular season Cooper was one of the finest hitters in the game, but October was a different story. After going 4-for-10 against Oakland in the 1975 ALCS, Cooper had mustered seven hits in his next fifty-seven postseason at bats, including an 0-for-2 performance thus far in Game Five. On top of that, he'd made a critical error that led to a run.

Mauch discussed the options on the mound with Sánchez, but the move to make was fairly obvious. Take Sánchez out and bring Hassler in. Cooper hadn't had a lot of success against Hassler, but he wasn't alone. Over the course of the 1982 season left-handed batters hit .152 off Hassler.

"Gene Mauch comes to the mound and he doesn't call in Andy Hasler, the 6'5" lefty that Cecil wants no part of," recalled DeCinces. "He left Sanchez in. I remember standing there and I'm going, 'what?' I just walked off the mound."

"Everyone in the American League knew Hassler terrorized left-handed hitters," said John in his autobiography. "Gene never made the move. He visited the mound but did not remove Sanchez. Cecil was probably the most surprised man in the park, aside from about 20 or so Angels. I was thinking, 'this is nonsense. Gene must have something up his sleeve.'"[40]

Mauch's decision was one strike from paying off when Cooper took an outside fastball and sent it to the down the left field line. Seven years earlier, Red Sox catcher, and Cooper's teammate at the time, Carlton

Fisk had famously waved his arms trying to keep a ball fair in Game Six of the 1975 World Series. As Cooper broke out of the box, he watched the ball and thrust his arms downward. Like Fisk had done, he was willing the ball to stay fair. It did. Moore and Jim Gantner scored to give the Brewers their first lead of the game.

"I'd heard County Stadium get loud before," said Molitor. "But I can honestly say there was a distinct difference in what that place sounded like after Cecil got that hit. It felt like it was vibrating, and with that facility, it probably actually was. It was something pretty special."[41]

Vuckovich gutted out seven innings, but Kuenn replaced him in the eighth with lefty Bob McClure. Kuenn also pulled Gorman Thomas, replacing him with the speedy Marshall Edwards. Thomas was essentially playing on one leg after injuring his right knee in a play at the plate in Game Four. Now, in the late innings with his team clinging to a 4–3 lead, Kuenn opted for defense first. McClure retired Lynn to lead off the inning and bring Don Baylor, whose grand slam in Game Four had given him an ALCS record ten RBI, to the plate.

"McClure's going to have to put the ball in a good spot to the next three hitters because they can all go downtown," observed Weaver.[42] The count went to 2–2 when McClure made a mistake and Baylor hammered it.

"Baylor hits it to left, the wind helps it out there," said Keith Jackson.[43]

"I knew Don Baylor," recalled Edwards. "I was playing a little deeper than normal. He was trying to make his name, too, trying to produce in that situation. When the ball came off the bat, I knew he had hit it well."[44]

"Marshall Edwards to the wall . . ." said Jackson.[45]

"It was like everything was in slow motion," said Edwards, "like you always hear about in moments like that. I saw it in the last five feet. There it was. I saw it plain as day."[46]

". . . makes the catch! If Gorman Thomas is in center field, that ball's off the wall for extra bases," said Jackson.[47]

"I remember losing my balance after the catch and going down," said Edwards. "I tossed the ball to Benji (Oglivie) and he threw it back in. That was my moment."[48]

Neither team scored in the eighth inning, and when Ron Jackson led off the top of the ninth with a single, Kuenn went to Pete Ladd to close it out. With two out, a runner on second, and the season on the line, Ladd faced future Hall of Famer Rod Carew. Ladd was eight years old when

Carew made his big-league debut in April of 1967. Now, with All-Star closer Rollie Fingers out with an elbow injury, it was up to Ladd to stop Carew and get the Brewers to the World Series.

"The place was going absolutely nuts," said catcher Ned Yost. "When it got down to one out in the ninth, I'm in my own little world in the bullpen, thinking, 'one out to the World Series.' Then I hear over the PA, 'Now batting for the California Angels, Number 29, Rod Carew.' My heart just sunk. I'm thinking, 'Oh my gosh we've got the best hitter in the American League and a runner on second.'"[49]

"Here's a man who's hit .300 fourteen years in a row," said Palmer. "We've always said on the bench it seems like he can get a hit any time he wants to."[50]

"And they're going to let Peter Ladd pitch to him," said Jackson.[51]

"That's why I retired," said Weaver, "to get away from those types of decisions."[52]

In his sixteen-year career, Carew had made the playoffs three times. All three times he came up short. All three times his team had lost to Weaver, Palmer, and the Orioles. In the Angels dugout, DeCinces, a former Oriole, watched Carew foul off multiple pitches and thought, "if there's ever a chance Rodney's gonna go (to the World Series) we need one of those balls to fall."

Ladd ran the count to 1–2 before throwing a thigh-high fastball on the outer half of the plate. Carew went with it and hit it to the left side of the infield.

"Carew hit a one hopper right to Robin (Yount) at short," recalled Yost. "It was smoked but Robin caught the ball, took a step and when he threw the ball to first, he raised his arms right away. I saw it and started jumping up and down. Before the ball even got to Cooper, I had jumped the fence and was sprinting to the mound."[53]

The Brewers were going to the World Series for the first time in team history while the Angels, who led the series two games to none, were left wondering what happened.

"I felt terrible for Rod," recalled DeCinces. "I remember standing there. I waited for him to come off the field. I felt terrible for everybody, but I was also angry at how that finished. I grabbed Rod and gave him a hug and said, 'You hit the crap out of that ball. Eight feet either way and we're still playing.' That's just what baseball does to you. I can remember coming into that clubhouse and it was just tough. Really, really hard."

DeCinces had been in a similar situation just a few years before. In 1979 his Orioles team was up three games to one over the Pittsburgh Pirates in the World Series. Pittsburgh came back to win the series in seven. "This one was just tougher," DeCinces continued. "There we just so many questions. So many things that were taken out of the players' hands. Somebody who wasn't on the field (Mauch) made a decision that affected all the guys that played the game."

"Gene knew the rule book better than anyone in baseball," said Tommy John. "He was a brilliant strategist and one of the most astute bench managers I ever saw. He had been managing since 1960, but he never won a pennant because he didn't understand pitching. That's what killed him in 1964 with the Phillies, and with the Angels in 1982."[54]

As the champagne flowed in the Brewers clubhouse, Vuckovich sang the praises of his teammates, saying "This club cannot be intimidated. They just keep coming at you. If you're a pitcher on this team, you have to try your damnedest because these guys won't let you give anything else."[55]

"This is a group of 25 guys who are molded into one," said Kuenn.[56] What he didn't say, but everyone knew, was that he was the one who had done the molding.

There was far less drama in Atlanta. The Cardinals scored four times in the top of the second inning of Game Three and cruised to a 6–2 win over the Braves. Atlanta's dream season was over, but now Whitey Herzog had to face the monster he had created by trading Simmons, Fingers, and Vuckovich to Milwaukee. There's no doubt that the Cardinals wouldn't have been where they were without Herzog, but the same could be said for the Brewers. The true winner of the seven-player deal between the Brewers and Cardinals on December 12, 1980, would be decided in the 1982 World Series, and it would take all seven games to get an answer.

10. THE WORLD SERIES

This Could Be the Best Year of My Life

John A Murphy, the . . . energetic head of Philip Morris' Miller brewing Co. keeps a voodoo doll named "August" (after Anheuser-Busch chairman August Busch III) in his Milwaukee office. Under his desk is a small rug bearing Anheuser-Busch's eagle trademark. For six years now, Murphy's Miller has been walking all over St. Louis' Anheuser-Busch.
Forbes, August 1978

When Phillip Morris bought Milwaukee-based Miller Brewing in 1969, the company was producing approximately seven million barrels of beer per year. By 1978, that number had jumped to 31 million.[1] Miller was a force that Anheuser-Busch needed to deal with, lest they lose their spot as the number one brewer in the United States, a position they had held since 1957. In an early summer meeting with some Anheuser-Busch distributors in 1981, August Busch III, son of St. Louis Cardinals owner Gussie Busch, approached Andy Steinhubl, Anheuser-Busch's vice president of brewing and chief brewmaster, and whispered, "I want you to make me up a recipe for something we will call Budweiser Light."[2]

Busch had spent the past five years watching Miller eat into his market share, and he'd had enough. Anheuser-Busch products Michelob Light and Natural Light had failed to make an impact in the market, and Busch felt it was time to put the family name on a light beer. Steinhubl produced a recipe by the end of the meeting, and the result, Budweiser Light, hit shelves in March of 1982. The new brew was launched with a multimillion-dollar ad campaign and a new slogan, "Bring Out Your Best." The new beer, coupled with an advertising blitz, effectively shut down Miller's challenge to Anheuser-Busch's dominance. Rather than feature ex-athletes in the commercials, Anheuser-Busch showcased a young Clydesdale horse named Baron, who was raised on the estate of chairman August Busch III, accompanied by a royal sounding voice-over.

> Born of tradition . . .
> Nurtured by pride . . .
> A light beer worthy of the Budweiser name.

At the time, Budweiser's market share in the United States stood at approximately 32 percent, while Miller was growing. But the release of Budweiser Light ended Miller's threat, and they finished the year with a market share of 20 percent.[3] Milwaukee-based Miller would remain behind St Louis-based Anheuser-Busch in the beer wars. Where the two cities would finish on the baseball field was up for debate.

"Let's call this the Word Beeries," joked St. Louis mayor Vincent C. Schoemehl.[4] His pun was a bad one, but it was apt, and he reinforced it by betting Milwaukee mayor Henry Maier a case of Budweiser against a case of "mixed brews" from Milwaukee on the outcome of the series.[5]

"It's good to have two Midwestern cities represented," said baseball commissioner Bowie Kuhn of the 1982 World Series. "We like to see the Series move around geographically. And it's great for fans in both cities who have supported both clubs. It's a good matchup. We've got the shining distinction of the power club like the Brewers against a hit-and-run club like the Cardinals."[6] The 1982 World Series was a contrast in styles. It was the first time in Series history that the team with the most home runs in the major leagues (Milwaukee–216) faced the team with the fewest (St. Louis–67). By contrast, the Cardinals stole 200 bases (second only to Oakland's 232), while the Brewers swiped just 84, with just one player (Paul Molitor) reaching double digits in steals. It was power vs. speed, with each team expertly designed for their home ballpark. "Just watching them [the Cardinals] on TV, I can see they've got the personalized Whitey Herzog stamp on them," said Milwaukee's Game One starter Mike Caldwell. "They have a lot of speedsters and a lot of guys who don't strike out. I don't want to get dizzy watching them run around the bases."[7]

Donned in a red ten-gallon Stetson hat, with a matching outfit, including red cowboy boots and string tie, Gussie Busch, the eighty-three-year-old owner of the Cardinals, and former head of Anheuser-Busch, threw out the ceremonial first pitch of the 1982 World Series. As St.

Louis starter Bob Forsch took the mound in the top of the first inning to face Paul Molitor, NBC color commentator Tony Kubek offered a piece of advice. "It has been said by almost every American League club that if you can keep Molitor and Yount off the bases, you can beat this ballclub," he said.[8] That may have been so but was easier said than done. Yount's 212 hits led the American League while Molitor's 201 were third. Between them on the leader board was first baseman Cecil Cooper with 205, meaning the top-three men in the Milwaukee order recorded more than 600 hits in 1982.

Forsch managed to keep Molitor off the bases by getting him to ground out, but Robin Yount drew a walk and came around to score as part of a two-run top of the first inning for the Brewers. That would prove to be the last time the Cardinals were able to keep Molitor off base that evening, as the Milwaukee third baseman set a single-game World Series record with five hits. Yount added four more, and Caldwell was masterful in a runaway 10–0 Brewers win. It was, as Herzog said, "a good old-fashioned butt kicking. There's nothing else you can say about it. We could have played until three in the morning and not scored."[9]

Caldwell was briefly a member of the Cardinals organization, having spent spring training with the team in 1977 before being dealt to Cincinnati. Six weeks later, the Reds sent him to Milwaukee for two minor leaguers. When Caldwell entered the Milwaukee clubhouse, he gave a small speech. "There's only 24 guys I like in baseball and that's you guys," he's reported to have said, "and if I ever get traded, I'll hate every one of you."[10]

The speech earned him the nickname "Mr. Warmth." It was a moniker Caldwell embraced, so much so that he wore a T-shirt under his uniform that read, "Mr. Bleeping Warmth."[11] But his mood was considerably brighter after his Game One victory.

"I look grumpy tonight?" he asked reporters.[12]

"The Cardinals have amazing speed," said Molitor. "By getting the lead early, we took away what they do best. If it's close or a tie game, their speed can run you right into the ground."[13]

"The lead helped immensely," said Caldwell. "Our team hadn't been hitting well the last few weeks, but I knew nobody could keep these guys down indefinitely. Paulie started it off, and the other guys just picked it up from him."[14]

Kubek's words in the top of the first inning had been prescient. In twelve plate appearances, Molitor and Yount reached base nine times, scored twice, and drove in four. The result was an easy victory and a 1–0 Series lead.

"This game, the score you saw tonight, with Paulie getting five hits and Robin four, that was Milwaukee Brewers baseball," said designated hitter Don Money, who contributed a hit of his own. "I'm not going to say we can do this every night. The Cardinals have a great team. They're going to come back and play us very tough. But we won the first game," he added. "That takes some of the pressure off. And we've been under a lot of pressure for a long time."[15]

The pressure was squarely on the shoulders of the St. Louis Cardinals in Game Two. They could not afford to go down two games to none, especially at home, so they altered their approach after the Game One drubbing. "We had advance scouts who went out and put together these reports on the Brewers," said Bob Forsch. "Pitch this guy here, this guy is slow, pitch this way in this situation. Well, we pitched that way and it seemed like every base hit was a foot from somebody. The slow guys were beating out hits by a step. When the game was over, I remember Tommy Herr, Ozzie Smith, and a few others getting together and basically saying screw those reports and play the way we've played everyone else all season long."[16]

Forsch and his teammates had a point. The Brewers collected five infield hits in Game One, including one by Gorman Thomas, who was playing with a bad knee. The Cardinals changed things up in Game Two, and the NBC announcing crew of Joe Garagiola and Tony Kubek picked up on it immediately. When Paul Molitor led off the game, Kubek noted that Ozzie Smith was playing about ten yards closer to home plate than he had the previous night.

"You certainly don't want to minimize scouting reports," said Garagiola. "They're important. I guess the only guy who didn't really believe it was [General George] Custer. But until you play against these guys [Milwaukee] you really don't get the feel, and tonight it's a different defense they're setting up."[17]

That defense was put to the test right away when Robin Yount drew a one out walk from Cardinals starter John Stuper and advanced to third on Cecil Cooper's hit-and-run single. Stuper got out of the jam when Ted Simmons hit into an inning-ending double play, but the Brewers offense showed they were going to continue to pressure the Cardinals defenders no matter where they played. One inning later, Milwaukee took a 1–0 lead when Roy Howell scored on Charlie Moore's line drive double to left center. They tacked on two more when Molitor led off the third with a single and scored on Ted Simmons's homer to right, his second of the series. The Busch Stadium crowd was getting restless. Their team had been outscored 13–0 and had mustered all of three hits. The uneasy feeling spread to the St. Louis bench as well. "We were all ticked off and started screaming at each other," said first baseman Keith Hernandez. "At a certain point, a club reaches rock bottom. We didn't want to get swept in four games and make it look like a mismatch."[18]

Dane Iorg led off the bottom of the third inning with a single to bring up Willie McGee. Respecting McGee's speed, Molitor played in to take away the bunt. Instead, McGee swung away and hit a chopper to Cecil Cooper, who made a diving stop and threw out Iorg at second base. Instead of having no one out and runners on the corners, the Cardinals had one out and a man on first. But that man was the speedy McGee. Milwaukee had taken the Cardinals out of their game by grabbing an early lead in Game One, and Herzog was determined not to let it happen again. Even though they were down 3–0, Herzog sent McGee on the first pitch to Tommy Herr, and McGee responded by stealing second easily.

Herr was a standout high school basketball player in Lancaster, Pennsylvania, and had accepted an offer to play at Duke. But when the Blue Devils switched coaches, Herr's offer disappeared, so he attended the University of Delaware to play football, baseball, and basketball. He signed with the Cardinals in 1974 as an undrafted free agent, and he epitomized the kind of player Whitey Herzog loved. He was a good athlete, a solid defender, and could run. "The most amazing hitter I had those years might have been Tommy Herr," wrote Herzog in his 1999 autobiography, *You're Missing a Great Game.* "I can't think of a better example of how having a plan, a sense of the situation you're in, can help you succeed. If there was one guy I managed that I would want hitting for me in the stretch drive, in August and September, it would be hard to pick between George Brett and Tommy."[19]

With two outs and McGee on third, Herr turned on Brewers starter Don Sutton's offering and smoked it into the gap in right center field for a ground rule double. The Cardinals finally had a run, and it had come in typical Whiteyball fashion: a single, a stolen base, and a ball in the gap. Oberkfell followed with a line drive single past a diving Jim Gantner at second to score Herr and cut the Milwaukee lead to 3–2 before Hernandez fouled out to end the inning.

The joy lasted all of one inning before Milwaukee tacked on another run in the top of the fifth. Robin Yount led off the inning with a double and scored on Cooper's single to make it 4–2, but the Cardinals got

something going in the bottom of the sixth. With runners on the corners and two out, Darrell Porter smacked a double to left field to tie the
game at four. Doug Bair retired the first two men he faced in the top of
the seventh, but Cooper's double to right chased him from the game,
and Herzog brought in his stopper.

Bruce Sutter signed with the Chicago Cubs as an amateur free agent
in 1971 and nearly didn't get out of Single-A. After a 1973 season in
which he went 3–3 with a 4.13 ERA in the Midwest League, Sutter's
then manager, Walt Dixon, sent a season-ending report to his bosses
in Chicago that read, "Bruce Sutter will make the major leagues when a
communist regime is ready to take over this country."[20]

Unable and unwilling to await a coup attempt, Sutter instead enlisted
the help of Chicago's minor league pitching coach, Fred Martin, who
taught him the split finger fastball. Unlike a regular fastball, which is
gripped on the fingertips, the split is held between the index and middle
fingers of the pitching hand. When thrown correctly, the pitch looks like
a fastball but dives right before it gets to the plate. After nearly being
released in 1973, Sutter shot through the minor leagues, made his debut
in 1976, and won the Cy Young Award in 1979. Now he was the key
piece of the Cardinals bullpen and needed to retire Ben Oglivie with
runners on first and second in a tie game. Sutter threw Oglivie a 1–1
splitter, and Oglivie pounded it into the ground toward second base.
Just like he had done in the All-Star Game, Ozzie Smith charged across
the diamond and cut in front of his second baseman to snare the ball
and make a quick throw, nailing Oglivie by a step. "Ozzie Smith steals it
from Tommy Herr," said Kubek. "That man is the biggest rally stopper
in baseball."[21]

Smith did indeed "steal" the ball from Herr, but, had he not done
so, Oglivie likely would have beaten the ball out to load the bases for
Gorman Thomas. Most shortstops couldn't have reached the ball, but
Smith not only did, he also recorded an inning-ending out. It was the
type of play he had been brought to St. Louis to make, and it kept the
game tied at four.

It stayed that way until the bottom of the eighth inning. With George
Hendrick on first base and one out, Porter ripped a single up the middle
to put runners on first and second and chase relief pitcher Bob McClure.
With Sutter cruising and the Brewers in trouble, Rollie Fingers's absence
loomed large, and NBC cameras took a shot of him in the Milwaukee
dugout. Kubek commented that Fingers threw a pain-free bullpen

session and could be available for Game Three but was not available now, so Kuenn went with Pete Ladd against Lonnie Smith. Ladd ran the count full, and his payoff pitch was a thigh-high fastball.

"I knew I couldn't hit it," said Smith. "I had no chance of hitting it."[22]

"It was on the outside corner," said Ladd. "It was not even on the black. But (home plate umpire Bill Haller) said it was completely outside. I knew he blew the call. There are many other things I could say, but I'm not going to say them."[23]

"I was pretty surprised," said Smith, "but the umpires are never wrong."[24]

The walk to Smith loaded the bases, and Ladd was fuming over Haller's missed call. He then did the one thing he couldn't do: he lost his cool and walked pinch-hitter Steve Braun to give the Cardinals the lead. Once he regained his composure, Ladd got McGee to line out for the second out and caught a break when Ozzie Smith's ground ball hit Braun in the heel for the third out of the inning, but the damage was done. Sutter shut the Brewers down in the top of the ninth to win the game and even the series.

It would have been easy to point fingers, either at Ladd or Haller, after the game, but the Brewers refused to do so. When asked about the call, Simmons responded, "We had a 3–0 lead. When you get three runs on a ballclub you should win. We got four and didn't score anymore. That's our fault."[25]

"The only thing I know is Lonnie Smith said it was a good pitch, and I respect his opinion," said Kuenn. "If the guy is called out, there's runners on first and second and two out, and it's a different situation," he continued. "But I don't think this will bother Ladd. He's a good kid. I thought he did a fine job."[26]

Ladd may have done a fine job, but the game underscored a glaring difference between the two teams. St. Louis had their stopper, and Milwaukee did not, and everyone knew what that meant. "We're the National League champions because of defense, just enough pitching, speed that constantly pressures the other team, and Bruce Sutter," said Herzog. "We give everyone heartburn, but we've won more games than anyone in the league."[27]

The series moved to Milwaukee for Game Three, and that meant a huge pregame tailgate party in the County Stadium parking lot. The smell of brats and burgers on the grill mixed with music and, of course, freely flowing beer as Milwaukee prepared for its first home World

Series game since 1958. During the regular season, Gorman Thomas was known to stop by and enjoy the company of the fans. "I'd show up for an afternoon game and the tailgating would be going on," he said. "I'd have a Coke and a brat. Then I'd come back after the game and have a beer."[28]

But Thomas had other things on his mind prior to Game Three, specifically how to succeed against St. Louis starter Joaquin Andújar. Milwaukee sent Pete Vuckovich to the mound, and both pitchers were outstanding through the early going, shutting out their opponents through the first four innings, but that changed in the top of the fifth.

Darrell Porter led off with a strikeout, but Lonnie Smith hit a ball in the gap in left center for a double. Dane Iorg bounced a ball to Cecil Cooper's right, and the ball kicked off his glove for an error. With one out and two on, Milwaukee catcher Ted Simmons set up in the middle of the plate with his glove at the bottom of the strike zone, but Vuckovich's pitch drifted up and away, and Willie McGee hit it over the wall in right field for a three-run homer.

It was still 3–0 in the top of the seventh inning when Smith hit the right-center field gap and legged out a triple. The relay throw hit him in the back and skipped into the third base dugout, and Smith was awarded home plate to make it a 4–0 Cardinals advantage. Two batters later, McGee stepped in again against Vuckovich. With McGee's previous home run in mind, Vuke's first pitch was up and in to knock McGee off the plate. The second pitch was low and in, but McGee backed off the plate a bit, which enabled him to barrel it up and send it down the right field line for his second home run of the game. McGee hit four home runs in 123 regular season games, but he'd now hit three in his last three postseason games, and the Cardinals had a 5–0 lead.

By the bottom of the seventh, a 5–0 lead seemed more than enough for Andújar. The twenty-nine-year-old righty from San Pedro de Macoris in the Dominican Republic turned in his finest season in 1982, winning 15 games. There was no doubting his talent, but his temperament had gotten him in trouble in the past. Andujar originally signed with the Cincinnati Reds as a sixteen-year-old in 1969 and made his major league debut for the Houston Astros in 1976. But it did not take long for him to wear out his welcome in Houston. The Astros nearly sent him to Philadelphia at the trade deadline in 1980 and ended up offering him to the Brewers in exchange for outfielder Dick Davis, but Milwaukee general manager Harry Dalton turned them down. By midseason 1981

Herzog entered the chase, but he was concerned about the reports that Andújar did not get along with Houston manager Bill Virdon. Herzog and Virdon had been friends since the 1950s, so when Astros general manager Al Rosen asked if Herzog was interested in Andújar, he called his buddy for the inside scoop.

"Bill, I hear Andujar don't like you," Herzog recalled saying to Virdon. "I've never known a ballplayer not to like you. I've never known a *person* not to like you. What's the problem with this guy?"[29]

"I'll put it like this," said Virdon.

The son of a gun wants to pitch every day. I'm not kidding you. I've got [Nolan] Ryan, I've got Vern Ruhle, I've got J. R. Richard, I've got [Joe] Niekro. Andujar pitched one Thursday. We got rained out on Friday and Saturday, so there weren't any games. And he comes into my office Sunday morning and he starts raising hell. He says he feels fine, he's ready to go again. He's ready! The other four guys ain't even been out to the mound yet, and he thinks it's his turn. Whitey, I'm telling you, this guy is out of his mind.[30]

Herzog took a chance and sent outfielder Tony Scott to Houston in exchange for Andújar, and the move panned out, thanks in large part to Cardinals pitching coach Hub Kittle. The Cardinals' new starter thrived under the tutelage of the sixty-five-year-old Kittle, whose professional baseball career dated back to 1937. After forty-five years as a player and coach, Kittle was the consummate teacher. Cardinals pitcher Dave LaPoint recalled once walking through a hotel lobby at 3 A.M. and seeing Kittle teaching a bellman how to throw a forkball. Andújar and Kittle clicked immediately, and Andújar's performance improved. After shutting out the Phillies in September, Andújar gave all the credit to his pitching coach. "The name of the game is to throw strikes," he said. "I'm not trying to overpower people anymore. I could throw it 95 or 97 miles per hour if I wanted to, but Hub Kittle convinced me that throwing strikes is the most important thing. Now I'm settling for 89 or 92."[31]

That strategy paid off, especially late in the season, when Andújar went 5–0 with a 0.98 ERA in the final month of the season. He followed that up with a Game Two win over Atlanta in the NLCS and was working on six and a third scoreless innings when Ted Simmons stepped to the plate in the bottom of the seventh and hit a hard one-hopper that bounced off Andújar's knee and sent him sprawling to the turf in pain.

"The pitch was a fastball away and Ted hit it hard," said Porter. "When it hit Joaquin in the knee, I thought it had a good chance to break something. The ball slips off that grass pretty fast and he just went down like a big old Oak tree."[32]

"It scared me to death," said Keith Hernandez. "(Cardinals Team Doctor Stan) London moved the knee around just a hair and (Andujar) was screaming. I was very concerned."[33]

After teammates carried Andújar off the field, he was taken to a local hospital for X-rays, which proved negative for a break, but his status for the rest of the series lay in doubt. The St. Louis bullpen escaped further damage in the seventh inning, but Milwaukee got something going in the eighth against Sutter. Robin Yount drew a two-out walk before Cooper hit an 0–1 splitter into the right field seats for a two-run homer. St. Louis added a run in the top of the ninth to make it 6–2 but had not yet finished the Brewers. Oglivie led off the inning with a hard ground ball down the first-base line that kicked off Keith Hernandez's glove for his second error of the series. Then Gorman Thomas crushed a ball to center field, but Willie McGee was off with the crack of the bat and timed his leap perfectly at the fence to steal a likely two-run homer. Sutter retired the final two batters to save the victory and give St. Louis a 2–1 lead in the series. After beginning the season in the minor leagues, Willie McGee's bat and his glove made him the star of the show on the game's biggest stage, all of which was a bit too much for the soft-spoken McGee. Twelve months earlier, he was buried in the Yankees minor league system. Now he was a World Series star. "I can't believe I'm here," he said. "But baseball is baseball, and anything is possible at any time."[34]

"I don't know anybody who ever played a better World Series game," said Herzog. "If he didn't make that catch in the ninth, Mr. Sutter could have been in trouble."[35]

The two teams hooked up again the following afternoon, and the Cardinals jumped out to an early lead, scoring one run in the first inning and three more in the second off Milwaukee starter Moose Haas. Cardinals starter Dave LaPoint, meanwhile, was having a much easier time against his former teammates. LaPoint was one of the players involved in the deal prior to the 1981 season that had sent Vuckovich, Fingers, et al., to the Brewers, but he did not earn a job out of spring training until 1982, when he broke camp with the Cardinals. St. Louis began the season against Houston, and when the Cardinals roughed up Nolan Ryan Opening Day, LaPoint wasn't sure if he belonged.

I said, "if Nolan Ryan gets beat 14 to 3, I don't stand a chance in this game. I'm not even going to unpack." The very first week, I was trying to leave after a game and Gene Tenace grabbed me by the collar and said, "Sit down kid. You're pitching this week, right? Sit down and listen. We're going to talk about the game and see if you learned anything tonight." We did that over and over. That's how I learned to pitch. That's how I learned to play the game.[36]

The lessons from Tenace paid off as LaPoint allowed only one run on four hits through the first six innings. Gorman Thomas led off the bottom of the second by fouling out to catcher Darrell Porter for the second time in a row, drawing boos from the home crowd. Ben Oglivie hit a high chopper to Hernandez at first base, who fielded it and threw to LaPoint, who was covering the bag for what should have been an easy out, but LaPoint dropped the ball. "When it hit my glove," he said afterwards, "it felt like a brick. And it fell like one."[37]

Don Money followed with a single to right field, but Charlie Moore popped out to Ozzie Smith at shortstop for the second out. Jim Gantner's double scored Oglivie and chased LaPoint from the game in favor of Doug Bair, who walked Molitor to load the bases to bring up Robin Yount. Michele Yount, Robin's wife, was pregnant with their son and was due at any time. Yount and the team had a plan in place to whisk her away to the hospital should she go into labor during the World Series. Fortunately, she was able to stay put to see her husband deliver a check-swing single to right field to score two runs to cut the Cardinals lead to 5–4. Herzog emerged from the dugout to pull Bair. Lefty Jim Kaat got Cecil Cooper to hit a high hopper to Keith Hernandez, who fielded the ball and stepped on the bag to end the inning. But, much to Hernandez's chagrin, umpires ruled the ball foul, and Cooper's at bat continued. He hit the next pitch past a diving Ken Oberkfell at third base for a single to score Molitor and tie the game.

Two batters later Thomas came to the plate again, this time against Cardinals reliever Jeff Lahti. The Brewers slugger was behind in the count 1–2, but, when Lahti threw a fastball on the outside corner, Thomas reached out and hooked it into left center field to drive home two and give the Brewers a 7–5 lead. Just seven outs away from being down 3–1 in the Series, Milwaukee now had a lead. Don Money lined out to end the inning, but the Brewers had sent twelve men to the plate and scored six runs to breathe life back into the home crowd as well as their World Series hopes.

Back from a commercial break for the top of the eighth inning, the NBC broadcast team speculated if Fingers might be available, and, seemingly on cue, the injured reliever got up and began to throw in the Milwaukee bullpen. Since his injury, he'd been bombarded with advice and home remedies, including one letter suggesting he tie an onion to his elbow to facilitate healing. But no home remedies could fix his elbow. "St. Louis knew I hadn't been in a ball game in three or four weeks," said Fingers. "If you don't pitch after three or four weeks, you know something's wrong. Guys aren't that stupid. I couldn't pitch. It was just too sore."[38]

Bob McClure held the Cardinals scoreless over the final two innings to seal the victory, and the Series was tied at two. After the game, reporters asked Herzog about LaPoint's error, and he didn't hold back.

"LaPoint ran 2 steps for that ball," said Herzog. "I don't know how he dropped it. It looked like an easy inning. It turned out to be a nightmare. We only needed one more out and seven straight hitters got on base."[39]

Those seven batters meant that Game Five would not be an elimination game, as Haas feared. "I got the feeling that it might be three games to one going to the fifth game the way things were going," he said. "Nothing seemed to be going our way."[40]

Nothing seemed to be going Gorman Thomas's way either. Ever the streaky hitter, Thomas was in the midst of a 3-for-29 slump in the postseason. His clutch double came at exactly the right time, for him *and* his team.

"The fans here know me, he said. "When I go into one of my slumps, it's legendary. When I'm cold, who cares? Anybody can get me out. The fans feel as disgusted as I do."[41]

"I started out the inning with a pop up to the catcher so, hey, maybe you could say I started the rally," he continued. "But then Benji [Ben Oglivie] got on on an error and then it was like an avalanche. The noise on our bench kept increasing in magnitude and volume, and then the fans got into it. When the fans here get into it, they can do damage and rattle you. I think the fans played a big part in it."[42]

A crowd of more than 56,000 packed County Stadium the following day for Game Five, and the pitching battle was a rematch of Game One, with Mike Caldwell going for the Brewers and Bob Forsch taking the mound for St. Louis. It was a sunny Sunday afternoon with temperatures in the mid-50s, but a strong wind blowing from right field to left field brought the wind-chill factor down to 37. Still, the hearty denizens of Milwaukee were undaunted as the stadium organist played "On Wisconsin" prior to the first pitch.

Inning after inning, Caldwell put men on base, and each time he wiggled out of trouble, often with the help of his defense. A diving stop by Jim Gantner saved a run in the third inning, Molitor started a double play to end the fourth, and Charlie Moore made a diving catch on a Lonnie Smith line drive in the fifth inning.

Milwaukee held a 3–1 lead in the top of the seventh when Ozzie and Lonnie Smith hit back-to-back singles to bring up Hernandez. The Cardinals first baseman began the series by going 0-for-15 in the first four games, but his bat heated up in Game Five, and he hit a ball hard to Cooper at first who flipped it to Yount at shortstop to try to start yet another double play. Lonnie Smith was bearing down on Yount at second, doing his best to break it up, and, while accurate, Yount's relay to first was just late. George Hendrick followed by singling up the middle to score Ozzie Smith, cutting the lead to 3–2 and bringing up Darrell Porter.

It was Porter's sixth inning two-out double to left field that proved to be the difference in Game Two, but the Brewers didn't think the left-hander swinging catcher could do it again and played him to pull. Mike Shannon noticed the strategy on the Cardinals radio broadcast. "Big gap down the left field line," he said. "He's burned this club once already like that. Here's the 1–1 delivery, ground ball into right field, GREAT diving stop by Cooper. He throws to first to get Porter and he SAVES the game."[43]

The play indeed saved at least one run, as Ozzie Smith would have certainly scored on the play. Cooper caught the ball when it was already past him and threw to Caldwell from his backside to quell the rally. Robin Yount homered to right field in the bottom of the inning to give the Brewers a 4–2 lead, and they won the game 6–4 to take a 3–2 lead in the series. Caldwell gave up fourteen hits in 8⅔ innings before being relieved by Bob McClure to pick up his second win of the series.

"That, for me, was one I was more proud of than the three hit shutout [in Game One]," said Caldwell. "I gave up 14 hits and still came within one double play ball of pitching a complete game. There were men on base the whole damn game. I got outs when I needed them. Charlie Moore made a great play in right field [and] Cecil Cooper made a diving play at first base."[44]

"Everyone said it would be Milwaukee's power against St. Louis' speed and defense," said Cooper. "Well, I think the world—not to mention the Cardinals—now knows that we're a lot more diversified than just a home run hitting team. The reasons we're one win away from the world championship are as much the top of the order and our defense as our home runs."[45]

Cooper's assessment was dead on. The top three hitters in the Milwaukee batting order, Molitor, Yount, and Cooper, combined for twenty-six hits through the first five games, and the defense had been outstanding. Yount was hitting a Series-high .524, but the humble short-stop deflected any praise sent his way. When asked if he had thought about being Series MVP, he said he already had two cars (the bonus for winning the award) and didn't need another one.

"He's just like that—all the time," said Molitor. "Two weeks ago, after we clinched the title against Baltimore, we had a players' party in the clubhouse. Everyone got a round Robin and started chanting 'MVP' and he started swinging at us. He hated that."

"There's no phoniness about the guy," Molitor continued. "He really, really doesn't care about himself—only about us."[46]

The series would shift to St. Louis for Game Six, and the Cardinals were hoping a change in venue would help turn things around after dropping two of three in Milwaukee. On the return flight to St. Louis, Bruce Sutter made a surprise announcement: "Party at the Forsch's house!"[47] Having gone 0–2 with a 4.97 ERA and with his team on the brink of elimination, Forsch was not really in the mood to attend a party, let alone host one. "Bruce, this is a bad idea," he said.[48] Undaunted, Sutter continued to spread the word about the upcoming soiree.

"Well, by the time the wheels landed in St. Louis, there was a party at the Forsch's. Whitey didn't know—thank God. We were in the back of the plane," recalled Forsch.[49]

"I guess Bruce figured everybody needed to relax," Forsch said. "He picked our house because it was the best venue. We had a basement with a full bar. The thing I was afraid of was: Here I was, losing Game 5, and all of a sudden there's a party at our house. What if I'm the reason we lose Game Six in the World Series, too!?"[50]

The party began Sunday evening and proved to be just what the team needed. After a day off to recuperate, St. Louis sent John Stuper to the mound, the first rookie to start two World Series games since another Cardinal, Dick Hughes, started Games Two and Six in 1967. "I was more nervous than I've been in my life for any athletic competition," he said after the game.[51]

Inning-ending double plays in the second and third innings helped calm Stuper's nerves, as did his teammates scoring twice in the bottom of the second inning. They added three more in the fourth and another two in the sixth on a Hernandez home run to chase Milwaukee starter Don Sutton, who allowed seven runs in 5⅓ innings.

"I had good stuff but bad location," Sutton said. "I have no excuses. I was sitting in the clubhouse icing my arm down, trying to come up with an excuse, but there are none."[52]

Fatigue may have been a factor for the thirty-seven-year-old Sutton. Entering Game Six, he had logged 227⅔ innings, his highest total since 1977. "There wasn't a whole lot left," he admitted years later. "I've always said I wish I could have given Milwaukee 'younger innings' in the World Series. It would have been fun."[53]

Just as Hernandez touched home plate, the drizzle that had been falling through much of the inning turned into a downpour and the game was delayed for nearly thirty minutes. When play resumed, the Cardinals blew the game open, scoring six runs in the bottom of the sixth inning, which was also delayed by rain. The game ended at 12:11 A.M., more than five hours after it began, and the Cardinals won it 13–1 to force a decisive Game Seven. Stuper sat through two rain delays to go the distance, allowing just four hits, and save the St. Louis bullpen.

"I just kept putting heat on my arm to keep the muscles supple in the delays," said Stuper. "Why not try to come back? It might be the biggest game I ever pitch. I wanted to come back and try to finish it after the second delay. The adrenaline kept me warm."[54]

The attention turned from Stuper to the scheduled mound matchup for Game Seven between Pete Vuckovich and Joaquin Andújar. Neither pitcher would be at their best. Vuckovich was dealing with what turned out to be a torn rotator cuff, and Andújar was still sore after being hit by a Ted Simmons comebacker in Game Three.

"It's not perfect," said Andújar of his leg, "but it feels better and when I threw on Monday, I knew I'd start. It's just another game. If I throw strikes, I'll win."[55]

"I'll be out there fighting as best I can," said Vuckovich. "I'm a survivor, and I plan to be the survivor pitching the biggest game of my life. This is something I've always wanted. Don't let anyone tell you it's just another game."[56]

The *St. Louis Post-Dispatch* pulled out all the stops with their head-line prior to Game Seven: "Cards Goal: Bury Brewers With Wounded Knee."[57]

Another capacity crowd packed Busch Stadium on a chilly night in St. Louis for Game Seven. The crowd of more than 53,000 brought the total attendance for the series to more than 384,000, among the highest in World Series history. Cardinals manager Whitey Herzog played it safe by having Dave LaPoint warm up in the bullpen in case Andújar couldn't go. As the two warmed up, LaPoint tried to gauge how his teammate was doing. "The biggest problem was you couldn't ask him anything," said LaPoint. "You'd say 'Joaquin how are you feeling?' and he'd answer 'Me one tough Dominican.'"[58]

The statement had become his catchphrase, and, in case anyone for-got, it was written on a banner that hung from the stands in right field, causing Ozzie Smith to ask Andújar if he had stayed up late making it. Banner or not, there was no way Andújar was going to let a sore knee keep him from taking the mound for the most important game of his career.

Pete Vuckovich had similar feelings in the visitors' bullpen despite his shoulder problems. He would win the American League Cy Young Award in 1982, but gutting it out through the final month of the sea-son proved costly. After winning 18 games over 223⅔ regular season innings in 1982, Vuke threw just 14⅔ innings in 1983 and missed all of 1984. He'd win eight more games over the course of his career. But the chance to pitch in Game Seven of the World Series was worth it. "It's the day you simulate as a young pitcher, whether you're throwing a ball off the wall or whatever," he said. "It's the game you dream of, going out and dominating and helping your team be World Champions."[59]

Both pitchers held the opponents scoreless through the first two innings, but the Cardinals put a man on in the first and left the bas-es loaded in the second. Roy Howell led off the top of the third with a ground ball to Hernandez at first base, who flipped to Andújar for the out, but the Cardinals starter came up limping after the play. It was obvious his leg was still bothering him, but he kept pumping fastball after fastball at the Milwaukee hitters, and they were consistently behind them. Hernandez walked with one out in the bottom of the third and advanced to second on a George Hendrick single through the right side of the infield. With two on and one man out, Darrell Porter lifted a fly ball to right field that took Charlie Moore to the warning track before he hauled it in. Both runners tagged and advanced, putting men on second and third with two out. NBC play-by-play man Dick Enberg noted that Vuckovich excelled at getting himself out of trouble, but color commentator Tony Kubek thought Vuke's luck may be running out. "How long can you keep up with that?" he asked Enberg.[60] The answer was at least one more inning, as Vukovich induced Dane Iorg to ground out to end the inning and strand two more runners.

Molitor led off the top of the fourth with a single through the hole at second base for his tenth hit of the series to bring up Robin Yount, who had eleven hits of his own. Yount hit a chopper to Oberkfell at third, who threw to Herr for a fielder's choice, leaving Yount on first with one out. Cecil Cooper followed with a single into right field, and Yount rounded second and headed for third. As he ran, George Hendrick scooped up the ball and threw to Oberkfell for a bang-bang play. Hendrick's throw was up the line toward left field, but Oberkfell dropped a knee to prevent Yount from reaching the bag and tagged him for the second out of the inning. Ted Simmons popped out to Darrell Porter to end the threat. Now it was the Cardinals' turn.

Willie McGee led off the bottom of the fourth with a single, and a hit-and-run play sent him to third with one out to bring former Phillie Lonnie Smith to the plate. Molitor played in at third base to take away the bunt and Smith hit a ball in the hole at shortstop. Had Molitor been playing at regular depth, the ground ball could have been an inning-ending double play. Instead, it turned into an infield single and gave the Cardinals a 1–0 lead. In the early innings, Andújar boasted to his teammates if they got him one run, they would be World Champs. Now he had his run, and the rest was up to him. Andújar was a remarkable 15–1 on the season when the Cardinals scored first, and he was full of confidence as Ben Oglivie stepped in to lead off the top of the fifth inning. Andújar's confidence faded a bit when Oglivie hit his first pitch into the right field stands for a game-tying home run. As time was called, Oberkfell, walked over to Andújar on the mound. "I said, 'what do you think now?'" Oberkfell recalled. "He said, 'I think we need two.'"[61]

Andujar settled down and got the final two outs of the inning, while Vuckovich held St. Louis scoreless in the bottom of the frame. It was game number 174 for the Brewers and 172 for the Cardinals, and it was tied at one with four innings to go.

Jim Gantner led off the top of the sixth inning with a double into the right center field gap. The Brewers led the major leagues in home runs and runs scored, but they could also play small ball, and Molitor dropped a beautiful bunt down the third base line. Oberkfell stayed close to the bag at third in anticipation of a play, and Andújar fielded the ball, but his throw caromed off Molitor's shoulder and into right field to score Gantner and give the Brewers a 2–1 lead. Yount then hit a high chopper to the right side. Both Hernandez and Herr broke for the ball, but Andújar didn't break for first. Herr fielded the ball but had no one to throw to, and Milwaukee had runners on the corners with no one out. Cecil Cooper lined out to deep left to score Molitor, and the Cardinals found themselves down 3–1 with just nine outs left in their season.

Tommy Herr bounced out to open the bottom of the sixth inning, but Ozzie Smith sliced a single to left over a leaping Molitor to get the crowd going once again. Throughout the season, Yount would often relay pitch selection to Molitor from shortstop, where he could see catcher Ted Simmons's signs. With Ozzie on first base, Simmons signaled for a changeup on the outer half. Because the crowd was so loud, Molitor couldn't hear Yount's call and did not adjust his positioning. Smith pulled the pitch down the line past the diving Molitor and into the left field corner for a double to send Ozzie to third with no one out.

"That was a small thing, but if I had been cheating a bit toward the line, it might have made the difference," said Molitor.[62] Kuenn trudged to the mound to remove his starter.

"Vuke, they got the lefties coming up, I'm gonna bring Bobby (McClure) in," he said. "You did a helluva job, big man. Super job."[63]

"Can I stay here and wish him the best?" asked Vuckovich. "Do whatever you want to do," replied Kuenn, who was joined by home plate umpire Lee Weyer and Simmons on the mound. "You can stay right here."[64]

"Anything on the ground, try to keep it in the infield," Vuckovich implored McClure.[65] With the lefty McClure in the game, Herzog countered with the right-handed Gene Tenace, who walked to bring Hernandez to the plate.

Hernandez grew up near San Francisco, the son of John Hernandez, who spent parts of six seasons in the minor leagues with the Dodgers, Cardinals, Yankees, and Indians. When Keith was just five years old, his father cut down a Little League bat to make it easier to handle and threw him batting practice. The work paid off as Hernandez became a star at Terra Nova High School, where he was teammates with McClure, before transferring to Capuchino High. He made his major league debut in 1974 and hit .344 with 11 homers and 105 RBI in 1979 to split MVP honors with Pittsburgh's Willie Stargell. By 1982, Hernandez was a bona fide star, one of the slickest fielding first basemen in the major leagues and a perennial .300 hitter. Now he was facing his former high school teammate with the bases loaded. It also happened to be his twenty-ninth birthday.

The two had faced off in Game Two with McClure coming out on top. They also squared off in the minor leagues and back in Little League, when Hernandez played for Ed and Joe's 76 Service Station and McClure was a pitcher for Sun Valley Dairy Barn.[66] The stakes were a bit higher this time.

With the count 3–1, McClure threw an inside fastball, and Hernandez sent it into right center field for a single that scored both Ozzie and Lonnie Smith to tie the game and bring Hendrick to the plate. McClure got ahead of Hendrick 1–2 before the Cardinals cleanup hitter fouled off back-to-back pitches. Despite being behind in the count, Kubek cautioned that Hendrick was still a dangerous hitter. "Hendrick is one of the only cleanup hitters that I know who can adjust when he gets behind in the count, alter his swing, and just peck away the opposite way. Most cleanup hitters are there for one thing: to take a big cut."[67]

McClure's next pitch caught the outer portion of the plate, but Hendrick leaned forward, all his weight on his front foot, and poked the ball off the end of the bat into right field for a single to score the go-ahead run, just as Kubek predicted. Milwaukee got out of the inning, but the damage was done.

Police officers accompanied by German shepherds assumed positions around the perimeter of the field as the game headed into the top of the seventh. Andújar retired the first two hitters before surrendering a single to Charlie Moore. Jim Gantner was up next, having delivered four hits against the Cardinals starter in two games. Gantner swung at Andújar's first pitch and sent a comebacker to the mound, which Andújar fielded and threw to first with his usual flair to end the inning. Andújar had made a habit of being demonstrative on the mound, sometimes pointing at hitters when he struck them out and doing other things many hitters regarded as showboating. Trailing in the seventh inning and having experienced Andújar's act in the minor leagues, Gantner was in no mood to take in the show.

"You're still a hot dog!" Gantner yelled.[68] Andújar whirled and challenged the Milwaukee second baseman, and fans nearly experienced something rarely seen, a Game Seven World Series bench-clearing brawl. Fortunately, home plate umpire Lee Weyer, who stood six foot six and weighed more than 250 pounds, wrapped Andujar in a bear hug and pushed him toward the St. Louis dugout while others intervened to calm the situation.

"I think Gantner knows that when I get mad, I don't have as good control," said Andújar. "I think he was trying to make me mad to help his team. But I don't take no bull from anybody. He called me a hot dog. I told him where to go. He wanted a piece of me. I told him come on, because I was ready."[69]

St. Louis went down 1–2–3 in the bottom of the frame, and Herzog called on Sutter for the final six outs. The bearded closer had been untouchable early in the postseason. He threw 4⅓ perfect innings against Atlanta in the National League Championship Series and followed that with a scoreless outing in Game Two of the World Series. But Milwaukee banged out four runs on three hits and two walks against the Cardinals closer in Games Three and Five. Sutter retired the top of the Brewers lineup in order in the top of the eighth, and his teammates gave him some breathing room by tacking on two insurance runs in the bottom of the frame.

In the top of ninth inning, Game Seven of the 1982 World Series—the "Suds Series," Sutter retired the first two Milwaukee hitters on ground balls to bring up Gorman Thomas who, with a bum knee and in the midst of a horribly timed slump, was 3-for-25 in the series. The count went full before Thomas fouled off three straight pitches. But Sutter's tenth pitch of the at bat was a fastball that Thomas swung through to end the game and the Series. Nine years earlier, Sutter's career was nearly over. Now, in front of 53,273 fans, he'd just fulfilled the dream of hundreds of thousands of young boys; striking out a batter to win the seventh game of the World Series. Fireworks erupted over Busch Stadium as the scoreboard flashed, "We Win." The Cardinals were World Champions.

"This was the big one, and I was going to be the hero or goat," said Sutter in a raucous Cardinals clubhouse after the game. "But I want it to be the one out there pitching. That's been my job all year long."[70]

Sutter had been masterful at that job. In 102⅓ innings pitched, he'd won nine games and saved 36 more, enough to lead the National League in that category for the fourth consecutive year. He began the postseason with 6⅔ scoreless innings, then suddenly appeared human when he had back-to-back rough outings in Games Three and Five of the World Series. But when his team needed him the most, Sutter bounced back to throw two perfect innings, the two biggest innings of his life, to secure the Cardinals' first World Series title since 1967.

"For my money, there's nobody I'd rather have out there than Bruce Sutter," said Jim Kaat. "Even when he was struggling this year, when the fans were hollering 'Boos' instead of 'Bruce,' I said that I don't care how many he loses, I can't think of another pitcher I'd rather have on the mound with a one-run lead."[71]

Sutter's performance underscored the absence of Rollie Fingers. There is little doubt that a healthy Fingers would have changed the dynamic of the series, if not the outcome. One had to look no further than Pete Ladd's rough outing in Game Two for evidence. But the Brewers weren't going to use that as an excuse. "I have never said once, 'Gee, do I wish I had Rollie Fingers," said Harvey Kuenn. "That's because I knew I didn't have him."

"I've had him up in the bullpen to see how he felt," Kuenn continued. "But what made it tough was whenever you have Rollie up, you have to have another man up with him, not knowing whether or not he'd be able to go into the game."[72]

A stoic, and also injured, Pete Vuckovich took his loss in Game Seven hard, saying, "I feel like I let down my teammates, all Milwaukee. But tomorrow's another day and next year's another year."[73]

It wasn't quite that easy for Vuckovich, though. The damage done by pitching with a torn rotator cuff throughout September and October forced him to miss most of 1983 and all of 1984. After winning 71 games from 1978 through 1982 he was never the same. He won just eight more games, and his career was over after the 1986 season.

"It could be said I gave up my career for Harvey Kuenn," said Vuckovich years later. "I probably pitched more than I should have. He had an awful lot to do with that. He walked around on one leg. He was as game as any man I've ever met in my life, and it kind of rubs off on you."[74]

After talking to the media, Vuckovich made his way to the home clubhouse to congratulate some of his former teammates, among them Keith Hernandez, who hit .583 (7-for-12) over the final three games of the series. Hernandez had been through some lean years with St. Louis, but he pointed out the difference between the 1982 Cardinals and teams of the past.

"This year, for the first time, I played with 25 guys where there were no big egos, no one or two or four people who always want headlines," he said. "Whitey deserves the credit for that. We have guys who will take the lead, and 25 guys who will sacrifice for 25 guys."[75]

Hernandez's performance could have earned him the Series MVP award, but that honor went to catcher Darrell Porter, who hit .286 with a home run and five RBI. It was the culmination of a remarkable rebound for the thirty-year-old. Two years earlier, he left the Royals to go into rehab for a serious drug and alcohol problem. Now he was the MVP of the World Series sitting in his locker, a bottle of non-alcoholic champagne in his hand, and he couldn't believe his good fortune.

"Lordy, Lordy, I ain't never had so much fun playin' ball," he said. "I've got me a beautiful wife, a little baby who's gonna be a looker, I haven't had a drink in two years and no pills or pot or whatever. I'm a happy man."[76]

There were lots of happy men and women outside the winning clubhouse as well. Fans across the city enjoyed copious amounts of Budweiser at their favorite night spots. Beers were just fifty cents at Ronayne's Restaurant and Pub on the South Side, and patrons definitely got their money's worth. "Elated would be the calm way of expressing it," said one customer. "When our bill came for $80, nobody argued, somebody just paid it."[77] At Kennedy's 2nd Street Company, one fan urged his fellow celebrants to elect Dane Iorg as president while at Uncle Sam's Plankhouse the band adapted rock and roll tunes to include the names of Cardinals players, at one point singing about "Bad, Bad Willie McGee."

As the team's theme song, Kool and the Gang's "Celebration" blared from the stadium speakers, nearly five thousand fans poured onto the field after the final out and overwhelmed the police officers stationed to prevent just such an occurrence. Fans grabbed anything they could get their hands on as souvenirs. One man scooped dirt from one of the bases into a horn he'd brought while others simply took the bases. When the field was finally cleared, Busch Stadium's head groundskeeper Ken Ragan took in the wreckage. The jubilant fans had done "thousands, and thousands, and thousands and thousands"[78] of dollars of damage to his field. When asked what the worst part was, he said, "everything."[79] St. Louis assistant chief of police William E. Brown approached Gussie Busch to apologize for the damage done to the field. His team had a plan in place but were simply outmanned by the fans. Busch just smiled, pondered his team's success, and told Brown, "I really don't give a damn right now."[80]

CONCLUSION

Nearly 100,000 people jammed the streets of St. Louis to celebrate with the World Champion Cardinals. It had taken Whitey Herzog just over two and a half years with the franchise to turn a group of underachievers into the kings of the baseball world, and the parade that began at Fourteenth and Olive Streets, made its way down Broadway, and ended at Busch Stadium was the culmination of the 1982 season, but that Cardinals team saw no reason why they shouldn't remain on top. "We've got the talent for that," said infielder Mike Ramsey. "If we don't win, we should be close. We've got a low-key ballclub, guys with a great sense of humor. They're not egotistical and very unpretentious."[1]

St. Louis slipped to fourth place in the NL East in 1983 but rebounded to win two more pennants in the 1980s, losing to the Royals in the 1985 World Series and the Twins in 1987. Since then, they've won two more World Series titles: one in 2006 and another in 2011, while reaching the Fall Classic in 2004 and 2013.

For the Milwaukee Brewers, 1982 remains the club's high-water mark. They moved to the National League prior to the 1998 season, and, despite multiple playoff appearances, they have yet to win another post-season series. In the eyes of Milwaukee, the 1982 Brewers will be forever special. The team boasted Hall of Famers Rollie Fingers, Don Sutton, Paul Molitor, Robin Yount, and Ted Simmons. Players like Gorman Thomas, Ben Oglivie, Pete Vuckovich, and Cecil Cooper remain fan favorites forty years later.

Despite the fact that they came up short, the city of Milwaukee threw a parade for the Brewers as well at the end of the 1982 season. Initially, many of the players did not want to participate in it but ultimately did so, feeling they owed it to the fans who had supported them throughout the season.

"We were emotionally drained," said pitcher Jim Slaton. "We didn't understand the effect we had on the city that year. It was the most unbelievable feeling, just seeing the fans' faces. We wondered why we affected these fans in that way. You kind of get in your own little world, your baseball world, and you don't realize how you affect other people.

"You're going through the streets and they're shaking your hand and thanking you. You were going, 'Yeah but we lost.' They didn't care. They welcomed us home like champions."[2]

By the end of the 1980s, baseball was beginning a transition from the Cardinals slashing style of play to the bashing style of the Brewers. In 1987, major league baseball teams combined to steal 3,585 bases, the most in the history of the game.[3] By 2021, despite the addition of four teams (Florida, Colorado, Arizona, and Tampa Bay), stolen base totals were down nearly 40 percent while home runs over the same period jumped 25 percent.[4]

Baseball may never again see a team like the 1982 Cardinals, a team that won a World Series despite hitting just 67 home runs. With the rise of analytics, most teams deem stolen bases a statistical risk not worth taking, but they sure made the game exciting.

Notes

INTRODUCTION

1. "1881 NL," *Walk Like a Sabermetrician* (blog), August 11, 2008, http://walksaber.blogspot.com/2008/08/1881-nl.html.

2. Von der Ahe's birth year is often listed as 1851, but in his book, *The Summer of Beer and Whiskey* (New York: Public Affairs, 2014), Edward Achorn lists it as 1848, saying Von der Ahe lied about his age to make him ineligible for military service in Prussia.

3. Achorn, "Summer of Beer and Whiskey," 14.

4. Achorn, 16.

5. Von der Ahe's Browns became the Perfectos in 1899 and the Cardinals in 1900. The American League version of the St. Louis Browns began as the Milwaukee Brewers in 1901 and moved to St. Louis for the 1902 season.

6. Achorn, 83.

7. Whitey Herzog and Jonathan Pitts, "You're Missing a Great Game," New York: Simon & Schuster, 1999, 37.

8. Mike Shropshire, "Seasons in Hell," Lincoln, NE: Bison Books, 2005, 171.

9. Herzog and Pitts, *You're Missing a Great Game,* 3.

10. Whitey Herzog and Kevin Horrigan, *White Rat: A Life in Baseball,* New York: Harper & Row, 1987, vi.

11. Herzog and Horrigan, 74.

1. THE OFF-SEASON

1. Tom Cushman, "George's Bombers Were a Big Dud," *Philadelphia Daily News,* October 29, 1981.

2. Dick Young, "Reggie: 'I have nothing to apologize for,'" *New York Daily News,* October 29, 1981.

3. Thomas Boswell, "Expos' Vote Swings Baseball into Split Season," *Cincinnati Enquirer,* August 7, 1981.

4. Tim Sullivan, "It's Over, And The Best Team Watches," *Cincinnati Enquirer,* October 5, 1981.

5. Jayson Stark, "Phils won't stay with status quo in Giles' regime," *Philadelphia Inquirer,* December 1, 1981.

6. Bill Conlin, "Phils Deal Catches Flak," *Philadelphia Daily News,* November 20, 1981.

7. Conlin.

8. Conlin.

9. Dallas Green and Alan Maimon, *The Mouth That Roared: My Six Outspoken Decades in Baseball*, Chicago: Triumph Books, 2013, 168.

10. Green and Maimon.

11. Ralph Bernstein, "Have the Phillies' pockets been picked by former boss?" *Morning Call*, December 9, 1981.

12. Frank Dolson, "Phils' wisdom is in question," *Philadelphia Inquirer*, December 9, 1981.

13. John Sullivan, "Transplanted odd couple: A new cure for the Cubs?" *Pittsburgh Post-Gazette,* February 1, 1982.

14. Frank Dolson, "Bowa doing a not-so-slow burn about Phillies' breach of faith," *Philadelphia Inquirer,* December 23, 1981.

15. Bill Conlin, "Green Light for Bowa," *Philadelphia Daily News,* January 28, 1982.

16. Ryne Sandberg and Barry Rozner, *Second to Home: Ryne Sandberg Opens Up*, Chicago: Bonus Books, 1995, 32–33.

17. Jerome Holtzman, "DeJesus traded for Bowa, rookie," *Chicago Tribune,* January 28, 1982.

18. Herzog and Pitts, *You're Missin' a Great Game*, 90.

19. Brad Balukjian, *The Wax Pack: On the Open Road in Search of Baseball's Afterlife*, Lincoln: University of Nebraska Press, 2020, 51.

20. Herzog and Pitts, *You're Missin' a Great Game*, 91.

21. Herzog and Horrigan, *White Rat*, 137, 139.

22. Herzog and Horrigan, 139.

23. Robert Ward. "The Day a Shit-Talking Reggie Jackson Tore Apart the Yankees," *Deadspin*, March 25, 2015, https://thestacks.deadspin.com/the-day-a-shit-talking-reggie-jackson-tore-apart-the-ya-1693602629.

24. Bill Madden, "Yanks get Winfield for 10 years, $15M," *New York Daily News,* December 16, 1980.

25. Madden.

26. Tim Tucker, "Come spring, think Zuvella," *Atlanta Constitution,* January 17, 1982.

27. Reggie Jackson, with Mike Lupica, *Reggie: The Autobiography*, New York: Villard Books, 1984, 316.

28. Jackson, 136.

29. "Turner Meets with Jackson," *Atlanta Constitution*, January 15, 1982.

30. Jerry Green, "Remembering Reggie," *Ithaca Journal*, July 23, 1987.

31. Tim Tucker, "Ted offers Reggie $100 Million—for 100 years," *Atlanta Constitution,* January 17, 1982.

32. Tucker.

33. "Jackson Derby Continues," *Atlanta Constitution,* January 21, 1982.

34. Jackson, *Reggie*, 322.

35. "1980 Major League Attendance & Team Age," https://www.baseball-reference .com/leagues/MLB/1980-misc.shtml.

36. John Strege, "The New Reggie: A Quiet Angel," *Sporting News,* March 6, 1982.

37. Ross Newhan, "Reggie Jackson Says He'll Play for Angels," *Los Angeles Times,* January 23, 1982.

38. Newhan.

39. Bill Dwyre, "Jackson Deal: Brilliant Stroke or Last Straw?" *Los Angeles Times,* January 23, 1982.

40. Dwyre.

41. "Aaron, Robinson in Hall of Fame," *Atlanta Constitution,* January 14, 1982.

42. Gary Deeb, "The big-brother act of late-night TV," *San Francisco Examiner,* January 29, 1982.

43. sopchoppy217, "Hank Aaron on Late Night with David Letterman, 1982," You-Tube video, 9:33, October 30, 2011, https://www.youtube.com/watch?v=kyADLqlm xrU.

44. sopchoppy217.

2. SPRING TRAINING

1. "Reopening Of Belushi Case Urged," *Daily Oklahoman*, June 29, 1982.

2. "Comedian John Belushi is found dead," *Chicago Tribune*, March 6, 1982.

3. Saturday Night Live, "Don't Look Back in Anger—Saturday Night Live," YouTube video, 4:22, October 3, 2013, https://www.youtube.com/watch?v=64LJXqyZCek.

4. Vic Wilson, "Fernandomania," Society for American Baseball Research, https: //sabr.org/research/fernandomania.

5. "They Said It," *Sports Illustrated,* February 1, 1982.

6. "Valenzuela's Contract Renewed," *St. Louis Post Dispatch*, March 2, 1982.

7. Scott Ostler, "His Fans Turn Faster Than His Screwball," *Los Angeles Times,* March 3, 1982.

8. Jim Murray, "Fernando's Support Seems to Be Missing," *Los Angeles Times,* March 2, 1982.

9. Mark Purdy, "And Batting Forth for Cincinnati . . . George Foster," *Cincinnati Enquirer*, February 2, 1982.

10. Tom Condon, "Athlete$: Take the $$ and run," *Chicago Tribune,* February 9, 1982.

11. Gary Long, "Bob Horner: Home Run Potential Still Untapped!" *Baseball Digest*, June 1982.

12. Tony Schwartz, "Horner: Turner A 'Jerk' For Demotion," *Atlanta Constitution,* April 29, 1980.

13. Schwartz.

14. Schwartz.

15. George Cunningham, "Horner Wanted Out Months Ago," *Atlanta Constitution*, March 23, 1982.

16. Ken Murray, "Agent Woy bucking management," *Fort Worth* Star Telegram, July 1, 1979.

17. Cunningham, "Horner Wanted Out."

18. Tim Tucker, "Braves Are Leaning on Horner, Murphy," *Sporting News,* April 24, 1982.

19. Tim Tucker, "Dale Murphy: A Brave Leader Hits His Stride," *Baseball Digest,* August 1982.

20. Tucker, "Braves Are Leaning."

21. Tucker.

22. Carl Clark Jr., "Writers Call for Rematch in Pennant Picks," *Sporting News,* April 10, 1982.

23. Rick Hummel, "Expos Favored," *St. Louis Post Dispatch,* April 4, 1982.

24. Ian McDonald, "The Complete Player," *Sporting News,* September 19, 1981.

25. "Ron LeFlore Alleges Expos, Fans, Racist," *Wilmington Morning News*, August 29, 1980.

26. "Ron LeFlore Alleges."

27. "Ron LeFlore Alleges."

28. Allen Lewis, "Raines to make run for Brock's stolen-base record," *Philadelphia Inquirer,* April 4, 1982.

29. "Expos' Carter Gets $14 Million," *St. Louis Post Dispatch,* February 16, 1982.

30. George Cunningham, "A Confident Millionaire," *Atlanta Constitution,* February 24, 1982.

31. Ian McDonald, "Bad Luck Piles Up For Expos' Rogers," *Sporting News,* February 20, 1982.

32. Charley Feeney, "Bucs to Speed Up Bid to Deal Parker," *Sporting News,* February 27, 1982.

33. Charley Feeney, "Agent Reich 'Disruptive,' Says an Angry Tanner," *Sporting News,* March 20, 1982.

34. Feeney.

35. Charley Feeney, "Keystone Combo Holds Bucs' Key," *Sporting News,* April 10, 1982.

36. George Cunningham, "Braves Are Best—In Spring," *Atlanta Constitution,* March 19, 1982.

37. Joseph Durso, "Herzog the Dealer Going For Jackpot," *New York Times,* March 15, 1982.

38. Rick Hummel, "Cards Being Watched On Bases," *St. Louis Post Dispatch,* March 11, 1982.

39. Hummel.

40. Rick Hummel, "Green 'Overwhelming' in Cards' Win," *St. Louis Post Dispatch,* March 12, 1982.

41. Hummel.

42. Rick Hummel, "Lonnie Smith Expects To Be Catalyst For Redbirds," *St. Louis Post Dispatch,* March 7, 1982.

43. Tim Tucker, "Tim Tucker's Inside Baseball," *Atlanta Constitution,* March 21, 1982.

44. "Topps Found Guilty of Monopoly in Bubble-Gum Baseball Cards," *Associated Press,* July 1, 1980.

45. "Judge turns card market 'Topsy-turvy,'" *Daily Dispatch,* July 2, 1980.

46. Michael Zhang, "Keith Olberman Was the Photographer Behind Bad Photos on 1981 Baseball Cards," *PetaPixel,* January 25, 2016, https://petapixel.com /2016/01/25/keith-olbermann-was-the-photographer-behind-bad-photos-on-1981-baseball-cards/.

47. Dick Perez, interview with author, October 19, 2021.

48. Perez.

49. "Not for kids only; Baseball card collecting attracts 250,000 hobbyists—some do it for the money," *Associated Press*, September 12, 1982.

50. "Not for kids only."

51. "Not for kids only."

52. Ken Nigro, "Weaver May Alter Retirement Plans," *Sporting News,* February 27, 1982.

53. Doug DeCinces, interview with author, February 8, 2021.

54. DeCinces.

55. Jack Ireland, "Traded DeCinces has been like real guardian Angel for Ripken," *News Journal,* February 2, 1982.

56. Ken Nigro, "'King Cal' rules at hot corner," *Baltimore Sun,* February 26, 1982.

57. Phil Pepe, "Yanks: 'We Can Win Without Reggie,'" *Sporting News*, February 13, 1982.

58. Dick Kaegel, "Spring Notebook," *Sporting News*, March 20, 1982.

59. Phil Pepe, "Nettles genuine Yank captain," *Daily News,* January 30, 1982.

60. Pepe, "Yanks."

61. Pepe.

62. Rob Zaleski, "No Sun City siesta for Paul Molitor," *Capital Times,* March 1, 1982.

63. Herb Anastor, "Don Money: Brewers' Bouncing Ball," *Daily Journal,* February 25, 1982.

64. "Brewer boss won't change his methods," *Spokesman-Review,* September 16, 1981.

65. Rob Zaleski, "Honest ol' Buck Shoots from the hip," *Capital Times,* March 4, 1982.

66. Zaleski.

67. Tom Haudricourt, *Where Have You Gone '82 Brewers?* Stevens Point, WI: KCI Publishing, 2007, 132.

68. Haudricourt, 119.

69. "1979 Oakland Athletics Statistics," *Baseball Reference,* https://www.baseball -reference.com/teams/OAK/1979.shtml.

70. Glenn Schwarz, "Martin, Minton discontented," *San Francisco Examiner,* February 24, 1982.

71. Gerry Fraley, "Brett's Tarnished Image," *Atlanta Constitution,* March 17, 1982.

72. Fraley.

73. Ross Newhan, "A Frustrated Brett Involved in Altercation," *Los Angeles Times,* September 16, 1981.

74. Newhan.

75. John Strege, "The New Reggie: A Quiet Angel," *Sporting News*, March 6, 1982.

76. Tom Barnidge, "Beware of Baseball Optimism In Spring," *St. Louis Post Dispatch*, February 26, 1982.

77. Jim Reeves, "Zimmer's Glowing Over Pitching Staff," *Sporting News,* March 6, 1982.

78. Gil Lebteton, "Sorry Joe. Eddie and Zim Can't Wait," *Fort Worth Star-Telegram,* April 2, 1982.

79. Lebteton.

80. Joseph Durso, "Mets Receive Two Pitchers," *New York Times,* April 2, 1982.

81. Joseph Durso, "Says Mets May Regret Trading Him to Rangers," *New York Times,* April 3, 1982.

3. APRIL

1. Dick Pothier, "The Colleges Love Pac-Man," *Philadelphia Inquirer*, May 9, 1982.

2. Steve Stecklow, "Pound Foolish over Pac-Man," *Philadelphia Inquirer,* April 4, 1982, 91.

3. Tom Nugent, "Video Games: Suburban Menace?" *Baltimore Sun,* February 25, 1982.

4. Jerome Holtzman, "Cubs break the pattern for opener," *Chicago Tribune,* April 6, 1982, 53.

5. Susan Reimer, "Ripken revels in storybook homer," *Baltimore Sun,* April 6, 1982, 21.

6. Ken Nigro, "4 Oriole homers flatten Royals," *Baltimore Sun,* April 6, 1982, 21.

7. Reimer, "Ripken revels," 24.

8. Brian Bragg, "Trammell in stitches after accident in bar," *Detroit Free Press,* April 9, 1982, 43.

9. Bragg.

10. Bragg, 39.

11. Bragg.

12. Peter Gammons, "Going Nowhere?" *Boston Globe,* June 28, 1981, 65.

13. Jay Weiner, "Mariners Torpedo Twins," *Minneapolis Star Tribune,* April 7, 1982, 52.

14. Weiner.

15. Weiner, 45.

16. Gary Libman, "Smalley traded to Yankees," *Minneapolis Star Tribune,* April 11, 1982, 27.

17. Libman.

18. Joe Soucheray, "Smalley traded to Yankees," *Minneapolis Star Tribune,* April 11, 1982, 27.

19. "Turner Flips over Braves' Chances," *Wisconsin State Journal,* March 12, 1982, 25.

20. George Cunningham, "'82 Braves: Time To Put Up Or Shut Up," *Atlanta Constitution,* March 12, 1982, 81.

21. Tim Tucker, "Guess who harvests most down on the farm," *Atlanta Constitution,* April 11, 1982, 46.

22. George Cunningham, "Mahler Two-Hits San Diego as Braves Win Opener 1–0," *Atlanta Constitution,* April 7, 1982, 21.

23. Bob Dart, "Hotlanta's Hotbraves," *Atlanta Constitution,* April 19, 1982, 11.

24. Dart.

25. Steve Wulf, "Braves' New World," *Sports Illustrated,* April 26, 1982, 16.

26. George Cunningham, "Don't Celebrate Yet, Reds Warn Braves," *Atlanta Constitution,* April 14, 1982, 23.

27. George Cunningham, "4–2 Win Is No. 12 In A Row," *Atlanta Constitution,* April 21, 1982, 21.

28. George Cunningham, "The Streak Ends," *Atlanta Constitution,* April 23, 1982, 101.

29. San Heys, "It Had To End: Braves Lose," *Atlanta Constitution,* April 23, 1982, 1.

30. Rick Hummel, "Cards' Opening Act Hard to Top," *St. Louis Post-Dispatch,* April 7, 1982, 21.

31. Frank Dolson, "Smith making the Phils' faces red," *Philadelphia Inquirer,* April 18, 1982, 59.

32. Tim Sullivan, "Padres' High-Fiving Leaves Dodgers Irked," *Cincinnati Enquirer,* April 25, 1982, 26.

33. Sullivan.

34. Sullivan.

35. Mark Heisler, "Padres Do a Number on Dodgers," *Los Angeles Times,* April 19, 1982, 41.

36. Heisler.

37. Ross Newhan, "Torborg Next Yankee Manager?" *Los Angeles Times,* May 2, 1982, 44.

38. Vic Feuerherd, "Brewers Rip Toronto 15–4," *Milwaukee Sentinel,* April 10, 1982, 6.

39. Feuerherd.

40. Ted Miexell, "Montreal explodes to rout the Phillies," *Morning Call,* April 11, 1982, 41.

41. Bill Livingston, "Carter takes beating but strikes back with the bat," *Philadelphia Inquirer,* April 11, 1982, 8E.

42. Jayson Stark, "Schmidt on Expos: 'They can't hit with us . . . play defense with us,'" *Philadelphia Inquirer*, April 11, 1982, 9E.

43. Stark.

44. "Schmidt angers Expos," *Montreal Gazette,* April 12, 1982.

45. "Trade Shocks Carlton," *St. Louis Post Dispatch,* February 25, 1972, 21.

46. "Trade Shocks Carlton."

47. Jayson Stark, "Carlton takes 4th loss as Expos trip Phils 5–2," *Philadelphia Inquirer,* April 22, 1982, 45.

48. Bill Conlin, "Rose, Phils are no Party for L.A.," *Philadelphia Daily News,* April 29, 1982, 82.

49. Tim Tucker, "Steinbrenner rides while Reggie waits," *Atlanta Constitution,* May 2, 1982, 61.

50. Phil Pepe, "Steinbrenner is wearing out the script: Hit panic button and change managers," *New York Daily News,* April 26, 1982, 42.

51. Pepe.

52. "We're likely to be around for a long time," *New Paris News,* November 22, 1978, 7.

53. Ross Newhan, "All in All, Reggie Would Rather Not Be In New York," *Los Angeles Times,* April 27, 1982, 45.

54. Newhan.

55. Peter Gammons, "When fools (with checkbooks) rush in," *Boston Globe,* May 2, 1982, 81.

4. MAY

1. Erik Brooks, "Born in Chicago, raised in Milwaukee: A New Look at the Origins of Miller Lite," *Beer & Beyond: Molson Coors Blog,* October 8, 2018, https://www.molsoncoorsblog.com/features/born-chicago-raised-milwaukee-new-look-origins-miller-lite.

2. Brooks.

3. Brooks.

4. maxcareyhof, "1980 Brooks Robinson Frank Robinson Miller Lite Commercial Baltimore Orioles," YouTube video, 0:29, February 19, 2012, https://www.youtube.com/watch?v=LOz9JIPjAMk.

5. Letters to the Sports Editor, *Baltimore Sun,* May 2, 1982.

6. Cal Ripken Jr. and Mike Bryan, *The Only Way I Know How*, New York: Viking, 1997, 85.

7. "Ripken Comes Through For Orioles, *Daily Times,* May 9, 1982.

8. Barry Bloom, "The King of Grease," *Sport Magazine,* August 1982.

9. Bloom.

10. Bloom.

11. Rick Hummel, "Cards Suffer Double Loss—Game and Green," *St. Louis Post Dispatch,* May 8, 1982.

12. Bill Conlin, "N.L. Beat," *Sporting News,* May 31, 1982.

13. Patrick Ruesse, "Twins Rookie Battles a Nervous Disorder," *Sporting News,* May 17, 1982.

14. Ruesse.

15. Ruesse.

16. Dan Shaughnessy, "A rookie's battle," *Boston Globe,* May 5, 1982.

17. Patrick Ruesse, "Chaos, Anger in Minnesota," *Sporting News,* May 24, 1982.

18. Peter Gammons, "Is Griffith Selling the Twins?" *Boston Globe*, May 16, 1982.

19. Patrick Ruesse, "'Who' Member Hrbek Keeps Twins Fans Glued to Their Seats," *Sporting News,* May 24, 1982.

20. Ruesse.

21. Tom Gage, "Scrapper Rozema Lost for Season," *Sporting News,* May 31, 1982.

22. Bill Lee and Dick Lally, *The Wrong Stuff,* New York: Viking, 1984, 212.

23. Lee and Lally.

24. Ian McDonald, "Lee Takes Stroll And Then a Hike," *Sporting News,* May 24, 1982.

25. McDonald.

26. Moss Klein, "Mayberry Takes Yankees Hot Seat," *Sporting News,* May 17, 1982.

27. Bill Madden, "Yankees Close To Mutiny," *Daily News,* May 6, 1982.

28. Steve Wulf, "This Time George Went Overboard," *Sports Illustrated,* May 9, 1982.

29. "Winfield will shed quiet image," *Pensacola News Journal,* May 20, 1982.

30. Jim Reeves, "Rangers' DH Job Angers Mazzilli," *Sporting News,* May 17, 1982.

31. Jim Reeves, "Left Fielders Unite Over 'Idiot' Quote," *Sporting News,* May 24, 1982.

32. Tim Sullivan, "For Any of Several Reasons, Reds' Attendance Lagging," *Cincinnati Enquirer,* May 9, 1982.

33. Jim Reeves, "Rangers' DH Job Angers Mazzilli," *Sporting News,* May 17, 1982.

34. Reeves.

35. Don Zimmer with Bill Madden, *Zim, A Baseball Life*, Kingston, NY: Total Sports Publishing, 2001, 154.

36. Zimmer.

37. Jim Reeves, "Parrish Struggles, Gropes, and Hopes," *Sporting News,* May 31, 1982.

38. Reeves.

39. Steve Pate, "One thing Chiles can't keep secret is record," *Fort Worth Star-Telegram,* May 25, 1982.

40. Peter Gammons, "A.L. Beat," *Sporting News,* June 7, 1982.

41. Gammons.

42. Kit Stier, "Brock's Theft Mark On Henderson's Mind," *Sporting News,* May 17, 1982.

43. Glenn Schwarz, "The Rickey Watch," *Sporting News,* June 14, 1982.

44. Schwarz.

45. Kit Stier, "Loss of McCatty Depletes A's Staff," *Sporting News,* June 14, 1982.

46. Jim Peterik, interviewed by Malcolm Jack, "Survivor: How we made Eye of the Tiger," *Guardian,* January 27, 2020, https://www.theguardian.com/music/2020/jan/27/how-we-made-eye-of-the-tiger-rocky-iii-survivor-sylvester-stallone.

47. Tom Haudricourt, *Where Have You Gone, '82 Brewers?* Stevens Point, WI: KCI Publishing, 2007, 141.

48. Haudricourt, 142.

49. "Augustine starts, but allows 12 runs," *Herald Times-Reporter,* May 12, 1982.

50. "Augustine starts."

51. "Rollie points finger at Rodgers," *Wisconsin State Journal,* June 2, 1982.

52. "Rollie points finger."

53. "Rollie points finger."

5. JUNE

1. Christopher Connelly, "Still Life," *Rolling Stone,* June 1, 1982, https://www.rollingstone.com/music/music-album-reviews/still-life-188697/.

2. Connelly.

3. Don Zimmer with Bill Madden, *Zim: A Baseball Life,* Kingston, NY: Total Sports Publishing, 2001, 156.

4. Zimmer.

5. Zimmer.

6. Zimmer, 157.

7. "Rangers Fire Eddie Robinson," *Odessa American*, June 11, 1982.

8. Zimmer, 157.

9. Zimmer.

10. Zimmer.

11. Mark Heisler, "Reuss Retires 27 Reds After Leadoff Double," *Los Angeles Times*, June 12, 1982.

12. Gordon Verrell, "Garvey's Future a Question Mark," *Sporting News,* June 21, 1982.

13. "Caught on the Fly," *Sporting News,* June 28, 1982.

14. "E.T. the Extra-Terrestrial," *Box Office Mojo,* https://www.boxofficemojo.com/release/rl995132929/weekend/.

15. "Jurassic Park," *Turner Classic Movies,* 2022, https://www.tcm.com/tcmdb/title/80025/jurassic-park/#notes.

16. John Stark, "One of the most magical films ever," *San Francisco Examiner*, June 11, 1982.

17. "Poltergeist," *Box Office Mojo,* https://www.boxofficemojo.com/release/rl107709953/weekend/.

18. Hal Bodley, "Phils' Rise Linked to Swift Dernier," *Sporting News,* June 14, 1982.

19. Bill Conlin, "Lefty Fans 16; To Top Cubs," *Philadelphia Daily News,* June 10, 1982.

20. Conlin.

21. Frank Dolson, "Rose's eternal youth for all fans to savor," *Philadelphia Inquirer*, June 23, 1982.

22. Dolson.

23. Terry Francona and Dan Shaughnessy, *Francona: The Red Sox Years*, New York: Houghton Mifflin Harcourt, 2013, 18.

24. Francona and Shaughnessy.

25. Francona and Shaughnessy.

26. Tim Raines with Alan Maimon, *Rock Solid: My Life in Baseball's Fast Lane*, Chicago: Triumph Books, 2017, 7.

27. Raines, 7–8.

28. Dick Williams and Bill Plaschke, *No More Mr. Nice Guy: A Life of Hardball*, New York: Harcourt, 1990, 211.

29. Williams and Plaschke, 212.

30. Raines, 3.

31. John Strege, "Emotion Puts Zing in Angels," *Sporting News*, July 5, 1982.

32. Don Baylor with Claire Smith, *Don Baylor: Nothing But the Truth: A Baseball Life*, New York: St. Martins, 1989, 178.

33. Strege, "Emotion Puts Zing."

34. John Strege, "Cheers Heat Reggie's Bat," *Sporting News*, July 5, 1982.

35. John Strege, "Rejevenated Boone is Angels Leader," *The Sporting News*, June 21, 1982.

36. Mel Durslag, "Singing Praises of Angels," *Sporting News*, July 5, 1982.

37. Joe Giulotti, "Even the Medics Are Mystified By Yaz. Over-40 Standout Hitter," *Sporting News*, June 28, 1982.

38. Peter Gammons, "Winning Pair, Sullivan, Houk," *Sporting News*, June 28, 1982.

39. Gammons.

40. Gammons.

41. Peter Gammons, "Sox outstanding in the outfield," Boston Globe, May 23, 1982.

42. Moss Klein, "*Piniella tunes out Yankee Excuses*," *Sporting News*, June 28, 1982.

43. Klein.

44. Klein.

45. Drew Silva, "Bob Sheppard, The Voice of God: 1910-2010," NBC Sports, July 11, 2010, http://hardballtalk.nbcsports.com/top-posts/bob-sheppard-the-voice-of-yankee-stadium-1910-2010

46. Silva.

47. "*Big-Apple Blooper*," *St. Louis Post Dispatch*, June 25, 1982.

48. Peter Gammons, "*A.L. Beat*," *Sporting News*, June 21, 1982.

49. Gammons.

50. Gammons.

51. Gammons.

52. "Brewers keep hammering," *Green Bay Press Gazette*, June 27, 1982.

53. "Oglivie learns to relax, goes on home run binge," *Green Bay Press Gazette*, June 28, 1982.

54. "Oglivie learns."

55. Tom Flaherty, "Crises Nothing New for Kuenn," *Sporting News*, June 21, 1982.

56. "Braves' Murphy Modest About On-Field Heroics," *Daily News*, June 26, 1982.

57. "Braves' Murphy."

58. Stan Isle, "Caught on the Fly," *Sporting News*, June 14, 1982.

59. Tim Tucker, "Streaky Braves Defy All Maxims," *Sporting News*, June 28, 1982.

60. Earl Lawson, "Reds Can't Smile as Losses Mount," *Sporting News*, June 21, 1982.

61. Lawson.

62. Lawson.

63. "Voice of the Fan," *Sporting News*, June 28, 1982.

64. "Voice of the Fan,."

65. Joseph Wancho, "George Hendrick," *Society for American Baseball Research,* https://sabr.org/bioproj/person/george-hendrick/.

66. Russell Schneider, "Aspro-Hendrick Cold War Interrupted by Silent Truce," *Sporting News*, September 28, 1974.

67. Dick Young, "Why it's Robby and not Doby," *New York Daily News*, September 29, 1974.

68. Rick Hummel, "Cardinals Hit Their Way Back Into First," *St. Louis Post-Dispatch*, June 30, 1982.

69. Jim Thomas, "Dodgers longest day ends with a split," *News-Pilot*, July 1, 1982.

70. Chris Cobbs, "Bevacqua: 'Fine Lasorda, Too,'" *Los Angeles Times*, July 4, 1982.

71. ScrippsRanchOldPros, "Tommy Lasorda meltdown about Kurt Bevacqua," YouTube video, 1:38, August 5, 2009, https://www.youtube.com/watch?v=fzjWQF1oP2M.

72. Phil Collier, "Padres Making Pluses Pay Off," *Sporting News*, June 21, 1982.

73. Collier.

74. Phil Collier, "Airtight Pitching Padres' Hallmark," *Sporting News*, June 28, 1982.

75. Phil Collier, "Best of the West? Padres Think So," *Sporting News*, June 14, 1982.

76. Collier.

6. JULY

1. MemoryMuseum, "Bob Uecker 1982 Miller Lite Beer Commercial," YouTube video, 0:30, https://www.youtube.com/watch?v=-CFqMeYsudM.

2. Tom Flaherty, "Brewers Shoot for HR Record," *Sporting News*, July 19, 1982.

3. Flaherty.

4. Tom Flaherty, "Brewers Having a Blast," *Sporting News*, August 9, 1982.

5. Stan Isle, "Caught on the Fly," *Sporting News*, August 9, 1982.

6. Stan Isle, "Caught on the Fly," *Sporting News*, July 26, 1982.

7. Phil Musick, "Lasorda grieves for missing 'stars,'" *Pittsburgh Post Gazette*, July 12, 1982.

8. "A.L. Out to Break All-Star Hex," *Pittsburgh Post Gazette*, July 12, 1982.

9. "A.L. Out to Break All-Star Hex."

10. Joseph Durso, "National League Wins 11th Straight All-Star Game," *New York Times*, July 14, 1982.

11. Tim Sullivan, "Concepcion Wins MVP as N.L. Whips A.L. 4–1," *Cincinnati Enquirer*, July 14, 1982.

12. Ian Ward, "1982 MLB ASG Film," YouTube video, 23:45, May 21, 2015, https://www.youtube.com/watch?v=03Khu0C2V_U.

13. Ward.

14. ClassicPhilliesTV, "1982 MLB All Star Game--@mrodsports," YouTube video, 4:00:23, September 27, 2016, https://www.youtube.com/watch?v=loTK8sD_Vyo.

15. ClassicPhillies TV.

16. Steve Howe, with Jim Greenfield, *Between the Lines: One Athlete's Struggle to Escape the Nightmare of Addiction* (Grand Rapids, MI: Masters Press, 1989), 124.

17. Ward.

18. Michael Farber, "Just a ho-hum NL win in a dull All-Star Game," *Montreal Gazette*, July 14, 1982.

19. "Oliver delights Montreal fans," *Nanaimo Daily News*, July 14, 1982.

20. "Oliver delights."

21. "Speier expects Fanning will get axe," *Montreal Gazette*, July 14, 1982.

22. "Speier expects."

23. Brian Kappler, "Oliver takes his manager's side in latest Fanning-must-go debate," *Montreal Gazette*, July 15, 1982.

24. "Speier apologizes to Fanning," *Montreal Gazette*, July 16, 1982.

25. Ian McDonald, "Expos Take Hope from Big Innings," *Sporting News*, August 2, 1982.

26. McDonald.

27. Hal Bodley, "Charging Phils Silence Critics," *Sporting News*, July 12, 1982.

28. Hal Bodley, "Corrales is Quiet, But in Command," *Sporting News*, July 19, 1982.

29. Hal Bodley, "Carlton Knocks Our Rumors of Demise," *Sporting News*, August 9, 1982.

30. Kit Stier, "A's Give Kingman Another Chance," *Sporting News*, June 21, 1982.

31. Stier.

32. Kit Stier, "Kingman Buries Woes with a Win," *Sporting News*, July 19, 1982.

33. "Martin wins 1,000th against nemesis," *Petaluma Argus-Courier,* July 9, 1982.

34. Kit Stier, "Bullpen is Blamed for A's Tumble," *Sporting News*, July 26, 1982.

35. Stier.

36. Kit Stier, "Henderson Rated A 'Triple Threat'," *Sporting News*, August 9, 1982.

37. John Strege, "Bottom Falls Out of Angels Hitting," *Sporting News*, July 19, 1982.

38. Strege.

39. John Strege, "Goltz Earns Spot as Angels Starter," *Sporting News*, July 12, 1982.

40. Strege.

41. Strege.

42. John Strege, "Angels Give Mauch Taste of 'Big Ball'," *Sporting News*, August 2, 1982.

43. Chris Mortensen, "Garvey sits, but string alive in Dodgers' loss," *Daily Breeze*, July 11, 1982.

44. Mortensen.

45. Mortensen.

46. "'A Mockery'," *Los Angeles Times*, July 10, 1982.

47. Gordon Verrell, "Newcombe Denies Drug Quote," *Sporting News*, July 26, 1982.

48. Russell Bergtold, "Don Newcombe," *Society for American Baseball Research,* https://sabr.org/bioproj/person/don-newcombe/.

49. Verrell, "Newcombe Denies Drug Quote."

50. Howe, *Between the Lines,* 121.

51. Howe.

52. Gordon Verrell, "Mets Bring Out Worst in Dodgers," *Sporting News*, August 2, 1982.

53. Gordon Verrell, "Home Has a Sour Taste for Dodgers," *Sporting News*, July 19, 1982.

54. Steve Dolan, "Wiggins of Padres Enters Drug Treatment Program Following Cocaine Arrest," *Los Angeles Times*, July 22, 1982.

55. Dolan.

56. "Padre rookie will return—soon," *Orlando Sentinel*, April 1, 1982.

57. "Williams pegs Padres .500," *Arizona Republic*, March 30, 1982.

58. Bill Conlin, "N.L. Beat," *Sporting News*, August 2, 1982.

59. Conlin.

60. Tim Sullivan, "Reds Fire McNamara," *Cincinnati Enquirer*, July 22, 1982.

61. Earl Lawson, "Reds' Fall Costs McNamara Job," *Sporting News*, August 2, 1982.

62. Lawson.

63. Zimmer, *Zim,* 158.

64. Zimmer.

65. Zimmer.

66. Zimmer.

67. Zimmer, 159.

68. Zimmer.

69. Zimmer.

70. Zimmer, 160.

71. Peter Gammons, "A.L. Beat," *Sporting News*, August 9, 1982.

72. Jim Reeves, "Zimmer Fires Parting Shots," *Sporting News*, August 9, 1982.

73. Dave Winfield and Alan Parker, *Winfield: A Player's Life*, New York: W. W. Norton & Co., 1988, 165.

74. Moss Klein, "Did George Ignite Winfield's Surge?" *Sporting News*, July 19, 1982.

75. Klein.

76. Klein.

77. Stan Isle, "Caught on the Fly," *Sporting News*, July 19, 1982.

78. Moss Klein, "Yanks Slide Linked to John, Guidry," *Sporting News*, July 26, 1982.

79. Moss Klein, "Spot Starter John Fights with V.P.," *Sporting News*, August 9, 1982.

80. Phil Pepe, "Tommy John wants out of Bronx Zoo," *York Daily Record*, August 3, 1982.

81. Tommy John, with Dan Valenti, *T. J.: My 26 Years in Baseball*, New York: Bantam Books, 1991, 235.

82. John.

83. Pepe, "Tommy John wants out."

84. Pepe.

85. Ken Nigro, "O's Murray a 'Regular' Superstar," *Sporting News*, May 10, 1982.

86. Ken Nigro, "Spotty O's Certain They'll Speed Up," *Sporting News*, July 19, 1982.

87. Ripken and Bryan, *Only Way I Know How*, 91.

88. Ripken and Bryan, 92.

89. Mark Heisler, "Something Missing with Dodgers," *Los Angeles Times*, July 30, 1982.

90. Jesse Outlar, "Torre takes a cautious stance," *Atlanta Constitution*, July 30, 1982.

91. I. J. Rosenberg, "Whatever Happened To . . . Chief Noc-A-Homa," *Atlanta Constitution*, September 4, 2016.

7. AUGUST

1. Stanley Meisler, "Fans in Toronto Can Now Toast Team With Beer," *Los Angeles Times*, August 1, 1982.

2. "First beer sold at Blue Jays game," *Toronto Star*, July 31, 1982.

3. "Blue Jays fans quaff beer for first time; 'It's good. It's great,' spectator says," *Globe and Mail,* July 31, 1982.

4. "Baseball and Beer—and the Blue Jays even won," *Leader-Post*, July 31, 1982.

5. Herschell Nissenson, "Yankee hot seat has a new occupant," *Ithaca Journal*, August 4, 1982.

6. Nissenson.

7. Nissenson.

8. Baylor, *Don Baylor*, 201.

9. Bill Madden, "Shift last-ditch try to salvage season," *Daily News*, August 5, 1982.

10. Madden.

11. Dan Shaughnessy, "Child struck by line drive," *Boston Globe*, August 8, 1982.

12. Shaughnessy.

13. Peter Gammons, "Lansford's Return Fires Up Red Sox," *Sporting News*, August 30, 1982.

14. "Reeling Astros Fire Manager Bill Virdon," *Santa Cruz Sentinel*, August 10, 1982.

15. Harry Shattuck, "Everybody Lauds Departed Virdon," *Sporting News*, August 23, 1982.

16. Kevin Thomas, "New Talent Featured In 'Fast Times,'" *Los Angeles Times*, August 13, 1982.

17. Thomas.

18. Richard T. Kelly, *Sean Penn: His Life and Times*, Edinburgh, Scotland, 2004, 90.

19. Kelly, 94.

20. Kelly, 94.

21. Kelly, 95.

22. "Fast Times at Ridgemont High," *IMDb,* https://www.imdb.com/title/tt0083929/?ref_=nv_sr_srsg_0.

23. Mark Heisler, "Cubs Hit the 'Wall' in a marathon, 1–1," *Los Angeles Times*, August 18, 1982.

24. Heisler.

25. "Valenzuela Glad To Play the Field," *Philadelphia Daily News*, August 19, 1982.

26. Mark Heisler, "Dodgers Are Winners at both 21 and 9-Ball," *Los Angeles Times*, August 19, 1982.

27. Jerry Reuss, *Bring in the Right-Hander!: My Twenty-Two Years in the Major Leagues,* Lincoln, NE, 2014, 185.

28. Reuss.

29. Reuss.

30. Gordon Verrell, "Now Even Lefties Beat the Dodgers," *Sporting News*, August 9, 1982.

31. Tim Tucker, "Braves Stumble Again," *Atlanta Constitution*, August 5, 1982.

32. Tim Tucker, "Braves fall out of 1st place," *Atlanta Constitution*, August 11, 1982.

33. Tim Tucker, "It wasn't Braves' day in sun," *Atlanta Constitution*, August 16, 1982.

34. Tucker.

35. Tim Tucker, "Montreal puts Braves to bed with 12–2 win," *Atlanta Constitution*, August 19, 1982.

36. Gerry Fraley, "Garber wondering when it all will end," *Atlanta Constitution*, August 19, 1982.

37. Tim Tucker, "The night Pascual Perez got lost—and found a spot in Braves history," *Atlanta Constitution*, May 14, 2020.

38. Tim Tucker, "Perez, Braves on road back," *Atlanta Constitution*, August 21, 1982.

39. Tucker.

40. Rick Hummel, "Kittle's Batting Tips Help Andujar Win," *St. Louis Post Dispatch*, August 13, 1982.

41. Hummel.

42. Rick Hummel, "Oberkfell Delivers Most Important Hit," *St. Louis Post Dispatch*, August 13, 1982.

43. *Celebrate 1982 World Champion St. Louis Cardinals,* LP, St. Louis Cardinals Baseball Club, 1982.

44. Rick Hummel, "Brummer Steals A Game For Cardinals," *St. Louis Post Dispatch*, August 23, 1982.

45. Terrence Moore, "Robby: Umpires are bush," *San Francisco Examiner*, August 23, 1982.

46. Moore.

47. Hummel, "Brummer Steals."

48. Hummel.

49. "Umpire nabs Gaylord Perry grease-handed," *Spokane Chronicle*, August 24, 1982.

50. Peter Gammons, "Aging Gaylord a Flagrant User of Spitter," *Sporting News*, September 6, 1982.

51. Gammons.

52. "Umpire nabs."

53. "Umpire nabs."

54. Rickey Henderson, with John Shea, *Off Base: Confessions of a Thief*, New York: Harper Collins, 1992, 73.

55. Henderson, 75.

56. King Thompson, "Henderson just misses 118th steal," *San Francisco Examiner, August 25, 1982.*

57. Brian Bragg, "A's shortstop charged with theft of integrity," *Detroit Free Press*, August 25, 1982.

58. Bragg.

59. Thompson, "Henderson just misses 118th steal."

60. Bragg, "A's shortstop charged."

61. Glenn Schwarz, "No rest for Rickey after record," *San Francisco Examiner*, August 28, 1982.

62. Schwarz.

63. Glenn Schwarz, "Murph shares in the glory," *San Francisco Examiner*, August 28, 1982.

64. Kit Stier, "'I'm Glad It's Over'—Henderson," *Sporting News*, September 6, 1982.

65. Schwarz, "No rest for Rickey."

66. "Rickey 'Relieved' after record 119," *St. Louis Post Dispatch*, August 28, 1982.

67. Schwarz, "No rest for Rickey."

68. "Wathan sets new record, Royals win," *Springfield News-Leader*, August 25, 1982.

69. Mike McKenzie, "Slick-Fielding White Swings Torrid Bat," *Sporting News*, August 19, 1982.

70. McKenzie.

71. McKenzie.

72. Bob Carter, "Tigers claw Royals, Gura in 7–1 win," *Chillicothe Constitution-Tribune*, August 5, 1982.

73. Carter.

74. John Strege, "DeCinces Joins An Elite Circle," *Sporting News*, August 23, 1982.

75. Strege.

76. "Fight a draw; A's win the game," *Press Democrat*, August 16, 1982.

77. "Fight a draw."

78. John Strege, "'Even if he's 51' Angels Try Tiant," *Sporting News*, August 19, 1982.

79. Ross Newhan, "History Doesn't Favor the Angels," *The Los Angeles Times*, August 22, 1982.

80. Pete Donovan, "Angels Lose in 9th and Fall Out of First Place," *Los Angeles Times*, August 16, 1982.

81. John, *T. J.*, 237.

82. John.

83. John.

84. John Strege, "Angels Get Shot In Arm With T. J.," *Sporting News*, September 13, 1982.

85. Tom Flaherty, "Hill Ace Vuckovich 'Locked in a Bubble,'" *Sporting News*, August 16, 1982.

86. Flaherty.

87. Tom Flaherty, "Ladd Stands Tall On His Big Night,'" *Sporting News*, August 23, 1982.

88. "Brewers win 2, lead by 5 1/2'" *Green Bay Press-Gazette*, August 13, 1982.

89. "Sutton Traded to Brewers for 3 minor leaguers," *Los Angeles Times*, August 31, 1982.

8. SEPTEMBER

1. "McLauchlan only good; Rush pleasant," *Ottawa Citizen*, October 15, 1982.

2. Jeff Miers, "Why do so many rock critics hate Rush?" *Buffalo News,* April 18, 2013, https://buffalonews.com/news/why-do-so-many-rock-critics-hate-rush/article_9a5898dc-32ed-59bb-88af-3b3eca01fe7a.html.

3. Raj Bahadur, "Rush Takes Off: The Geddy Lee Interview," *Power Windows,* originally published in *Northeast Ohio Scene,* October 28-November 3, 1982, http://www.2112.net/powerwindows/transcripts/19821028scene.htm.

4. Jayson Stark, "Phils Fall to Bucs 4-2 and find Race Growing Tighter," *Philadelphia Inquirer,* September 14, 1982.

5. Stark.

6. Jayson Stark, "Carlton overpowers Cards, 2-0," *Philadelphia Inquirer*, September 14, 1982.

7. Stark.

8. Stark.

9. "Redbirds Put Philadelphia Into A Funeral-Like Mood," *St. Louis Post Dispatch*, September 14, 1982.

10. Arnold Irish, "Phillies Unhappy With Critical Call," *St. Louis Post Dispatch*, September 21, 1982.

11. Rick Hummel, "Many Chapters in Cards' story," *St. Louis Post Dispatch*, September 28, 1982.

12. Mike McKenzie, "Twins, Howser see two different sides to slumping Royals," *Kansas City Star*, September 20, 1982.

13. McKenzie.

14. Ross Newhan, "Tie-Breaker is Next as Angels Get Even," *Los Angeles Times*, September 20, 1982.

15. Newhan.

16. Ross Newhan, "Zahn's True Grit Puts Angels on Top," *Los Angeles Times*, September 22, 1982.

17. Mike McKenzie, "Angels surprise package keeps Royals in AL West tailspin," *Kansas City Star*, September 22, 1982.

18. Newhan, "Tie-Breaker is Next."

19. Newhan, "Zahn's True Grit."

20. Ross Newhan, "Angels Help Quisenberry Realize His Fear, Lead by 2," *Los Angeles Times*, September 22, 1982.

21. Mike McKenzie, "Sconiers pins 2-1 loss on Royals with his first hit," *Kansas City Star*, September 22, 1982.

22. Mike McKenzie, "Royals' skid goes on despite good work of pitching staff," *Kansas City Star*, September 22, 1982.

23. Tim Tucker, "Reds prolong Braves' Agony," *Atlanta Constitution*, September 18, 1982.

24. Tucker.

25. Tucker.

26. Mark Heisler, "Red-Faced Dodgers Lose Lead to Braves," *Los Angeles Times*, September 29, 1982.

27. Tim Sullivan, "Jittery Dodgers Try Partying," *Cincinnati Enquirer*, September 29, 1982.

28. Tim Tucker, "Inside Baseball," *Atlanta Constitution*, April 11, 1982.

29. Haudricourt, *Where Have You Gone,* 130.

30. Lou Matter, "Medich helps save life of heart attack victim," *Baltimore Sun*, July 18, 1978.

31. Haudricourt, *Where Have You Gone,* 113.

32. Thomas Boswell, "Shelby Throws Orioles Back Into East Race," *Washington Post*, September 27, 1982.

33. Boswell.

34. John Hughes, "Shelby? Remember That Name," *Wisconsin State Journal*, September 27, 1982.

35. Boswell, "Shelby Throws."

36. Kent Baker, "Birds Romp, 8-3 and 7-1," *Baltimore Sun*, October 2, 1982.

37. Baker.

38. Tim Tucker, "Niekro does it!" *Atlanta Constitution*, October 2, 1982.

39. Tucker.

40. Tucker.

41. John Hillyer, "After Monday, maybe no Sunday for Giants," *San Francisco Examiner*, October 2, 1982.

42. Hillyer.

43. Mark Heisler, "Reuss, Dodgers Leave the Giants Thinking Monday," *Los Angeles Times*, October 2, 1982.

44. Heisler.

45. Hillyer, "After Monday/"

46. Hillyer.

47. Haudricourt, *Where Have You Gone,* 41.

48. Alan Goldstein, "Sutton calm for big test today," *Baltimore Sun*, October 3, 1982.

49. Kent Baker, "11-3 rout takes race to final day," *Baltimore Sun*, October 3, 1982.

50. Haudricourt, *Where Have You Gone,* 50.

51. Tim Tucker, "Braves stop San Diego 4-2 to near title," *Atlanta Constitution*, October 3, 1982.

52. Tucker.

53. John Hillyer, "Dodgers Eliminate Giants," *San Francisco Examiner*, October 3, 1982.

54. Mike Littwin, "Not All Giants Had Given up as Score Hit 10-0," *Los Angeles Times*, October 3, 1982.

55. Littwin.

56. Mark Heisler, "Dodgers Finish Off Giants in 15-2 Rout but Need Help Today," *Los Angeles Times*, October 3, 1982.

57. Haudricourt, *Where Have You Gone,* 43.

58. Haudricourt, 42.

59. Haudricourt, 43.

60. Jim Palmer and Jim Dale, *Together We Were Eleven Foot Nine: The Twenty-Year Friendship of Hall of Fame Pitcher Jim Palmer and Orioles Manager Earl Weaver*, Kansas City, MO: Andrew McMeel, 1996, 155.

61. Palmer and Dale, 156.

62. Palmer and Dale, 156.

63. Palmer and Dale, 156.

64. Bob Sudyk, "'Steiner' to Ask More Pay for Playing Less," *Sporting News*, October 18, 1975.

65. Classic MLB1, "1982 10 03 ABC Brewers at Orioles," YouTube video, 3:08:55, February 7, 2019, https://www.youtube.com/watch?v=-qNR_wC_6Qo.

66. Palmer and Dale, *Together We Were Eleven Foot Nine*, 155.

67. Palmer and Dale, 157.

68. Jay Jaffe, "A Gripping Saga: 11 tales of pitchers using spitters, sandpaper and scuffing," *Sports Illustrated*, May 3, 2013.

69. Alan Goldstein, "Did Sutton chicanery take title from Birds?" *Baltimore Sun*, October 4, 1982.

70. Classic MLB1, "1982 10 03 Dodgers at Giants," YouTube viceo, 3:01:06, June 26, 2017, https://www.youtube.com/watch?v=I887fGKRvWI.

71. Classic MLB1.

72. Classic MLB1.

73. Classic MLB1.

74. Classic MLB1.

75. Classic MLB1.

76. Bucky Walter, "'We want Joe,' a chant for next season," *San Francisco Examiner*, October 4, 1982.

77. Tim Tucker, "Braves Win It!" *Atlanta Constitution*, October 4, 1982.

78. Tucker.

79. Childs Walker, "He embodied Orioles Magic," *Baltimore Sun*, August 21, 2007.

80. Classic MLB1, "1982 10 03 ABC Brewers at Orioles."

81. Classic MLB1.

82. Classic MLB1.

83. Classic MLB1.

84. Classic MLB1.

85. Haudricourt, *Where Have You Gone,* 137.

86. Classic MLB1, "1982 10 03 ABC Brewers at Orioles."

87. Classic MLB1, "1982 10 03 Dodgers at Giants."

88. John Hillyer, "Morgan gives L.A. lesson in humility," *San Francisco Examiner,* October 4, 1982.

89. Classic MLB1, "1982 10 03 Dodgers at Giants."

90. Classic MLB1.

91. Tucker, "Braves Win It!"

92. Classic MLB1, "1982 10 03 ABC Brewers at Orioles."

9. THE PLAYOFFS

1. Thomas M. Stinson, "Court pulls plug on WTBS' plans to show Playoffs," *Atlanta Constitution*, October 5, 1982.

2. Stinson.

3. Classic MLB1, "1982 ALCS Game 1 – Brewers @ Angels," YouTube video, 2:40:39, October 26, 2018, https://www.youtube.com/watch?v=uqhmbRVqdPc.

4. Classic MLB1.

5. John, T. J., 241.

6. Gerry Fraley, "Downing's Heart Still In It," *Chicago Tribune,* June 26, 1991.

7. Classic MLB1, "1982 ALCS Game 1 – Brewers @ Angels."

8. Bill Brophy, "Baylor belts Brewers," *Wisconsin State Journal*, October 6, 1982.

9. Brophy.

10. Bill Dwyre, "Brewers Send a Ladd to Do a Man's Work," *Los Angeles Times*, October 6, 1982.

11. Dwyre.

12. Tim Tucker, "Rain Washes Niekro shutout with Braves in the lead 1–0," *Atlanta Constitution*, October 7, 1982.

13. Tucker.

14. Peter Gammons, "A.L. Beat," *Sporting News*, August 27, 1981.

15. Bob Verdi, "Close calls all go Vuckovich's way," *Chicago Tribune*, March 18, 1982.

16. Ross Newhan, "Kison and Angels Have Right Stuff, 2–0 Playoff Lead," *Los Angeles Times*, October 7, 1982.

17. Newhan.

18. Newhan.

19. Classic MLB1, "1982 NLCS Game 1 Braves at Cardinals," YouTube video, 2:40:29, October 26, 2018, https://www.youtube.com/watch?v=mD-iphG4Nk4.

20. Classic MLB1.

21. Classic MLB1.

22. Tim Tucker, "Cards sprint to a 1–0 lead; Forsch stars," *Atlanta Constitution*, October 8, 1982.

23. Tucker.

24. Jesse Outlar, "Torre's rain-soaked rotation: Niekro, Niekro, Niekro," *Atlanta Constitution*, October 9, 1982.

25. Outlar.

26. Classic MLB1, "1982 ALCS Game 3 Angels at Brewers," YouTube video, 2:20:58, October 26, 2018, https://www.youtube.com/watch?v=BF6zfpai0yk.

27. Doug DeCinces, interview with author, February 8, 2021.

28. Pete Donovan, "John to Pitch Game 4 Today," *Los Angeles Times*, October 9, 1982.

29. Donovan.

30. John, *T. J.*, 241.

31. Classic MLB1, "1982 ALCS Game 4 Angels at Brewers," YouTube video, 2:51:58, October 26, 2018, https://www.youtube.com/watch?v=DNHCWBnqbu0.

32. Ross Newhan, "The Ghosts of '64 haunt Mauch, and Series Is Tied," *Los Angeles Times*, October 10, 1982.

33. Newhan.

34. Newhan.

35. Tim Tucker, "Braves fall 4–3; Cards looking for NL Sweep," *Atlanta Constitution*, October 10, 1982.

36. Tucker.

37. Baylor,*Don Baylor,* 187.

38. Haudricourt, *Where Have You Gone*, 85.

39. Mike Littwin, "For Once, Cooper Takes Advantage of an Opportunity," *Los Angeles Times*, October 11, 1982.

40. John, *T. J.*, 187.

41. Haudricourt, *Where Have You Gone,* 146.

42. Classic MLB1, "1982 ALCS Game 5 Angels @ Brewers," YouTube video, 2:29:59, October 26, 2018, https://www.youtube.com/watch?v=LWzjkzcoUxE.

43. Classic MLB1.

44. Haudricourt, *Where Have You Gone,* 100.

45. Classic MLB1, "1982 ALCS Game 5 Angels @ Brewers."

46. Haudricourt, *Where Have You Gone,* 100.

47. Classic MLB1, "1982 ALCS Game 5 Angels @ Brewers."

48. Haudricourt, *Where Have You Gone,* 100.

49. Haudricourt, 19.

50. Classic MLB1, "1982 ALCS Game 5 Angels @ Brewers."

51. Classic MLB1,.

52. Classic MLB1.

53. Haudricourt, *Where Have You Gone,* 19.

54. John, *T. J.*, 240.

55. Bill Brophy, "Brewers St. Louis Bound," *Wisconsin State Journal*, October 11, 1982.

56. Brophy.

10. THE WORLD SERIES

1. "Miller Brewing Company," *Encyclopedia.com*, May 21, 2018, https://www.en cyclopedia.com/social-sciences-and-law/economics-business-and-labor/ businesses-and-occupations/miller-brewing-company.

2. William Knoedelseder, *Bitter Brew: The Rise and Fall of Anheuser-Busch and America's King of Beer*, New York: Harper Business, 2012, 183.

3. Knoedelseder, 272.

4. Fred W. Lindecke, "Series Business," *St. Louis Post-Dispatch*, October 12, 1982.

5. Lindecke.

6. Kevin Horrigan, "Baseball's Big Brass Has Its Party Under The Arch," *St. Louis Post-Dispatch*, October 12, 1982.

7. Rick Hummel, "It's Brewer Might Vs. Cardinal Speed," *St. Louis Post-Dispatch*, October 12, 1982.

8. Classic MLB1, "1982 World Series Game 1 Brewers at Cardinals," YouTube video, 2:02:58, February 6, 2019, https://www.youtube.com/watch?v=QooJ-f0LRto.

9. Rick Hummel, "Cardinals Embarrassed" *St. Louis Post-Dispatch*, October 13, 1982.

10. Mark Heisler, "Mike Caldwell gives Cardinals nothing to hit but birdseed," *Los Angeles Times*, October 13, 1982.

11. Heisler.

12. Heisler.

13. Mike O'Brien, "Cardinals and the nation get to see 'real' Milwaukee Brewers," *Los Angeles Times*, October 13, 1982.

14. O'Brien.

15. O'Brien.

16. Rob Rains and Alvin Reid, *Whitey's Boys*, Chicago: Triumph Books, 2002, 12–13.

17. Classic MLB1, "1982 World Series Game 2 Brewers at Cardinals," YouTube video, 2:18:09, February 6, 2019, https://www.youtube.com/watch?v=tVOeqJ7Pksk.

18. Rick Hummel, "Whitey Plays His Ace: Sutter Baffles Brewers," *St. Louis Post-Dispatch*, October 14, 1982.

19. Whitey Herzog and Jonathan Pitts, *You're Missin' a Great Game*, Ne York: Simon & Schuster, 1999, 129–30.

20. Tyler Kepner, *K: A History of Baseball in Ten Pitches*, New York: Anchor, 2020,125.

21. Classic MLB1, "1982 World Series Game 2 Brewers at Cardinals."

22. Hummel, "Whitey Plays His Ace."

23. Mike O'Brien, "Brewers bemoan 'bad call,'" *Daily Tribune*, October 14, 1982.

24. Hummel, "Whitey Plays His Ace."

25. O'Brien, "Brewers bemoan 'bad call.'"

26. O'Brien.

27. Hummel, "Whitey Plays His Ace."

28. Haudricourt, *Where Have You Gone*, 44.

29. Herzog and Pitts, *You're Missin' a Great Game,* 134.

30. Herzog and Pitts.

31. "White Sox streak to 6, Cardinals to 7," *Tampa Bay Times*, April 18, 1982.

32. Phil Pepe, "Andujar injury bring back memories," *New York Daily News*, October 15, 1982.

33. Rick Hummel, "Wonderous Willie Puts Cards One Wing Up," *St. Louis Post-Dispatch*, October 15, 1982.

34. Mike Lupica, "Another Willie steals glory in Series with bat & glove," *New York Daily News*, October 15, 1982.

35. Tony Walter, "McGee rips Brewers," *Green Bay Press-Gazette*, October 15, 1982.

36. Rains and Reid, *Whitey's Boys,* 65.

37. Peter Gammons, "Error helps Brewer rally; Series tied 2–2," *Boston Globe*, October 17, 1982.

38. Rains and Reid, *Whitey's Boys,* 131.

39. Rick Hummel, "Error Opens Floodgates, Birds Drown, 7–5" *St. Louis Post-Dispatch*, October 17, 1982.

40. Hummel.

41. Leigh Montville, "It was cold, then Stormin'," *Boston Globe*, October 17, 1982.

42. "Thomas wasn't worried," *Green Bay Press-Gazette*, October 17, 1982.

43. "Celebrate 1982 World Champion St. Louis Cardinals," LP, St. Louis Cardinals Baseball Club, 1982.

44. Haudricourt, *Where Have You Gone*, 35.

45. Peter Gammons, "Yount has 4 hits, again," *Boston Globe*, October 18, 1982.

46. Mike Smith, "Milwaukee Shortstop Gets Four Hits Again" *St. Louis Post-Dispatch*, October 18, 1982.

47. Bob Forsch, with Tom Wheatley, *Tales from the St. Louis Cardinals Dugout: A Collection of the Greatest Cardinals Stories Ever Told*, New York: Sports Publishing, 2013, 173.

48. Forsch, 174.

49. Forsch.

50. Forsch.

51. Rick Hummel, "Cards On Brink Of World Title" *St. Louis Post-Dispatch*, October 20, 1982.

52. Hummel.

53. Haudricourt, *Where Have You Gone*, 44.

54. Peter Gammons, "Stuper 4-hitter sets up Game 7," *Boston Globe*, October 18, 1982.

55. "Game 7 pits best vs. best," *Boston Globe*, October 18, 1982.

56. "Game 7 pits best vs. best."

57. Neal Russo, "Brummer's Feeling Of Emptiness: 8—Bottles Of Champagne Drained," *St. Louis Post Dispatch*, October 22, 1982.

58. Ranes and Reid, *Whitey's Boys,* 5.

59. Haudricourt, *Where Have You Gone,* 23.

60. MLB Vault, "1982 World Series, Game 7: Brewers @ Cardinals," YouTube video, 2:33:20, September 30, 2010, https://www.youtube.com/watch?v=veJj5iI4TM8.

61. Ranes and Reid, *Whitey's Boys,* 5.

62. Haudricourt, *Where Have You Gone,* 145.

63. Luigi Aguilera, "MLB 1982 World Series Highlights," YouTube video, 37:23, April 21, 2016, https://www.youtube.com/watch?v=qfN14H5kUaY.

64. Luigi Aguilera.

65. Luigi Aguilera.

66. "A Boyhood Pal Of Hernandez's," *St. Louis Post-Dispatch*, October 21, 1982.

67. MLB Vault, "1982 World Series, Game 7: Brewers @ Cardinals."

68. Haudricourt, *Where Have You Gone,* 63.

69. Larry Whiteside, "'Hot dog' with a hot hand," *Boston Globe*, October 21, 1982.

70. Mike Smith, "Cards' Ace Emotional," St. Louis Post Dispatch, October 21, 1982.

71. Smith.

72. "Arm Problems Kept Fingers Sidelined," *St. Louis Post Dispatch*, October 21, 1982.

73. Neil Russo, "Brewers Credit the Cardinals, And Vuckovich Takes The Blame," *St. Louis Post Dispatch*, October 21, 1982.

74. Russo, 25.

75. Kevin Horrigan, "Clutch Base Hits Came in Bunches," *St. Louis Post Dispatch*, October 21, 1982.

76. Dave Kindred, "Porter reaps his just reward," *Washington Post*, October 21, 1982.

77. Robert L. Koenig and Dennis Hannon, "Fans Go Wild, Wilder At Moment Of Victory," *St. Louis Post Dispatch*, October 21, 1982.

78. Koenig and Hannon.

79. Koenig and Hannon.

80. Bill McClellan, "Police: Why Didn't They Win In Milwaukee?" *St. Louis Post Dispatch*, October 21, 1982.

CONCLUSION

1. Russo, "Brummer's Feeling Of Emptiness."

2. Haudricourt, *Where Have You Gone*, 76.

3. "MLB League by League Totals for Stolen Bases," *Baseball Almanac,* https://www.baseball-almanac.com/hitting/hisb3.shtml.

4. "League by League Totals for Home Runs," *Baseball Almanac,* https://www.baseball-almanac.com/hitting/hihr6.shtml.

Index

About the Author

Jonathan "J." Daniel spent twenty years working in sports, both in front of and behind the camera, producing five seasons of *Rays Magazine*, a weekly television show about the Tampa Bay Rays, and working as a sports producer in Cincinnati, Tampa, and Chicago. He is the author of *Phinally!: The Phillies, the Royals, and the 1980 Baseball Season That Almost Wasn't* and blogs at www.80sbaseball.com.

Photo by Paul D'Andrea